Cybercash

By the same author:

Reforming Money and Finance: Financial Institutions and Markets in Flux (Armonk, NY: M.E. Sharpe), 1989

How Credit-Money Shapes the Economy: The United States in a Global System Flux (Armonk, NY: M.E. Sharpe), 1994

Reforming Money and Finance: Toward a New Monetary Regime, 2nd edn (Armonk, NY: M.E. Sharpe), 1997

CYBERCASH

The Coming Era of Electronic Money

Robert Guttmann

palgrave
macmillan

First published 2003 by
PALGRAVE MACMILLAN
Houndmills, Basingstoke, Hampshire RG21 6XS and
175 Fifth Avenue, New York, N.Y. 10010
Companies and representatives throughout the world

PALGRAVE MACMILLAN is the global academic imprint of the Palgrave
Macmillan division of St. Martin's Press, LLC and of Palgrave Macmillan Ltd.
Macmillan® is a registered trademark in the United States, United Kingdom
and other countries. Palgrave is a registered trademark in the European
Union and other countries.

ISBN 0–333–98730–6 hardback

This book is printed on paper suitable for recycling and made from fully
managed and sustained forest sources.

A catalogue record for this book is available from the British Library.

Library of Congress Cataloging-in-Publication Data

Guttmann, Robert, 1951–
    Cybercash : the coming era of electronic money / by Robert Guttmann.
      p. cm.
    Includes bibliographical references and index.
    ISBN 0–333–98730–6
      1. Electronic funds transfers. I. Title.

HG1710 .G88 2003
322.1'0285—dc21

2002068339

Editing and origination by Aardvark Editorial, Mendham, Suffolk

10 9 8 7 6 5 4 3 2 1
12 11 10 09 08 07 06 05 04 03

Printed and bound in Great Britain by
Creative Print & Design (Wales), Ebbw Vale

This book is dedicated, with much love,
to my wife Gina Philogène and our children,
Alexandre and Maxine

CONTENTS

LIST OF FIGURES AND TABLES

Figures

Tables

PREFACE

Invitation to a Voyage

Attention readers! This book is important!

Robert Guttmann's *Cybercash* is important because it deals with an ensemble of 'major' innovations capable of triggering a powerful wave of change. These innovations concern money – arguably the institution through which our social ties manifest themselves in a most consistent and indispensable fashion. The book thus analyzes innovations which, in all likelihood, will profoundly affect all aspects of social life.

As the author reminds us, money possesses a 'public' dimension beyond its private usage by all of us. We value it and use it only because collectively we know with certainty that everyone else will consider it as good as does each one of us. Thus, changing the form of this link by introducing new intermediaries in acts of exchange means transforming social life itself. With cybercash – the new type of money that circulates on the internet in several forms – this is precisely what we get: a revolution in the support structure of market exchanges and even in the dynamic of the exchange process itself.

Robert Guttmann deserves to be thanked for having given us this detailed and precise analysis of the birth of a new type of money – its first forms, its first uses – and for having accomplished this task in such a profound, yet thoroughly readable fashion. He dissects with care the new business models of online firms such as Yahoo!, eBay, or E*Trade, and elaborates on the reasons why these firms fascinate us as harbingers of the future. With the same sharp edge he analyzes the failures, the victims of the e-crash. Under the direction of Robert Guttmann this constantly shifting and sometimes strange world of the internet is rendered intelligible and transparent. He presents a radical innovation, in the Schumpeterian sense of triggering powerful waves of 'creative destruction', as if it were a riddle in a detective story whose resolution he guides us to step by step.

A key merit of the book lies precisely here, in the way its author analyzes the microeconomics of internet-based actors, in particular those engaged in online financial transactions and services. He examines in great detail three generations of cybermoney (Chapter 5), both in their strengths and weaknesses. While at the moment blocked, these monetary innovations are bound to develop and expand a great deal over the next couple of decades because they have given birth to new concepts and models. Take, for example, Flooz or Beenz, both truly private monies put into circulation by e-enterprises and used by millions, which could not withstand the storm of the dot-com crash of 2000–01. A second important dimension of the book is to have pushed this microeconomy, in the context of the birth of cybercash, all the way to the macroeconomic problems which that new money form will undoubtedly bring in its wake. The book focuses in particular on problems of monetary policy, mostly related to the setting of interest rates and control over the money supply, as well as on the problem of risk management. Both types of problem threaten to wrong-foot the central banks themselves by eventually shattering the maladjusted policy instruments currently in use.

Guttmann's key argument, developed throughout the book, is that on the internet we find not only firms using stored money and those hooked up to the banks online, but also we find true issuers of cybercash, creators of money and loans, willing to place their bets on security portfolios and to protect their risk exposure across the entire spectrum of derivatives. If they can manage to overcome the disadvantage of their late entry in terms of reverse network externalities, these new financial operators have serious economic arguments as to why they should enter into competition with banks and the traditional credit card companies. That development is entirely rooted in the monetary history of the last two decades. Financial deregulation, the automation of payments and the securitization of credit have already prepared us at length for the arrival of electronic money. The irresistible spread of the internet has created the locus where this new money will inevitably grow and progress. Both the money creation monopoly of the banks and the Fed's control over the payments system are thus bypassed, threatened and rendered less efficient, a fact that will push us towards a reform of the public policy apparatus dealing with the management of money.

From the micro-phenomenon of online money used or created between internet-based actors – already appearing in different forms within the P2P, B2C and B2B segments of e-commerce – the author derives a macroeconomic dimension. He sees the integration of money and finance on the internet feeding the formation of fictitious capital on a very large scale. The lessons of the e-crash, briefly but brilliantly analyzed in Chapter 3, are well presented. They pervade the entire book ensuring that it never sinks to the level of simplistic, oracle-like announcements.

The final part of the book, comprising Chapters 7 and 8, takes a forward-looking view that is strongly optimistic about the ability of cyber-cash to find a large number of socially useful applications in the world of exchange and production. That projection closes, however, with an analysis of the collapse of Enron, presented here not as 'the imperfect child of an otherwise healthy system', but more likely as 'the perfect child of an unhealthy system'. All this makes the point that the potential embodied in cybercash does not develop spontaneously or automatically. Whether it concerns security and privacy (two issues crucial to its devel-opment, as argued forcefully in Chapter 4), risk management or control over money creation, cybercash gives rise to difficult and generic prob-lems in the form of qualitatively new market failures that only the visible hand of the government as regulator can confront effectively. Policy makers will gradually develop responses to these challenges. The last part of the book that is dedicated to the 'internet-based economy' will captivate the reader. Describing a combination of opportunities and major risks – qualified here as systemic – which arise out of the fusion between money and the internet, it gives us a sense of tomorrow's economy.

Therein lies one of the most fascinating aspects of this book. Through the analysis of cybercash the author introduces the reader to a veritable social history of capitalism. A voyage not only through those nanoseconds in which cybercash moves through huge electronic networks connecting financial operators across the world, but also through those long periods during which the complex social forms and institutions underlying mone-tary exchange evolve.

In short, a captivating book on a topic of major importance, written with a level of care and knowledge that is a credit to the author. A book whose quality, density and novelty of information presented provokes reflection.

BENJAMIN CORIAT
(Professor of Economics, Université Paris-Nord)
Sartène, Corsica

ACKNOWLEDGMENTS

While this book is very much the product of my own thinking, it would have never been written without the input of many friends and colleagues. I would like to thank in particular François Chesnais, Suzanne De Brunhoff, Martin Kenner, Pascal Petit, Dominique Plihon, Dominique Perrut, Stephan Schulmeister and Claude Serfaty for their valuable help and patient advice. My thanks extend also to the organizers of the Columbia University Seminar, Hofstra University's Economics Club, the ARC2 Seminar at CEPREMAP (Paris), and the Faculty Seminar at Université Paris-Nord for giving me the opportunity of presenting various aspects of this book. Finally, I wish to express my gratitude to Stephen Rutt, my editor at Palgrave Macmillan, for his support and insights.

The author and publishers wish to thank the Federal Reserve Bank of Kansas City for permission to use Table 1.1.

Every effort has been made to trace all the copyright holders but if any have been inadvertently overlooked the publishers will be pleased to make the necessary arrangements at the first opportunity.

LIST OF ABBREVIATIONS

ACH	automated clearing-house
AES	advanced encryption standard
ALM	automated loan machines
API	application program interface
ARPA	Advanced Research Projects Agency
ATM	automated teller machine
BIS	Bank for International Settlements
B2B	business-to-business
B2C	business-to-consumer
CA	certification authority
CBOT	Chicago Board of Trade
CD	Certificate of deposit or cassette disk
CFTC	Commodities Futures Trading Commission
CHIPS	clearing house interbank payments system
C-SET	chip-secured electronic transaction
DES	data encryption standard
DIA	Depository Institutions Act
DIDMCA	Depository Institutions Deregulation and Monetary Control Act
DSL	digital subscriber line
EBPP	electronic bill presentment and payment
EBT	electronic benefits transfer
ECB	European Central Bank
ECML	electronic commerce modeling language
ECN	electronic communications network
ECP	electronic check presentment
EFT	electronic fund transfer
ERP	enterprise resource planning
EU	European Union
FASB	Financial Accounting Standards Board

FCC	Federal Communications Commission
FDIC	Federal Deposit Insurance Corporation
FSMA	Financial Services Modernization Act
FSML	Financial services markup language
FSTC	Financial Services Technology Consortium
FTC	Federal Trade Commission
GATS	General Agreement on Trade in Services
GPN	global production network
IASB	International Accounting Standards Board
IPO	initial public offering
ISP	internet service provider
IT	information technology
JEPI	joint electronic payments initiative
LIFFE	London International Financial Futures Exchange
MNC	multinational corporation
M2M	machine-to-machine
NAI	network advertising initiative
NASDAQ	National Association of Securities Dealers Advanced Quotation
NIST	National Institute of Standards and Technology
NOW	negotiable order of withdrawal
NYCE	New York Cash Exchange
NYSE	New York Stock Exchange
OBI	open buying on the internet
OECD	Organization for Economic Co-operation and Development
OPEC	Organization of Petroleum Exporting Countries
OTC	over-the-counter
OTP	open trading protocol
PC	personal computer
PDA	personal digital assistant
PIN	personal identification number
POS	point-of-sale
P2P	peer-to-peer
P3P	platform for privacy preferences project
R&D	research and development
RM	remote monitoring
SEC	Securities and Exchange Commission
SET	secure electronic transaction
SSL	secure sockets layer

SWIFT	Society for Worldwide Interbank Financial Telecommunications
TCP/IP	transmission control protocol/internet protocol
TNB	transnational bank
VAT	value-added tax
WAP	wireless applications protocol
WTO	World Trade Organization

PART I

Money and the Internet

CHAPTER I

Electronic Money

Ever since its inception about 15,000 years ago, money has been subject to ongoing change – both in its form and modus operandi. Such changes have in turn typically brought about major transformations in the functioning of our economy. Given money's strategic position in the organization of economic activities, it is not surprising to see changes in the monetary process having major repercussions for exchange, production and credit. This is especially true when new money forms rise to the fore.

Today we face precisely such a situation with the shift from paper money to electronic money. Having gradually replaced central bank notes and bank checks with plastic cards, electronic fund transfers and auto-mated clearing-houses, the world is now readying itself for the next step in the automation of money. Electronic commerce conducted on the internet is bound to spur a variety of online-payment mechanisms, and such cyber-cash may very well multiply the uses of the internet as marketplace, in production, and for financial transactions. We are at the threshold of a new industrial revolution, fuelled by the proliferation of digital-money forms. That revolution and the role of cybercash in it are the subject of this book.

We begin our exploration in this opening chapter with a closer look at the phenomenon of electronic money. First we examine how the penetration of computer and communication technologies in banking has already transformed the way we handle money and make payments (section 1.1). Having thus set the stage for further automation of the monetary process, banks are now using the emergence of the internet as a launching pad for cybercash as the ultimate form of electronic money. Given its hetero-geneity, high-tech features and immaterial nature, cybercash promises to be radically different from any other form of money we have known heretofore. As such it deserves being defined as a qualitatively new money form (section 1.2). The far-reaching implications of a change in money form can only be fully appreciated if we conceptualize money as a social institution central to the organization of economic activities (section 1.3). Such a theoretical grounding enables us to identify the historic evolution of money as one of its progressive dematerialization (section 1.4) and to take a closer look at money's contradictory nature as a key factor behind changes in its form (section 1.5). The chapter ends with a brief look at the emergence of cybercash and the driving forces underlying its proliferation (section 1.6).

1.1 The Beginnings of Electronic Money

Today about half of all the transactions in the US economy are still paid for in cash (currency bills and coins). The other half involves noncash transactions of which about 70 percent involve payment by check. While accounting for only 30 percent of noncash transactions, electronic-payment methods involving credit cards, debit cards, wire transfers and automated clearing-houses (ACHs) have been growing much more rapidly than the number of transactions conducted by cash or check (see Table 1.1).

Traditional forms of paper money still offer users certain unique advantages. For instance, *cash* ensures anonymity which makes it the money form of choice for tax evasion and illegal activities, such as drug trafficking. Cash denominated in 'hard' currencies is also popular in places where the local currency is not trusted (for example dollars in Latin America or euros in Russia). Access to cash has been bolstered greatly by the dramatic increase in automated teller machines (ATMs) whose number has tripled in the United States over the last decade from 75,000 terminals

Table 1.1 Noncash payment types, United States				
Type	Number of transactions (billion, 1997)	Average annual growth (1993–97) %	Share of total (1993) %	Share of total (1997) %
Checks	66.09	2.3	79.1	72.2
Credit cards	16.88	7.8	16.4	18.4
Debit cards	3.91	53.3	0.9	4.3
ACH	4.55	15.5	3.4	5.0
Wire transfer	0.15	7.3	0.1	0.2

Source: Weiner (1999, p. 55). By permission

in 1989 to 235,000 in 1999. These ATMs, which lower the operating costs of banks, allow bank customers to conduct various banking activities with the help of computers which operate faster, more reliably and more cheaply than human bank tellers. By linking their ATM networks, banks have found a way to bypass geographic branching restrictions (for instance the long-standing US prohibition against interstate banking) and operate nationwide, even globally organized banking networks.

The other dominant form of paper money, namely *checks* backed by demand deposits at banks, still remains by far the preferred form of noncash payment among consumers. Having been around for over a century, they are familiar, widely accepted and fairly convenient. Anyone writing a check has the feeling of 'hands-on' control over a given payment, a significant psychological advantage compared to less tangible payment methods using computers. Like cash, checks enable individuals to make payments to other individuals. Checks, however, are very expensive to process. The check-clearing mechanism set up by the Federal Reserve, the US central bank, in 1918 is a cumbersome and costly affair. Checks travel from the bank, in which the check was deposited, via the regional Federal Reserve banks to the bank on which the check was drawn, and back. Each of these steps demands a good deal of paperwork from the parties concerned. Since checks have to be physically moved from bank to bank, they also involve considerable transportation costs, including the operation of a large fleet of airplanes and trucks deployed each day by the regional Federal Reserve banks for the movement of checks between states. The costs of printing, handling and delivering the 60 billion checks written each year in the United States by individuals and corporations exceed US$50 billion, nearly $1 per check. In addition to these direct costs we have to consider indirect costs which are harder to measure. For instance, the possibility of processing delays is quite high in an air traffic system which is already stretched to capacity and vulnerable to extreme weather conditions. Any delay in check-processing creates a loss of income which could have been earned from investing cash earlier. This opportunity cost has become more important now that (deregulated) interest rates tend to be fairly high.[1]

In recent years the banking sector has intensified its efforts to automate the check-collection process. The most promising step in this direction so far has been the use of *electronic check presentment* (ECP) technology in which the payment information on a paper check is transmitted by computers between the banks involved to make the check collection process faster, more efficient and less costly. Today already roughly one in five checks is presented electronically. Driving check electronification one step further, the Fed is currently experimenting with *electronic checks* which have become possible because of dramatic improvements in digital-imaging technology. It has launched pilot programs offering digital images of truncated checks to ECP customers over the internet. E-checks may eventually evolve into a popular and convenient payment mechanism for online transactions (see section 5.4).

Even though cash and currency remain dominant, America is certainly moving in the direction of paper-less electronic payments. On the retail level, for instance, we can witness the rapid growth of *credit-card* transactions. Such credit cards, of which there are now over half a billion in circulation within the United States alone, essentially represent a revolving line of credit to consumers. Their use in transactions authorizes funds to be moved over large electronic networks linking card-holders, merchants, their respective banks and the credit-card companies operating those networks (for example Visa, MasterCard, American Express, Discover). An agreement in February 1996 between MasterCard and Visa, the two dominant credit-card companies, to introduce a single 'secure electronic transaction' (SET) format for credit-card purchases on the internet paved the way for the take-off of e-commerce.[2]

Another increasingly popular means of electronic payments on the retail level are *debit cards* of which there are already 250 million in the United States. These can be used for ATM transactions and in point-of-sale (POS) transactions at retail stores equipped with specially fitted terminals. Having the convenience of combining ATM and POS capabilities on a single card, such debit cards can be presented to a merchant just like a credit card for payment. But unlike credit cards, which involve credit, debit cards are linked to a customer's bank account from which the amount of the transaction is immediately debited. Such debit cards began with the spread of ATM networks which connected the ATMs of different banks for reciprocal use by their respective customers. Their use expanded to off-line retail purchases when Visa and MasterCard opened up their electronic fund-transfer networks for debit cards (alongside credit cards) in the early 1990s, prompting a rapidly growing number of merchants to equip their stores with POS terminals hooked to banks. Debit-card transactions finally moved online a few years ago, routed through the same networks as the banks' ATM transactions.[3]

The growing popularity of plastic cards has given Visa and MasterCard a powerful position in America's payment system. Together these two companies, which are associations owned by the banks issuing those cards, control about 75 percent of the US$1.3 trillion-per-year US credit-card market. The two companies have parlayed that market power into securing control over debit cards as well. Once use of those debit cards extended beyond ATMs to POS terminals at retailers, the banks came to depend on the processing networks run by Visa and MasterCard. Both then imposed 'honor all cards' rules which force merchants to accept any card bearing their logo, whether credit or debit card. Acting in effect as a duopoly, they have saddled merchants with considerable processing charges. In the case of credit cards these may reach 6.5 percent of the transaction whereas in the case of debit credits the charges can amount to 45 cents per transaction (compared to the 10 cents charged by smaller debit-card networks, such as NYCE).[4]

While plastic cards dominate retail banking, electronic-payments services in wholesale banking used by corporations, financial institutions and government agencies are entirely instruction-driven. Key in this area are so-called *wire transfers* for which we have created two distinct networks. Fedwire is operated by the Federal Reserve and used primarily to settle domestic interbank transfers. The clearing house interbank payments system (CHIPS), operated by a consortium of banks grouped together in the New York Clearing House Association, principally settles foreign-exchange transactions. Both of these networks specialize in high-value transactions, averaging $3 million and $6 million per transaction respectively. Each handles about $1.5 trillion in transfers on any given day.

A third type of electronic-payments system uses a network of *automated clearing-houses* through which financial institutions can transfer funds to each other on behalf of their clients, be they consumers, businesses, or government agencies. Such fund transfers, which average about $3000 per transaction, are processed, distributed and settled by a central clearing facility, the ACH operator. Today three private ACH networks (that is, Electronics Payments Network, American Clearing House Association, and VisaNet ACH) account for 20 percent of all ACH transactions in the United States while the Fed controls the rest. After a quarter of a century in existence, ACH transactions have become entrenched in a variety of payment arrangements, especially direct deposit of salaries and government benefits into the checking or savings accounts of individuals. Three-quarters of America's retirees receive their Social Security benefits that way, and half the US workforce gets paid through automatic payroll deposit in the employee's bank account. ACH networks make it easy for consumers to pay automatically recurrent mortgage and utility bills while businesses use ACHs to pay suppliers, contractors, or the government (for example taxes). Even the US Treasury sends most of its payments nowadays via ACHs. Given these widespread uses, ACH networks in the United States are (directly or indirectly) used by nearly half of all Americans, over 2 million businesses, and 20,000 financial institutions.

The arrival of the internet promises to boost the volume of ACH transfers, thanks to two innovations. The first is known as *check conversion* whereby a paper check is converted into an ACH transaction at the moment of payment so that a paper check never enters the system. Several web sites have recently begun to offer online check conversion services for e-commerce payments where the customer first provides check information after which the amount in question gets routed through the ACH network. The second innovation is *electronic bill presentment and payment* (EBPP) which enables utility companies, merchants and financial institutions to use the internet for transmitting bills and account statements to customers and receiving payments and remittance information from those customers in return. EBPPs are processed by ACH networks whereby they can be automatically debited from a customer's checking account or posted to a credit-card account. This technology promises to cut the average handling cost of $1.20 per bill sent by mail to $0.32, saving US businesses $20 billion per year.[5]

Spurred on by the growing use of computer and communication technologies, banks have brought us to the threshold of electronic money. Their efforts to automate fund transfers have penetrated our payment system and so prepared us for the introduction of cybercash. Cash has been transformed by ATMs which in turn have given rise to debit cards and POS terminals. Checks are in the process of being converted from paper into electronic format. As e-checks, they may evolve into an early version of cybercash capable of mass use. The widespread use of credit cards and debit cards has habituated the public to 'plastic money' to a point where a majority may be ready to accept so-called *smart cards*. Equipped with microprocessors and capable of network connectivity, such smart cards may soon become a key component of cybercash (see Chapter 5 for more). Electronic fund transfers already dominate the world of wholesale banking, notably wire transfers and ACH networks. The internet promises to extend the use of ACH fund-transfer technology from wholesale banking to the mass market of retail banking, coupled with the diffusion of electronic billing. All these innovations in the direction of automating our payments system have created a socio-technological infrastructure for a computer-based money form capable of replacing paper money, be it cash or checks.

1.2 Defining Cybercash

While electronic money ('e-money') is a broader concept referring to all computer-based fund-transfer mechanisms (for instance credit or debit cards, ACHs) and their access hardware (for example ATMs, POS terminals), cybercash is a more narrowly focused term applying to all fund-transfer systems routed through the internet. The delineation between these two overlapping characterizations of the new money form is fluid. It is hard to distinguish clearly between 'electronic money' and 'cybercash', because the former has set the stage for the latter and is now gradually merging into it. Those omnipresent plastic cards, for instance, will soon be turned into smart cards which can be connected with any access ramp to the internet, whether personal computers (PCs), cell phones, or personal digital assistants (PDAs). Paper checks can now be spared their costly and circuitous route through the Fed's traditional check-clearing process by being presented electronically and transferred over the internet. ACH-based transactions too will be conducted increasingly online, especially once electronic billing has taken hold among businesses and households.

Official definitions, provided by the world's leading central banks grouped together in the Bank for International Settlements (BIS) as their umbrella organization, ignore the distinction between 'electronic money' and 'cybercash' altogether. They only refer to the former, never to the latter. Dating to 1996–97 (Bank for International Settlements, 1996a; Group of Ten, 1997), these BIS definitions capture more than a decade of efforts by banks to automate their payment services through a variety of proprietary computer and communication networks. But these definitions came too early to reflect the emergence of cybercash as the next stage in the evolution of electronic money. The internet provides a centralized and global network which will eventually absorb and/or replace all the autonomous fund-transfer networks set up by banks during the first phase of money automation. E-money is about to be turned into cybercash.

Any technology-driven and innovation-rich object, such as electronic money or for that matter cybercash, is inherently difficult to define. You are faced with the problem of having to describe a dynamic phenomenon within a comparatively static framework. This dilemma is clearly evident in the official central bank definitions of electronic money supplied by the BIS. Those definitions always refer to three specific e-money variants which at the time had already emerged as coexisting alternatives, but which also represent different stages in the leap from electronic money to cybercash.

- The first and least advanced form of e-money is referred to as *access products* (Bank for International Settlements, 1996b, pp. 3–4). These are electronic means of communication, such as computers, which enable consumers to access otherwise conventional payments services. Credit-card payments on the internet would fall in that category, as would most online banking activities. Check conversion, which replaces paper checks with ACH transfers, would also qualify.

- The second type of electronic money consists of 'stored-value' cards with which to execute payments via POS terminals, through devices that are directly connected to each other, or over open communication networks such as the internet. Such prepaid cards, which sometimes are also referred to as *electronic purses*, store value inasmuch as they contain a record of spendable funds in the card-holder's possession. This type of electronic money involves hardware, specifically the cards and connection devices (for example POS terminals, card readers attached to PCs). The cards themselves may be equipped with a magnetic stripe, but will increasingly have a computer chip embedded in them instead. Endowed with greater technological capabilities, such smart cards are multi-functional and may offer a variety of services other than payments, such as personal identification or storage of medical information.[6]

- The third type of electronic money included in the BIS definitions of 1996–97 was at the time the least developed, but has the greatest potential to become the foundation for cybercash in the future. We are talking here about stored-value devices that operate via software installed on computers. Such software-based e-money products, also called 'digital cash', are typically designed to make payments through networks of interconnected computers, notably the internet. While software-based e-money does not involve the kind of hardware associated with card-based e-money and thus may be less costly to set up, it requires the distribution of software to consumers and/or merchants who will have to install it on their computers.

The complex technology underlying electronic money produces additional distinctions between its different variants. Some e-money systems may be balance-based, involving devices which manipulate a numeric ledger so that transactions can be booked as credits or debits to a balance. In contrast, other e-money systems employ devices which store electronic 'notes', sometimes referred to as digital coins or tokens. These notes come in fixed denominations and are identified by a unique serial number. In such note-based systems payments are made by transferring notes from the payor's device to the payee's device, and the balance consists of the sum total of notes accumulated in the user's device. We can further distinguish e-money variants on the basis of whether they are created by a single issuer or multiple issuers, whether they can be transferred directly between interacting parties or involve a third party, what kind of clearing and settlement procedure they follow, whether they require online authorization by a third party or not, and so forth.[7]

The technologically dynamic nature of cybercash is bound to render the already dated official definitions of e-money increasingly obsolete. Even after five years of rapid innovation we are still at the very beginning of the phenomenon (see Chapter 5). As we project forward the life cycle of cybercash beyond its current birth phase, we have to assume that major technological and organizational improvements have yet to occur. Smart cards will one day be very smart indeed, combining a multitude of applications which will turn this wallet-sized piece of chip-embedded plastic into an indispensable link to the outside world for its holders. No longer dependent on connectivity devices, these cards will be activated and operate on their own. They will identify users with the touch of a finger and store as well as process an amazing amount of information. Who knows what kind of financial services these cards will be able to offer in, say, ten years? Moreover, once money becomes software, the monetary process can be organized in entirely new and varied ways. The technological possibilities for the infrastructure of online-payment platforms and digital-money circulation are numerous, hence not fully predictable. We may have a considerable number of limited-circulation cybercash systems, each specifically designed for a particular online market or activity. At the same time we may also have a globally centralized payments system anchored in the internet in which money flows across a (cyber)world without borders at the speed of light. How this combination of centrifugal and centripetal forces underlying cybercash will be managed is a question worth pondering (see Chapter 6).

A first step towards addressing this question involves asking ourselves how such cybercash will be created. The official central bank definitions are of little help here. By defining electronic money solely in terms of stored-value devices, the monetary authorities represented by the BIS side-step this question altogether. The notion of storing value implies loading the e-money device with already existing funds that can be drawn from checking accounts, credit-card accounts, or other supplies of liquid funds. No new money is created in the process. Of course, the storage of value also implies that any e-money accumulating in the card-based or software-based device can be spent again without prior reconversion into physical cash, thereby assuring an autonomous circulation of e-money within its network sphere largely separated from the off-line circulation of paper money. Since all modern money forms are created in acts of credit extension (see section 1.4 below for more), we can imagine the BIS definition of e-money even allowing for the possibility that the value stored on the chip-embedded card or in digital cash was advanced as a loan by an online lender and thus represents newly created money. More difficult to foresee are other mechanisms by which the transfer of digital tokens from issuer to user gives rise to new e-money being created. For instance, new tokens may be offered as a gift or as a reward for specific activities undertaken online by the targeted recipient which are designed to enhance the revenues of the issuer or its network partners. Cybercash could thus become a terrific marketing tool promoting sales, brand recognition and customer loyalty while turning consumption-related activities from pursuit of leisure into paid 'e-work'.

Far from being just an auxiliary medium of exchange or electronic access device for traditional payment mechanisms (such as checks or credit cards) as implied by the BIS definitions of e-money, cybercash may evolve into an independent and fully fledged money form that is radically different from any type of money we have known so far. This qualitatively new money form will in turn open up new ways to organize exchange, production and credit through the internet as locus of economic activity. Money is central to our cash-flow economy, and each specific money form will create its own unique conditions for the activities underlying those cash flows. An economy dominated by cybercash can be expected to behave quite differently from an economy based on paper money. That argument necessitates some clarification of money's role in advanced capitalist economies such as ours.

1.3 Money as Social Institution

Before plunging into the complexities of cybercash, let us digress briefly into a discussion of the meaning of money to contextualize the coming era of electronic money. My overriding argument guiding the entire book, which I will try to substantiate in the remainder of this chapter, is the idea that changes in the form of money reverberate through the entire economic system and are capable of transforming markets, industry and finance. This vision of money's multi-faceted impact derives from a theoretical framework which explores this phenomenon more broadly and in more interdisciplinary fashion than is customary among my colleagues in the economics profession.

Economists offer only limited help in clarifying our understanding of money. Most of them analyze money as just another good, albeit one endowed with unique demand and supply functions. Alternatively, ever since Keynes (1936), some economists have viewed money as a financial asset which offers its owners liquidity and competes with other, less liquid financial assets, notably bonds.[8] While these two standard views of money contain some important differences in modeling and policy implications, they are similar in that they both treat money as an exogenous variable which exists alongside the rest of the economy. From this perspective, the key problem is how much money is needed to sustain a given level of economic activity. Neither the modalities of money's integration into the economy nor the form of money are considered important issues worthy of closer examination. Yet these are precisely the questions which gain a certain relevance with the imminent arrival of cybercash, a new form of digital money circulating on the internet which, over the next decade, may very well come to rival the coins, paper notes, checks, plastic cards and automated (wire or electronic) fund transfers we use today when making a payment.

The questions we are interested in, namely how money gets integrated into our economy and why its form matters in that context, demand a different theoretical approach. In that alternative, money is best defined as a man-made *social institution* at the center of our cash-flow economy. Money occupies this strategic place, because all our principal economic activities – exchange, production, credit – are nowadays organized as monetary circuits:

■ Exchange today is almost exclusively monetary exchange, meaning the swap of a good or service for a certain amount of money fixed by its price. In such monetary exchange the seller earns the income which the buyer spends.

■ Production involves the buying of inputs, their combining in the production process for creation of output, and the selling of that output at a price exceeding costs. This activity necessitates the spending of money now – for purchases of inputs – in order to make more money later – from the sale of output.

■ Credit also involves cash outlays preceding hopefully larger cash inflows. In this activity, the lender first transfers funds to the borrower in exchange for an income-earning financial asset. Whether that claim is an IOU from a loan or a security such as a bond or an equity share, the lender will subsequently cash it in to augment his income in the form of interest, dividends, or capital gains.

These monetary circuits are interdependent. Exchange transactions in the form of purchases initiate both production and credit activities either one of which is ended by a reverse exchange transaction in the form of a sale. Production, which creates more value and new income, involves cash outflows preceding cash inflows and thus requires a good deal of credit to bridge this cash-flow gap. In turn, production supports credit by generating the profit from which interest, dividends and to a less direct extent also capital gains are subtracted. None of these financial income forms associated with credit would exist without the income creation from production.

That interdependence of all monetary circuits forces different actors into relating to each other as buyers and sellers, workers and managers, creditors and debtors. Money thus organizes our space in terms of different social relations which we engage in while carrying out our economic activities. That spatial interdependence of our cash-flow economy becomes brutally obvious when some circuits get disrupted (for instance producers failing to sell profitably). Such disruption spreads immediately to other circuits (for instance producers laying off workers or defaulting on their debts), with the potential for some serious declines in economic activity.

Money structures not only space, but also time. All investments aimed at the accumulation of capital, whether based in production or credit, follow a temporal sequence of cash flows. Cash outlays are required now in order to generate more cash inflows later. In the meantime our money invested as capital is at risk. Given the impossibility of knowing in advance what the future holds, all investors face radical uncertainty. They must anticipate without knowing for sure what to expect. Economic actors have tried to meet the challenge of managing time as a cash-flow gap in three ways. First, they try to transform inherently intangible and unmeasurable uncertainty into calculable risk on the basis of anticipating different scenarios and assigning probabilities to each. When investors evaluate investment projects, they estimate returns derived from the different scenarios and then discount those expected future cash (in)flows to their present value. The rate at which we typically discount future cash flows to their present value is the prevailing rate of interest adjusted for risk.[9] Second, economic actors enter into contracts with each other in which future cash-flow commitments are predetermined in amount and date. Such *forward-money contracts*, as insurance, pension plans, bonds, futures, even the wage fixed in advance in collective-bargaining agreements, facilitate planning for the future by making outcomes less uncertain and more calculable. Finally, the value of contracts in the marketplace gives actors a signal concerning the general consensus opinion about the future as it specifically pertains to the asset contracted. Based on our interpretation of such price signals we buy or sell and so participate in the formation of that consensus. By facing the future together and communicating our anticipations of it, we make it collectively easier for each of us individually to cope with the uncertainty.

This ability of money to structure our time and space by forcing us into interdependent circuits of exchange, production and credit will surely gain additional force when money has become electronic. Circulating on computer networks that span the planet, cybercash transcends physical space and national boundaries. As such it will inevitably become a major force in fostering globalization, allowing individuals to engage in exchange, production and credit relations with actors across the globe. Flowing with the speed of light by means of the latest communication technologies (for example fiber optics or broadband), cybercash also compresses real time to an instance of seconds and thus greatly accelerates the pace at which things get done in the pursuit of economic activity. The virtual world operates with lightning speed, but will be intertwined with the inert structures and well-anchored norms of our physical world and so depend on the latter's slower time rhythms.

What is it about money that makes all economic activities be organized as flows of money between actors and over time? Why, in the process, does it acquire this magical power which we chase after most of our lives? Money possesses these irresistible qualities because of its three functions:

1. As a *unit of account* money makes all marketable goods and services commensurable on the basis of a single price standard, the money price. We use money to measure value. In the process we acquire a profound knowledge of what a particular good or service should cost and where it fits in the hierarchy of values we have constructed for our world of products. Markets force us to generate this process of price formation together, in competition with each other and in our interactions as buyers and sellers. Changes in nominal (that is, money) prices and in relative prices within the hierarchy serve as signals around which we orient our actions.

2. As a *medium of exchange* money allows goods and services to change
    hands. We can buy anything we desire with the right amount of money.
    But before we are able to buy, we need to sell something we own to
    earn the money we wish to spend. Its medium-of-exchange function
    transforms money into the sole representative of income and subjects
    everyone to a monetary constraint: the need to sell before being able to
    buy. Our ability to earn income thus depends on someone else's will-
    ingness to spend his or her income on what we have to offer, a source
    of interdependence which binds all of us into an endless web of
    exchange relationships with each other.

3. As a *store of value* money is capable of maintaining its purchasing
    power over time. This ability to preserve value allows money to be
    mobilized for investments whose completion takes time. Production,
    which adds value and so creates new income, requires money to be
    invested in inputs (that is, labor, plant and equipment), these inputs to
    be transformed into output, and such output to be sold for more money
    than initially spent on the inputs. The whole process starts with money
    and ends with money, hopefully more of it. The same can be said for
    financial investments involving credit. Since money acts as a store of
    value, it can be saved for spending later. In the meantime these savings
    can be loaned out to someone else whose spending intentions exceed
    current income levels. For the privilege of giving such deficit-spending
    units income to spend before they have earned it, the lenders will
    require a portion of the borrowers' future income gains. Both produc-
    tion and credit start with an outlay of cash and end with an influx of
    cash, because money represents the most liquid form of capital. The
    accumulation of money as capital is the ultimate goal of all investors,
    be they producers or financiers.

Because of its functions money thus comes to represent three objects of
desire to which we all relate intimately – value, income and capital. It is
this triple representation which enables money to give all economic activities their unique character as cash flows. Therefore, it stands to reason that
the precise modalities of the monetary process – involving the creation of
money, its insertion into the circuits of economic activity and its circulation within those – will have a significant impact on how we determine
prices, earn and spend income, organize production and transform savings
into credit.

In the case of cybercash, for instance, this may mean that a lot more
products will be priced through online auctions involving competitive

bidding procedures, as the phenomenal success of eBay suggests. Objects, which up to now have never been put up for sale, may become marketable in the online world of cybercash. Profitable selling of second-hand goods, liquidation of surplus inventories and leasing of excess productive capacity may all be possible when you can reach millions of new potential customers thanks to the internet and provide them with immediate access to online funds. Online markets thus have the potential to widen the scope and increase the scale of exchange, transforming in the process many hitherto illiquid objects into tradeable assets. The use of the internet and cybercash in the automation of the production process will transform the producers' relationships with suppliers as well as customers, greatly enhance their product development capabilities, make it easier for firms to change their output mix on short notice, centralize cash management and streamline the flow of production. As producers integrate the internet evermore tightly into their operations, they will find it opening up new avenues of capital accumulation. I am thinking here in particular of various intangible forms of capital which in the future may well become decisive for the competitiveness of firms (see Chapter 7). For instance, in-house use of the internet, the so-called *intranet*, will allow firms to tap the knowledge base of their employees much more effectively than has been the case so far. Access to cybercash will facilitate the online-automation efforts of producers, especially in their interactions with suppliers, customers, employees and partners. Cybercash will also transform finance by creating many more credit channels and spawning a variety of new financial contracts which fund online activity.

1.4 The Dematerialization of Money

The long-term impact of cybercash promises to be far-reaching. This is true for any new money form. To the extent that new forms of money alter the monetary process of its creation, insertion and circulation, they will trigger corresponding changes in the organization of exchange, production and credit. Even a cursory look at the historic evolution of money, which as a social institution is evidently subject to ongoing change, will confirm this. In the fifteen millennia of its existence, money has undergone a variety of changes in form, and each change has brought about dramatic transformations in the ways humans organized their economy.

Agrarian money, which dominated the prehistoric period of early settlements, centered on a variety of commodities which communities deemed useful and trusted because of their relatively stable value – barley, wheat, salt (in great demand as a means to preserve food), oxen, animal hides and many more. The transformation of these commodities into a medium of exchange required a collectively elaborated consensus as to their usefulness and intrinsic value, which came about in routine activities of social interaction – exchange, religious ceremonies involving sacrifices, the transfer of dowries to seal marriages and the imposition of fines as punishment for crimes in lieu of taking revenge in kind.[10] To the extent that agrarian money helped to replace communal ownership of land with private property, it enabled land-owning individuals capable of producing the money-commodity to gain a huge advantage over those not able to do so. Their temptation to produce as much of the money-commodity as possible must have led regularly to excess supplies which raised prices and so undermined the public trust placed in that money form.

In the fourth millennium BC agrarian money forms began to be replaced by pieces of metal. Public trust in the ability of metal pieces to serve as a medium of exchange centered around their physical characteristics, in particular their shapes and their metallic content (that is, their 'weight'). These elements of trust could be ensured much better after the invention of coinage in the 8th century BC. Metal coins could be standardized quite effectively in terms of their shape and weight. Since the mining of metal concentrated control over the supply of money and weapons in the hands of those owning the mines, the introduction of metal money centralized political power. Throughout antiquity – from the Pharaohs of Egypt to the Caesars of Rome – dynastic rulers built thriving economies and large territorial empires on the promise to maintain the value of the metal money issued in their name.[11] But equally often their successors, driven by megalomania and forced by large debts, reneged on that promise and debased their coins. These rulers had much to gain from issuing coins whose intrinsic value was far below their face value, but did so at the expense of undermining the public's trust in coins of inferior quality. By the time of Rome's collapse in 476 AD, metal coins had been so eroded that it took almost a millennium for them to revive and begin penetrating a feudal economy which for centuries had been predominantly based on payments in kind from serf to landlord.

When precious metals made a comeback in the Middle Ages, their storage generated deposit receipts which soon began to circulate as a medium of exchange in lieu of the underlying precious metals ('specie') they represented. From then on any gold, silver, or bimetallic standard included a considerable amount of paper claims on specie reserves which complemented the rather inelastic supply of these precious metals. As goldsmiths transformed themselves into bankers, deposit receipts became bank notes. The coexistence of these two (metal and paper) money alternatives was regulated by the convertibility guarantee which enabled holders of notes to redeem them on demand for specie at banks. Realizing that such redemptions would only be a fraction of available specie reserves on any given day, banks began to issue paper notes in excess of their specie reserves. This practice of *fractional-reserve banking* proved very attractive, since it enabled banks to earn more interest income from loaning out new paper notes. But whenever overextended banks suffered from financial problems, a worried public would rush to redeem their notes before it was too late. Such panic runs, which might sink even relatively healthy banks, would shrink the inflated money supply back to its metallic core in the wake of recessionary adjustments following such banking crises. It was only in the late 17th and early 18th century that the public – first in Holland, then in Britain – began to accept de facto irredeemable notes without panic. In the meantime, governments too had begun to issue their own notes whose convertibility with gold or silver was occasionally suspended in the face of war-induced budget deficits. Inconvertible notes by government were prone to hyperinflation and usually suppressed after the war in favor of a return to the gold standard.

In the 19th century Britain's leadership led to an international gold standard in which pounds served as a substitute form of world money and Britain's capital exports enabled other countries to industrialize. Despite this and other innovations loosening the link between gold reserves and paper notes, the gold standard eventually collapsed in September 1931. Its demise in the midst of the Great Depression brought to an end a system which no longer met the needs of a modern industrial economy. Gold proved ultimately too inelastic a commodity to support expanding volumes of production and trade. Scarce supplies of gold constituted a 'metallic barrier' to growth. Attempts to use paper-money substitutes invited recurrent banking crises when their convertibility with gold came to be doubted by the public. In those crises the gold standard left little discretion for governments to intervene, since it obliged them to keep their budget balanced and restricted their ability to inject new funds. Moreover, the specie-flow adjustment mechanism, which regulated the world economy through flows of gold reserves from countries with balance-of-payments deficits to countries with external surpluses, became over time less effective and more burdensome.[12]

The collapse of the gold standard necessitated far-reaching reforms to put in place a more effective replacement. Such monetary reform was first undertaken in the United States during Roosevelt's New Deal with the

Emergency Banking Act of 1933, Glass-Steagall Act of 1933, Securities Act of 1933, Securities Exchange Act of 1934, Gold Reserve Act of 1934, and Bank Act of 1935. It was then given an international extension with the Bretton Woods Conference of 1944 and adopted after the war by other industrial nations. Those initiatives marked the transition from commodity-money, where money was represented by a commodity such as gold, to *credit-money* in the form of bank checks and central bank notes created in acts of credit extension.[13]

How does this link between money creation and credit extension work? Whenever commercial banks take deposits, they gain an equivalent sum in reserves, a small portion of which is set aside to meet withdrawals. The rest, constituting so-called *excess reserves*, can be loaned out. Such loans take the form of an empty book of checks which the borrower is authorized to use for payments up to the amount of the loaned principal. This empty book of checks constitutes new money. The decommodification of money in the 1930s, surely one of the most important moments in its historic evolution, has thus turned money into something quite different – a credit relation. The central bank manages this new type of (credit-) money by manipulating the amount of excess reserves available to banks for lending. For that purpose it uses such monetary-policy tools as discount loans, open-market operations and reserve requirements. In addition, the central bank also backs private bank money by guaranteeing its automatic convertibility with central bank notes and by assisting its issuers when in crisis.

Roosevelt's monetary reforms stripped money of any intrinsic value and turned it into mere paper tokens which are nothing but a promise to pay. The public is willing to accept such pieces of paper as money, because it trusts their issuers, the banks, and the government guarantee backing those tokens. The insertion of new tokens into our cash-flow economy gets accomplished through a loan which transfers them from their issuer to users in whose hands they become money when the loan gets spent. This transfer mechanism ensures an *elastic* supply of money responding more or less automatically to the public's needs for liquidity. Whenever an actor wants to spend in excess of current income and manages to qualify for a bank loan, new money is made available by the banking system in support of that loan. Profit-seeking commercial banks obviously have an interest in making those loans, since such a transformation of their zero-yield excess reserves into interest-yielding loan assets earns them profit.

Tied to credit extension, money creation effectively monetizes a portion of new debt and in this way makes debt-financing less onerous. A capitalist economy necessarily encounters cash-flow gaps which need to be bridged by external funding. After all, its growth rests on investments, an activity involving cash outlays now in order to earn more money later. Such investment-related cash-flow gaps could henceforth be covered by automatic liquidity injections, with banks extending credit and thereby validating the future income-creating activities of their borrowers.[14] Roosevelt's monetary reforms thus gave us what Hicks (1974) characterized as an 'overdraft economy', in effect a *debt economy* propelled forward by continuous debt-financing of excess spending and its partial monetization through automatic liquidity injections by banks.

The debt economy made possible by the introduction of credit-money played a crucial role in the postwar boom of the 1950s and 60s:

- For one, it greatly facilitated large-scale investment projects associated with mass production technology (that is, assembly-line plants) by funding them amply at low-interest rates. In that sense the new monetary regime provided institutional support for a technological revolution in production which had begun decades earlier when the spread of electricity transformed the way we produced manufactured goods.[15]

- Consumers finally gained broad access to bank credit in the form of mortgages, car loans, student loans, personal loans and credit cards. Such debt-financed consumer spending provided the needed impetus for rapidly growing consumption centered on purchases of homes, cars and other large-ticket consumer goods which provided adequate aggregate-demand support for the much enhanced supply capacity of mass production technology.

- Being able to spread their considerable fixed costs ('overheads') over large production volumes, industrial enterprises enjoyed unit-cost reductions with growing output – a type of productivity gain known as *economies of scale*. But instead of being forced to match the value reductions from such productivity gains with price reductions enforced by overproduction conditions as happened recurrently in the era of commodity-money, elastic supplies of credit-money put companies in a position to resist such downward pressure on prices and instead use the productivity gains for increases in real wages. This change created a more stable balance between aggregate demand and supply in the economy which ultimately helped to sustain corporate profits more effectively.

- Moreover, in the postwar regime of credit-money governments found it much easier to finance budget deficits, even chronic ones. Such enhanced capacity for deficit spending enabled states to transform themselves into a Keynesian-type 'welfare state', redistributing income from rich to poor and offering a variety of income-maintenance programs (for example Social Security, unemployment compensation) to maintain aggregate demand.

■ Finally, in the international arena, the Bretton Woods system supplied the world economy with ample supplies of dollars via large-scale US capital exports through aid and assistance programs such as the Marshall Plan for Europe's reconstruction, massive US military outlays overseas in the context of the Cold War and rapidly increasing investment activity by US multinationals abroad. Thus within a decade, the dollar shortage of the immediate postwar years was turned into a dollar glut, a process facilitating the liberalization of international trade and the catching-up process of other industrialized nations (notably Japan and Germany) after the war.

1.5 The Dual Nature of Money

The introduction of credit-money marked a milestone in the historic development of capitalism, giving that system an elastic currency to accommodate its growth dynamic much more effectively. This advantage becomes especially evident when looking at the conditions of its general acceptability. Rather than deriving its status as money from its intrinsic value as a commodity (first agrarian, then metal), credit-money involves pieces of paper with promises to pay which a third party, a bank, will comply with as an order. The public accepts these promises, because it trusts the banks to honor them. If any commercial bank ever reneges on the promise and fails to pay, then it will be the central bank which assumes that responsibility.

This triangular arrangement, where a payment obligation of buyer to seller becomes a debt relation between their respective banks settled by the central bank or any other clearing-house arrangement, has made money more trustworthy than it was when still represented by a commodity. With a few exceptional situations of hyperinflation ravaging a nation's economy, the public has come to trust bank checks and central bank notes to such an extent that their presumed validity is taken for granted. Of course, money works best when anchored in automaticity. It is precisely when we do not have to ask ourselves where money comes from, how it circulates and who guarantees it that it has a chance to operate smoothly.

The moment we are forced to wonder about these questions because of unforeseen circumstances, our confidence in whatever money form is currently prevailing will erode. Without that public trust no money can function effectively. Of course, history is replete with examples where monetary instability (hyperinflation, for instance) or financial crisis (such as widespread bank failures shrinking the supply of private bank money) undermined this presumed automaticity or where a degraded money form had to be replaced by a better alternative.

The many instances of monetary instability are an indication that the insertion of money into our cash-flow economy is perhaps more problematic and less automatic than we presume. This is indeed the case. When analyzing money as a social institution, we are inevitably struck by two different aspects of money which may be incompatible with each other. On the one hand, money serves as a *public good* inasmuch as its proper functioning – in terms of the modalities of its creation, its smooth circulation and its stable valuation – yields such large social benefits that you would not want anyone to be deprived of those. It is precisely this quality of money as a public good benefiting us all which justifies the public trust and consensus of general acceptability vested in it. On the other hand, money may also contain elements of a *private commodity* to the extent that it gets created by agents seeking to benefit individually from that privilege.

This dual nature of money is contradictory to the extent that the private-commodity aspects of money, if allowed to manifest themselves unimpeded, may very well engender consequences which undermine the public-good qualities of money. There are at least three such troubling consequences rooted in the private-commodity nature of money:

1. If some market agents were empowered to create money and thereby were in a position to finance their spending with new money, they would gain a decisive advantage over all those market agents unable to do same. Today we have resolved this equal-access problem by locating the creation of money outside the marketplace, in the banking system. Banks issue mere tokens (for example an empty book of checks) and then transfer those via credit to borrowers in whose hands the tokens become money as soon as the loan gets spent on goods, services, or assets.[16] We still have a financial-exclusion problem violating the equal-access requirement of money as a public good. Banks continue to deny credit to many businesses considered less creditworthy, particularly the smaller and/or newer ones, while also depriving the poor of access to checking accounts.

2. Another destabilizing consequence of money's private-commodity dimension is the tendency for banks to overextend credit during boom periods in pursuit of greater income and then cut back lending sharply amidst the first troubling signs of overextension, such as in response to sudden defaults. This boom-bust pattern of bank lending gives rise to a markedly procyclical money supply which reinforces the business-cycle dynamic of ups and downs in our economy. Moreover, the propensity of credit overextension engenders recurrent financial crises which, if left unchecked, have the potential for serious disruption of economic activity.

3. Finally, the private-commodity aspect of money also manifests itself in the fact that in the hands of private issuers, competing with each other for market share and motivated by profit, money itself becomes an object of innovation and product development. Modern money is essentially a matter of contractual arrangements by banks on the liability side (deposits) and asset side (loans). Monetary innovation mostly involves changes in those contractual arrangements and is therefore implemented much more easily than innovation in industry aimed at altering tangible products or developing new ones from scratch. Compared to industrial research and development, monetary innovation involves few sunk costs and is less confined by physical limits. Such activity aims not only to lower transaction costs and facilitate exchange, sine qua non conditions for public acceptance without which no monetary innovation can succeed, but also to increase the money-creating capacity of banks seeking to earn more income this way.

To the extent that these private-commodity dimensions of money all threaten its public-good quality, they have to be kept in check. Otherwise money does not operate efficiently and undermines the stability of the economy. For centuries the dualistic nature of money was managed by its linkage to precious metals which regulated the supply of money and its insertion into the economy. After 1931 the ruthless discipline of gold gave way to a more flexible management of (paper) money by the state as the only nonmarket agent capable of counteracting market forces. The state's monetary authority, typically a central bank, was authorized to manage money's public-good quality with a combination of monetary-policy tools manipulating the money-creation ability of banks, financial regulations designed to affect the structure and behavior of banks, lender-of-last-resort mechanisms to counteract financial crises and international monetary arrangements which guide the participation of the national economy in the world economy.

1.6 The Emergence of Cybercash

Credit-money in the form of paper tokens, surely one of the great achieve-
ments of the New Deal, is now being gradually transformed into electronic
money. In the 1980s, banks began to experiment with emerging computer
and communication technologies to benefit from the technological revolution under way. Computerized payments systems, run by consortia of
commercial banks, could move money transfers beyond the reach of
central banks and so undermine their control over the monetary process.
Large-volume transfers between businesses were automated through a
network of bank-operated automated clearing-houses and electronic fund-
transfer technology. The banks also tried to push the electronic revolution
into retail banking by getting households accustomed to using automated
teller machines, paying with plastic (debit or credit) cards and conducting
their banking transactions at home on the computer.

The accelerating efforts by banks to develop electronic alternatives to
paper money are not just motivated by the desire to take advantage of
technological progress. They are also caused by the steady erosion of the
postwar regime of state-administered credit-money. In the next chapter we
will see how a new type of crisis, the stagflation of the 1970s and early
1980s, disintegrated that regime step by step. This process unleashed new
forces – notably the deregulation of money, the securitization of credit and
the computerization of finance – which prompted banks to invest much
more heavily in electronic money and banking.

Electronic money will soon experience an important push forward
through its applications on the internet. In Chapter 3 we will see how this
new medium of communication is transforming itself into a locus of
economic activity which demands access to online-payment facilities. E-
commerce on the internet drives electronic money towards cybercash. This
imminent development in the history of money will give us an entirely
new type of money, one even more immaterial than paper. Its intangibility
as something existing only virtually, as a flow of data over computer
networks, will shift the emphasis of public trust from confidence in banks
as third-party intermediaries making good on the promise to pay to the
technology of fund transfers and nonbank players getting involved in the
monetary process.

CHAPTER 2

The Monetary Regime in Transition

In the preceding chapter we made reference to the notion of monetary regimes. This concept describes an amalgam of institutional arrangements pertaining to the prevailing forms of money, the modalities of their coexistence and the management of their use. Not only can forms of money change, but so can the monetary regimes guiding their creation and circulation. When new money types emerge, they may prompt changes in the monetary regime to accommodate their presence. We have seen that happen with the transition from agrarian money to metal money over five millennia ago, during centuries of coexistence between metal coins and bank notes from the early Middle Ages to the British-led gold-exchange standard of the 19th century, and then again with the creation of a new regime centered on state-administered paper money following the collapse of the gold standard in the 1930s. Today we face yet another change in the monetary regime brought about by a new money form, in this case electronic money. Completing the trend towards the dematerialization of money, we have finally arrived at a point where money is nothing but a flow of data between interconnected computers. Such virtual money renders obsolete any regime designed for paper money and will therefore bring about major changes in the way we manage the monetary process.

That kind of change is gradual in nature. Prone to develop life-long routines in matters of money, people are highly resistant to any change in money form and payment habit. With so much public trust and habituation vested in the status quo, new money alternatives only have a chance to rise to the fore if hitherto prevailing money representatives have become burdensome or proven unreliable. Such is the case today. The postwar regime of state-administered credit-money, once a pillar for global expansion, experienced a structural crisis during the 1970s and early 1980s which tore apart its key components one after another (section 2.1). This piecemeal disintegration coincided with the deregulation of money (section 2.2) and triggered a financial revolution nourished by securitization of credit (section 2.3) and computerization of finance (section 2.4). These three structural changes in our credit system have prompted banks to reorganize and in the process bring us to the threshold of electronic money (section 2.5).

2.1 Stagflation Crisis

Most economists link the end of the unprecedented postwar boom to OPEC's oil-price hike in October 1973. I suspect that the boom had ended quite a bit earlier, with a steep decline in corporate profitability and rising inflation pressures during the second half of the 1960s. This sudden reversal in the fortunes of US industry can be explained by a variety of new constraints, be they saturation of demand in key 'growth' industries (for instance cars), a breakdown in the balance between wage increases and productivity gains, or intensifying competition from European and Japanese manufacturers.[1] Whatever its causes, the end of the boom was masked for several years by increased borrowing activity which helped to maintain aggregate spending levels even though income levels had begun to stagnate or even decline (see Figure 2.1).

This initial response set the pattern for the subsequent structural crisis. Central bank commitment to low-interest rates gave borrowers access to fairly cheap bank credit which they actively used to forestall any squeeze on spending in the face of stagnant income. US banks satisfied the increase in domestic credit demand not least by relying more and more on new money-market instruments, so-called *borrowed liabilities*, which allowed them to fund lending (and money-creation) activity beyond the confines of Fed-controlled deposit liabilities.[2] In the process the pace of money creation accelerated, providing a buffer against cumulative declines in incomes and spending. The movement away from inelastic commodity-money to elastic credit-money thus contributed to a fundamental change in the dynamics of a structural crisis. Whereas in the era of the gold standard we saw recurrent debt-deflation adjustments to overextension pushing us into depression (as described in Fisher, 1933), now we were spared such physical destruction of productive capital and mass unemployment of labor. In the regime of credit-money, banks provided an elastic currency to finance the budget deficits and private-sector borrowing needed to prevent aggregate demand from shrinking to the point of depression. What we got instead was long-term stagnation coupled with intensifying inflation, a

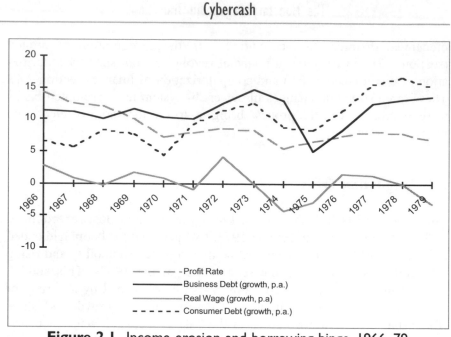

Figure 2.1 Income erosion and borrowing binge, 1966–79

Source: Grimm (1982, Table 2); Federal Reserve (2002a, Table L-1; 2002b,
Table L-1); Council of Academic Advisors (1990, Table C-44)

somewhat milder form of structural crisis running its course more gradually
(between 1969 and 1982). Such a *stagflation crisis* was more moderate than
depression by giving rise to rapid money creation in support of existing
spending levels. This process counteracted the physical destruction of
capital at the expense of a gradual devaluation of money, a process of debt
monetization which socialized (and thereby reduced) private risks and
losses by transferring them to everyone using the national currency.

Stagflation involved a dynamic of monetary accommodation to a debt-
inflation spiral. Once inflation became embedded in our minds, we would
foresee accelerating price increases and speed up planned purchases. Such
expectations of rising inflation would also prompt increased borrowing,
already fuelled by slowing income growth clashing with fairly rigid cash-
flow commitments. With interest rates generally lagging behind inflation,
the prospect of paying back the debt with devalued dollars proved quite
irresistible. Since increased debt also meant the faster growth of money
supply, expectations of rising inflation turned into a self-fulfilling prophecy.

Here we see paper money show its burdensome side. While it provides
us with a built-in safety net against the kind of depression we last experienced in the 1930s, any paper-money standard carries an inflationary bias.

And such inflation can become deeply embedded in the daily operations of a modern economy. This may be because an economy built on forward-money contracts can easily institutionalize the expectation of rising inflation (for instance cost-of-living adjustments in collective-bargaining agreements). Or it may be because an economy built on mass production technology carries a lot of fixed costs in the form of depreciation and debt-servicing charges which push up unit costs (that is, total production costs per unit of output) whenever output stagnates. Whatever the underlying source of inflationary pressures in a slow-growth economy, the debt-inflation spiral it sets off has two inevitable consequences – monetary instability and financial fragility.

As regards monetary instability, the inflationary pressures of the 1970s and early 1980s undermined the quality of paper money. Inflation, once allowed to intensify over time, eventually created a grave loss of public confidence in paper money that was continuously depreciating. Its ongoing degradation weakened each of its functions. Rapidly accelerating inflation made it impossible for money to serve as a reliable store of value and savings collapsed. Money's means-of-payment function also suffered as old debts got repaid with devalued dollars. Increasingly frequent price changes put stress on its unit-of-account function. In the end even its medium-of-exchange function came under threat, with people searching for more trustworthy money forms (for example the dollarization of hyper-inflation economies) or, in extreme cases, even reverting to barter.

As regards financial fragility, inflation fed credit demand while stagnation made debt-servicing more burdensome. Of course, in the early phase of the stagflation crisis, before 1974 and then again between 1977 and 1979, the growing burden of debt was masked by artificially low-interest rates and inflation-induced paper profits (from carrying assets on the books at historic costs). At some point, however, the level of leverage reached such proportions that highly indebted borrowers could meet their debt-servicing requirements only through additional borrowing. Such a vulnerable position sets the stage for acute financial crises (see Minsky, 1982). The true state of financial fragility in our stagflation-wrecked debt economy only became obvious in the final phase of that structural crisis, with the dramatic disinflation process of 1981–84 during which massive loan defaults in real estate, agriculture, energy and on sovereign loans to developing countries (especially Latin America) exploded into the face of overextended bankers.

The stagflation period of the 1970s and early 1980s actually saw a sequence of gradually intensifying financial crises, testimony to the growing stress in our credit system. These financial crises took the form of recurrent *credit crunches* near the cyclical peak when inflationary pressures, borrowing activity and the money supply were all rising rapidly. Whenever accelerating inflation pushed money-market rates above Fed-imposed rate-ceilings on bank deposits, customers would move funds out of banks into higher yielding money-market instruments (for example money-market funds). Such massive disintermediation of funds out of banks triggered typically a credit crunch which the Fed tended to reinforce through an anti-inflation policy of significant tightening. As the stagflation crisis unfolded, we witnessed recurrent credit crunches which became more serious with each cycle: 1966, 1969–70, 1973–75 and finally the climax during the double-dip downturn of 1979–82.[3] The Fed's price regulation in banking thus provided an automatic shutdown mechanism against inflationary overheating. Underlying the disintermediation of funds triggered by inflation rates exceeding low-interest-rate ceilings was a revolt of creditors against the declining quality of money and the losses imposed on them by negative 'real' (that is, inflation-adjusted) interest rates. Savers

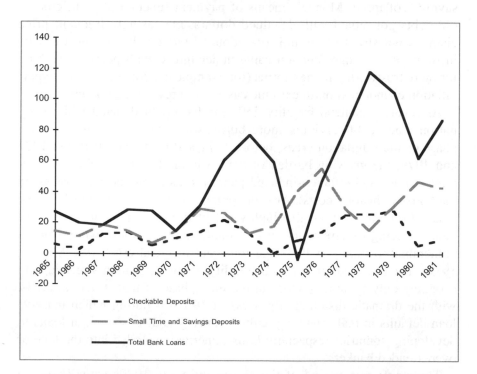

Figure 2.2 Credit crunches of US commercial banking, 1965–81

Source: Federal Reserve (2002a, Tables F-204, F-205, F-215; 2002b, Tables F-204, F-205, F-215)

refused to keep their money in low-yielding savings instruments, and bankers did not want to lend money at fixed rates so low that they would not even keep up with inflation (see Figure 2.2).

The sharply procyclical debt-inflation spiral described above tore the postwar regime of state-managed credit-money apart, bit by bit. Massive speculative attacks on the overvalued dollar forced the US government to suspend the gold convertibility of its currency on 15 August 1971.[4] The collapse of Bretton Woods was followed by an attempt to realign fixed-exchange rates no longer anchored in gold, the Smithsonian Agreement of December 1971. That agreement broke down amidst yet another major dollar crisis in March 1973 which ushered in the era of flexible-exchange rates. Once governments had lost control over exchange rates, it was only a question of time before they would experience the same fate with regard to interest rates – as Keynes (1936) had correctly predicted. In October 1979 the Fed abandoned its postwar policy of low-interest rates. Shortly thereafter rate-ceilings on bank deposits and loans were phased out. At the peak of the stagflation crisis, in the early 1980s, the US faced a serious banking crisis which forced significant extension of active lender-of-last-resort assistance both at home (with regard to banks specializing in farm loans, energy loans, or real-estate loans) as well as in the international arena after Mexico's quasi-default in August 1982.

2.2. The Deregulation of Paper Money

The key pillars of the postwar monetary regime, fixed-exchange rates and low-interest rates, depended on tight control over the money-creation process of private banks. For the central banks to exercise such control, they had to specify what type of money commercial banks could offer and then regulate the issue of that money. Since money creation was a major source of income for banks (in the form of interest income from loans generated in the process), they sought to escape this constraint. The means to do so was innovation, which in the case of money carries fewer sunk costs than industrial innovation involving tangible goods. Banks engaged in monetary innovation to evade central bank regulation and thereby use the space created for more income generation. That process was a fundamental aspect of the stagflation crisis, because it satisfied the increased demand for credit and the heightened need for debt monetization during that period.

As we have seen in our earlier discussion of stagflation, banks began to experiment with monetary innovation early on. In the early 1960s, they

introduced a variety of 'borrowed liabilities', such as federal funds, repur-
chase agreements, negotiable certificates of deposit and commercial paper.
Access to these money-market instruments enabled banks to fund their
lending (and money-creation) activity beyond their deposit base controlled
by the central bank. At the same time banks introduced the eurocurrency
market, a global private banking network offering deposits and loans in
any currency outside the country of its issue and thus beyond the regulatory reach of any nation-state.[5] The transnational banks operating in the
euromarket set up their own payments system, an interbank network for
electronic fund transfers known as SWIFT (Society for Worldwide Interbank Financial Telecommunications), to escape the reach of any central
bank. SWIFT, which is owned and controlled by the banks using it, is
basically a communication network which handles the electronic mail
containing the instructions for money transfers and other account-
settlement procedures between banks. It is used by more than 7000 banks
in 192 countries.

Representing a highly privatized form of bank money, eurocurrencies
can be expected to tilt the balance between money's public-good aspect
and its private-commodity nature toward the latter. In the four decades of
its existence, the eurocurrency market has indeed nourished all the private-
commodity aspects of money discussed in the previous chapter (see
section 1.5). Access to this market is confined to the world's leading banks
and corporations, the wealthy and states deemed sufficiently creditworthy
by the international financial community. Everyone else is excluded from
this vital source of global capital, and this exclusion has contributed to the
growing gap between the 'haves' and 'have nots' in the world economy. As
a global engine of liquidity creation and debt-financing, the euromarket
has also shown itself prone to overextension of credit. This tendency manifested itself most dramatically in the global debt crisis of developing countries during the 1980s. Finally, the euromarket has been a powerful
incubator of regulation-evading innovation by banks. Able to offer
competitive deposit and lending terms in the absence of regulatory restrictions, the unregulated euromarket has played a major role in the circumvention of domestic bank regulations and so rendered those increasingly
ineffective.[6]

For three decades now we have seen the eurocurrency market function
as the engine for the mushroom-like multiplication of short-term capital
flows in and out of currencies and countries. Connected through the euromarket, the world's leading multinational corporations (MNCs) and
transnational banks (TNBs) constantly communicate information about the
status of different currencies. When such collectively formed expectations

about a particular currency become sufficiently homogenized, these actors can easily launch massive attacks against the suspect currency and so turn their widely shared expectations into a self-fulfilling prophecy. In the late 1960s, the euromarket had evolved into a devastatingly efficient network for speculative attacks on the dollar and other overvalued currencies. It was ultimately the collection of players operating in the euromarket whose concerted and repeated runs out of the dollar forced Nixon's suspension of dollar-gold convertibility on 15 August 1971, the beginning of the end for the postwar monetary regime.

When the system of fixed-exchange rates broke down in the early 1970s, most economists and politicians hoped that the advent of flexible-exchange rates would remove external imbalances more rapidly while allowing central banks to focus their monetary policy on domestic conditions rather than defending fixed-exchange rates. But the reality turned out to be quite different. While giving the world economy much needed flexibility to absorb exogenous shocks (as in the case of OPEC's oil-price hikes), market-determined exchange rates have also turned currencies into an irresistible object of speculation. Widespread currency speculation has in turn fed trading volumes in the foreign-exchange market, the world's largest market, where national currencies are nowadays traded in massive quantities like commodities for short-term capital gains (or avoidance of capital losses).[7] This huge market operates with its own private payments system, known as CHIPS (clearing house interbank payments system) and based in New York, which is seamlessly connected to both the euromarket's SWIFT and the Fed's domestic payments systems (for example Fedwire).

Currency speculation, which has become a major profit center of transnational banks and multinational corporations, has proven fairly disruptive.[8] This activity has contributed to a great deal of currency-price volatility which disrupts trade patterns, increases transaction costs (because of the need for hedging) and exacerbates price risk to the detriment of long-term investments. Once speculative anticipations concerning an apparently overvalued currency have homogenized sufficiently to trigger a sell-off of that currency, the quantities of funds mobilized in such an attack have usually far outweighed the relatively meager foreign-exchange resources of central banks. While speculators do force exchange rates to realign in the desired direction, they overdo such readjustments. A currency, which may need a devaluation of, say, 20 percent, can easily lose 50 percent in the wake of such a concerted attack. The overshooting tendency is unfortunately reinforced by the perverse *J-curve effect* whereby currency devaluations at first increase a country's trade deficit (rather than reduce it) and so induce further sell-off pressures.[9]

Given the prevalence of speculation in currency markets, the regime of flexible-exchange rates has also subjected governments to the cold logic of the marketplace where bets are placed on currencies, thus on entire countries and their governments issuing that money, as if they were chips placed on a casino table. Policies opposed by currency traders get punished through orchestrated sell-offs of the currency in question. No government, not even the American (as Carter found out in 1978–79), can pursue a macroeconomic policy course which runs against the consensus of currency traders. During the first decade of the flexible-rate regime (1973–83), a number of governments tried to ignore this new reality and pursued competitive devaluation strategies as a form of monetary protectionism favoring domestic industry. But these governments found out painfully that such a 'soft money' strategy would leave them exposed to excessive devaluations, in the end causing higher inflation and interest rates than a 'hard money' strategy would have. Since March 1983, when France's Mitterand was forced into a 180-degree reversal of his stimulative policies by a massive attack on the franc, no major industrial nation has dared to ignore pressure from the foreign-exchange markets in favor of high-interest rates, lower budget deficits, deregulation of business, opening up of domestic markets for foreign goods or capital, and privatization of state-run enterprises. While this fact may be desirable in light of the conservative policies such a market constraint has imposed on every government in the world, try and tell that to the millions of long-term unemployed in Europe or the suddenly impoverished populations of Asia!

Once exchange rates had moved beyond the control of governments, it became much more difficult for central banks to maintain control over interest rates. If interest rates were too low, the currency would come under attack and so force such rates higher. In October 1979, amidst rapidly accelerating inflation and an intense year-long attack on the dollar, the Fed finally ended its postwar policy of keeping interest rates low. The abandonment of the Fed's low-interest policy was followed by the systematic abolition of interest-rate ceilings on bank deposits and consumer loans in the Depository Institutions Deregulation and Monetary Control Act (DIDMCA) of 1980 and the Depository Institutions Act (DIA) of 1982. In the aftermath of this deregulation, the banks introduced a whole new generation of interest-bearing checking deposits (for instance, NOW accounts, SuperNOW accounts) and savings deposits offering unregulated money-market yields (for instance money-market deposit accounts, consumer CDs).

Facing greater variability of interest costs on their liability side thanks to fluctuating deposit rates, the banks have tried to avoid fixed-rate loans on the asset side in favor of expanding their portfolio of adjustable-rate loans. This move to a variable-rate regime has had major repercussions for our credit system. On the plus side, banks no longer face the kind of disintermediation they experienced regularly when their deposit rates were controlled by the government. They can now bid for funds as long as they want to, provided they are willing to pay higher rates. By practicing cartel-like adjustments in their loan rates, the banks have found it easier in their deregulated environment to maintain positive yield spreads between deposits and loans and so defend their profit margins. Since any change in loan rates applies immediately to old adjustable-rate loans as well, such price adjustments affect a lot more borrowers than under the previous regime of fixed rates. The Fed and other central banks have for this reason pursued a gradualist policy of incremental interest-rate changes since 1982.

On the negative side, the new regime of variable-rate deposits and loans has perhaps opened the door for ultimately worse overextension of credit, since the availability of bank funds continues much longer without hitting a limit as it used to when the Fed's deposit-rate ceilings fell below the prevailing inflation rate. Moreover, banks have to compete for deposits by bidding up rates. They are then forced to invest those costlier funds in higher yielding assets which offer promising returns only because they also carry greater risks. The resumption of price competition in banking (at least on the deposit side) has therefore engendered a bias in favor of greater risk-taking among banks, leading to much more frequent bank failures during the 1980s and a system-wide banking crisis in 1990–91.[10] Finally, it is also worth noting that the new generation of variable-rate deposits introduced by banks in the 1980s has made it much more difficult, if not impossible, for central banks to target their nation's money supply. These deposits combine both transaction and investment motives which renders their interest-rate elasticity more variable and their velocity quite unstable. Not surprisingly, the Fed and other central banks have in recent years focused on interest rates rather than the money supply in their conduct of monetary policy.

The new variable-rate regime has also given us much steeper inflation-adjusted interest rates since 1981 (see Figure 2.3) by allowing lenders to charge higher risk and inflation premia. Such high 'real' rates have had significant redistributive effects, shifting income shares from wages via

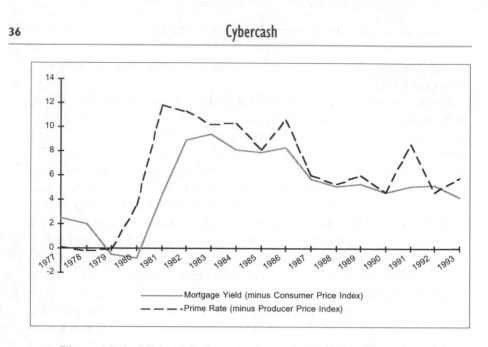

Figure 2.3 US real (inflation-adjusted) interest rates, 1977–93
Source: Council of Economic Advisors (2002)

industrial profit to interest income, with corporations squeezing labor to compensate for their greater interest burdens. Moreover, the prevailing interest rate defines the minimum rate of return required for investment projects to be considered profitable, and in the face of such elevated hurdle rates industry has invested more cautiously. High-interest rates also favor investments with a more rapid pay-off, a consideration which may help to explain why businesses have been willing to spend so heavily on information technology (IT), notably computer hardware and software. Both effects, high-hurdle rates and the bias in favor of the short term, are key factors behind the rapidly growing importance of financial portfolios among industrial enterprises which have found returns on financial assets often more appealing than on industrial assets. Since high-interest rates raise the opportunity costs of cash, firms have tried hard to make their cash-collection efforts more efficient and deploy the cash among higher yielding financial assets serving as liquid substitutes for cash.

Deregulation has made private bank money more expensive. The costs of bank funds, the raw material of money creation, have gone up amidst more intense price competition among banks on the deposit side. Those higher costs are then passed on to borrowers as banks reprice their adjustable-rate loans upwards whenever deposit rates rise. In addition, borrowers face much greater price risk from variable-rate loans than they used to when most of their loans still carried fixed rates. User costs associated with deregulated paper money have also gone up significantly during the last two decades. Ceilings on bank deposits had operated like a government subsidy to banks, giving those institutions cheap access to the nation's savings. Once these ceilings (set by the Fed under Regulation Q) had been phased out and banks had lost this hidden subsidy, they began to price the use of checks and other fund-transfer services explicitly, imposing a variety of service charges, user fees and minimum-balance requirements on the public to the chagrin of many.

It is this increasing social cost of private bank money in paper form which has opened the door for cheaper and more efficient money alternatives to emerge. Thanks to its progressive deregulation, paper-based credit-money has in recent years ended up imposing higher interest burdens, greater credit risk and substantial user fees on its users. In addition to these costs the very reliability of paper money has become questionable in the aftermath of the terrorist attacks on the United States during the fall of 2001. Facing first the shutdown of the entire domestic air traffic system ordered by the US government on 11 September 2001 and then anthrax-laced letters causing havoc with mail delivery, US corporations suddenly had to face the possibility that they would not be able to pay their bills or get paid on time. The traditional payment method of sending checks through the mail and using planes for their delivery suddenly looked vulnerable to massive disruption. The combination of terrorist attacks has dramatically accelerated efforts by suddenly security-minded corporate managers to develop online payment-and-billing facilities as a more reliable alternative to paper money.[11] As paper money becomes increasingly costly and risky, the search for a better money alternative in the form of cybercash intensifies.

Any such change in money form comes about only slowly, however, since the public gets very vested in whatever it has been using traditionally as money. In light of their deep roots, existing money forms do not get replaced easily. New money forms can only succeed if they manage to gain public acceptance because of obvious advantages in terms of convenience, safety, speed, anonymity, cost and trustworthiness. Still, those advantages are more readily acknowledged when the existing money form has begun to exhibit some obvious drawbacks, as has happened in recent years with paper money.

2.3. Securitization of Credit

The deregulation of private bank money in the wake of a disintegrating monetary regime has opened the door for the emergence of a new money form by increasing the social costs of paper money and spurring monetary innovation for a better alternative. At the same time the collapse of the postwar monetary regime has also given rise to broader structural changes in the credit system, a sort of financial revolution. These changes, specifically greater reliance on marketable securities (such as bonds, stocks) at the expense of loans as a primary credit channel and the growing penetration of information-processing technologies in financial markets and institutions, have provided additional impetus for the development of electronic money. Before discussing this new money form, it would behove us therefore to take a closer look at the securitization of credit and computerization of finance as key forces in its emergence.

Over the last fifteen years we have witnessed, first in the United States, then in other industrial nations, and now also across so-called emerging markets in Latin America, Eastern Europe and Pacific Asia, a fundamental change in the way credit is organized. The supply of external funds has increasingly moved away from bank loans to securities which are traded in financial markets (see Figure 2.4). While there have been many forces

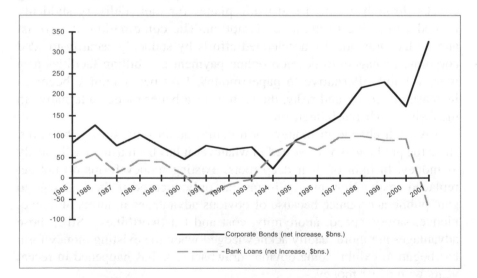

Figure 2.4 US corporate funding preferences

Source: Federal Reserve (2002c, Tables F-212, F-215; 2002d, Tables F-212, F-215).

behind this change, a key event boosting such securitization of credit was the resolution of the global debt crisis of developing countries in the late 1980s by transforming impaired loans into securities (for instance loan sales, debt-bond swaps, debt-equity swaps). Since then the securitization trend has accelerated. New debt instruments, such as commercial paper and junk bonds, have for the first time given many firms access to securities markets and reduced their traditional reliance on bank loans. Those securities markets have become much better organized thanks to greater volume and a vastly more efficient trading infrastructure, a clear example of *network economies* whereby the growing size of a network (such as a financial market) bestows its participants with more benefits (for instance liquidity, transparency). The stock market in particular has proven a deep source of capital for all kinds of businesses, including start-ups and relatively young high-tech companies with strong growth prospects. Trading volume in stocks and other securities has been boosted greatly by mutual funds and pension funds, both of which trade large bundles of securities across a variety of financial markets.

Compared to loans, securities have distinct advantages for both sides of the credit transaction. Lenders benefit from liquidity. With securities they can disengage from an investment at any time by selling it off, whereas illiquid loans do not offer such an exit option before maturity. Borrowers can tap a deeper supply of funds in securities markets which is consequently often cheaper than the interest they would have to pay on a bank loan. Many governments, for instance, have accepted securitization of their deficit-financing, because this has given them access to global capital markets and alternative domestic saving channels. And a growing number of firms in need of external funds have ended up preferring to deal with impersonal securities markets rather than intrusive bank loan officers. Finally, unlike loans, securities are priced daily in the marketplace. Such continuous market evaluation makes it easier for all sides to manage the underlying risk-return trade-off involved in any given credit transaction.

The credit-securitization trend has had many profound consequences. One has been the irresistible attractiveness of capital gains which have replaced interest and dividends as the primary form of income for financial asset-holders. Capital gains, amounting to the difference between the resale price and the initial purchase price, are earned when securities are resold at a higher price than the investor paid when acquiring them. Given booming stock markets and attractive conditions in bond markets, many investors have reaped sizeable capital gains over the last couple of decades. Such gains are not only attractive because they are taxed at a significantly lower rate than other forms of income (at least in the United States), but also because they are potentially much less limited than interest or dividends. While these latter two represent a more or less fixed portion of the borrower's eventual income gains, capital gains derive from the market's evaluation of the underlying future earnings potential of the agents issuing the securities. Under normal circumstances market psychology tends to be quite optimistic, reflecting a widely shared belief in continuous growth. Since such expectations are communicated and so collectively constructed among market participants, they may at times create a euphoria, in which case security prices rise rapidly and yield large capital gains (for instance the annual increases of the Dow and NASDAQ indices in excess of 20 percent during the 1997–2000 boom). When investors earn such large capital gains, there is a certain wealth effect, as the sense of being richer, even though only on paper, induces asset-holders to increase their spending. The wealth effect can also work in reverse, when stock or bond prices are tumbling. We do not know how large the wealth effect is.[12] We do know, however, that even major stock-market declines, as in October 1987 or in August 1998, often do not trigger recession. As long as the market rebounds rapidly and/or the decline remains fairly self-contained without spilling into the banking system, a robust economy will be able to shake off any damage to market psychology from such a sell-off.

Even though capital gains are quite risky in light of the price volatility found in most securities markets, their impressive growth in recent years has attracted millions of first-time investors into the securities markets. Today nearly half of all American households own securities, compared to only 12 percent in 1982. In the process, millions of middle-class households have been transformed into increasingly sophisticated investors, accumulating diversified securities portfolios through discount brokerages, mutual funds, pension funds and other tax-sheltered retirement vehicles. There are several other factors behind the emergence of this demographic group, most notably large income gains in many professional and managerial job categories, a widening of investment opportunities for the upwardly mobile middle class through deregulation, increasing use of securities to pay employees (such as stock options or 401(k) accounts), and the baby-boomers reaching an age where they start saving and worrying about retirement.

The emergence of this class of investors has had profound political consequences. An already powerful coalition of financial institutions, financial managers of industrial enterprises and central bankers is now gaining, through these new savers, a large voter-representation base in support of policies benefiting predominantly financial asset-holders. Such policies typically include long-term reductions in budget deficits, high 'real' interest rates, further deregulation of finance as well as certain key industries (as a catalyst for massive merger-driven restructuring in those sectors to boost stock-market valuations), privatization of public-sector enterprises (as yet another boost for the stock market), and tax benefits for financial investment portfolios (including capital-gains tax reduction and expansion of tax-sheltered investment vehicles). Those upwardly mobile investors are a global phenomenon. Already in the United States they comprise in excess of 50 million households. They are also growing rapidly in other industrial nations and some larger emerging-market economies (for example Brazil, and Mexico).

The proliferation of financial investors among the general population poses a threat to traditional banking, a situation which will make the coming battle over the control of cybercash that much more significant. As more and more of the nation's savings has been routed through mutual funds and pension funds rather than bank deposits, these so-called institutional investors have grown very rapidly and poured huge amounts of funds into the world's stock and bond markets. The securitization of credit has also benefited investment banks which specialize in market-making activities such as the brokerage, trading and underwriting of securities. The impressive expansion of these nonbank institutions heavily involved in the securities markets has come at the expense of banks (see Table 2.1).

In the face of such market-share erosion commercial banks have decided to join the trend of credit securitization. They have begun to repackage loans into marketable securities (for example mortgage-backed securities), supplied securities markets with credit (for example broker loans), diversified into investment banking or institutional investment activities and expanded their securities portfolios. These activities provide banks with fee income and commissions, more stable sources of income than the often volatile profits from interest-spreads between bank deposits and loans.

Banks have also participated actively in the credit securitization trend as counterparties to trades in *derivatives* which industrial corporations and financial institutions use to manage the price risk of their portfolios. Having become exposed to renewed price volatility in the financial markets following the deregulation of exchange and interest rates, investors have made increasing use of new hedging instruments shielding them from such price risk. These instruments are called derivatives, because their value is linked to some underlying financial instrument such as currencies, bonds, or stocks. They can be traded in special markets, as is the case with futures and options, or they can be specifically customized for individual portfolios, such as swaps or collars. These derivatives have become an essential ingredient for any large investor's risk-management strategy. While used

Table 2.1 Total financial assets of US financial institutions (in $bn)				
Year	Commercial banks	Insurance companies	Pension funds	Mutual funds	Security brokers and dealers
1985	2376.3	1094.7	1625.0	488.3	156.0
1986	2619.6	1259.5	1760.6	717.1	184.6
1987	2774.5	1410.3	1874.3	794.0	137.9
1988	2952.1	1578.9	2016.5	835.5	135.9
1989	3231.4	1748.5	2386.9	1014.3	236.6
1990	3337.5	1884.9	2435.1	1101.7	262.1
1991	3442.2	2055.3	2807.4	1304.5	332.5
1992	3654.9	2184.9	3011.6	1532.0	381.7
1993	3891.8	2397.4	3354.9	1935.0	478.8
1994	4159.7	2541.0	3548.0	2077.4	454.7
1995	4493.8	2803.9	4226.7	2594.1	568.1
1996	4710.4	3016.3	4745.7	3229.1	636.4
1997	5174.6	3358.3	5563.6	4031.9	779.2
1998	5642.2	3648.6	6232.4	4942.8	921.2
1999	5980.3	3942.8	6872.2	6117.3	1001.0
2000	6462.2	4007.3	6827.5	6246.7	1221.4
2001	6875.6	4186.9	6338.2	6377.1	1437.4

Source: Federal Reserve (2002c, Tables L-109, L-117 to L-122, L-130; 2002d, Tables L-109, L-117 to L-122, L-130)

for hedging purposes, derivatives also attract speculators betting on the movement of interest rates or exchange rates. For every hedger, there is a speculator. The high leverage permitted in the financing of derivative contracts, with investors often putting down less than ten percent of the contract's value, has made these instruments an irresistible object of speculation. While the derivatives have added liquidity to currency and securities markets, at times they have also proven a destabilizing force in the hands of highly leveraged speculators whose wrong guesses may oblige them to liquidate assets into a declining market. Notwithstanding occasional crisis situations involving derivatives (for example Orange County, Barings, Long-Term Capital Management), stock options, stock-index futures, bond futures, currency futures, interest swaps and other derivative instruments have greatly contributed to the expansion of the underlying securities markets by adding to the volume and allowing investors to manage their risk exposure better. In this way they have become an indispensable element in the securitization of credit. Banks have engaged very heavily in derivatives as a source of fee income and trading profits.

Another consequence of securitization has been with regard to the nature of financial crisis. When banks and their lending activity dominated the credit system, financial crises took the form of credit crunches during which shaky and overextended banks rationed their credit (for example the recurrent credit crunches in the United States at every cyclical peak between 1966 and 1982). But at the same time those kinds of financial crises were moderated by three factors:

1. The government's lender-of-last-resort interventions aimed at troubled banks (through deposit insurance, discount loans by central bank).

2. The possibility – in the absence of objective market valuation for loans – of using special accounting rules to boost otherwise impaired bank asset values.

3. Pressure on banks to stick with their customers through the provision of refinancing facilities or debt reschedulings, for fear of having to write off their loan assets at a heavy loss.

Now, with securities dominating the credit system, financial crises unfold much more swiftly via massive capital flight and immediate asset devaluation in the financial marketplace. While they may often be self-contained, these financial-market crashes do have the potential of hurting economic activity when they create large enough losses and/or depress credit-financing. In such a case those crises are not as easily managed by the monetary authorities who, unlike earlier during the era of bank loan domination, can only intervene indirectly in securities markets and vis-à-vis nonbank institutions. The contrast between the Mexican peso crises of August 1982 and December 1994 demonstrates very well the differences between the 'old' (loan-mediated) and 'new' (securities-mediated) types of financial instability. The Asian crisis of 1997 is an even more pertinent example of the new type of financial instability, a dramatic illustration of its swiftness and contagion capacity. That crisis started as a currency crisis, spilled rapidly into the economies of countries affected by paralyzing their domestic banking systems, and then proceeded over a period of 18 months to spread from country to country through Eastern Asia via Russia to Latin America.

2.4 Computerization of Finance

As securitization has driven more credit transactions into the financial markets, trading volume in all kinds of securities has surged over the last decade. Look, for instance, at the stock market. During the 1987 crash, the New York Stock Exchange (NYSE) experienced serious information-processing and settlement delays, as volume surged for the first time above 500 million shares on that fateful 19 October 1987 when the Dow Jones tumbled over 22 percent. Today, only fifteen years later, daily NYSE volume regularly exceeds 1 billion shares (and NASDAQ's share can easily top 1.5 billion shares on a given day) without any glitch in market operations. That doubling, in some instances even tripling, of trading volume in financial markets over the last decade has combined with increased complexity of intertwined transactions to nourish greater use of computers. Both these forces together have propelled a technological revolution in bond, stock and currency markets. Computerization has thrown these markets into organizational turmoil out of which they will all emerge radically transformed.

Take, for example, the nation's stock exchanges. In 1997 the Securities and Exchange Commission (SEC) introduced new rules which broke the near-monopoly of the NYSE (also known as the 'Big Board') and NASDAQ by authorizing so-called electronic communications networks (ECNs). Since then about a dozen of these networks have been launched, mostly by leading brokerage houses (Morgan Stanley and Salomon introducing MarketXT or Primex set up by Merrill Lynch and Goldman Sachs), market-information providers (for instance Reuter's Instinet, Bloomberg's Tradebook LLC), or online brokers (for instance Schwab's Redibook, Datek's Island). ECNs match stock trades electronically for customers who want to bypass the exchange floor. These computer-based alternatives to the traditional stock exchanges collect, display and automatically execute customer orders more speedily and at a lower cost than either the Big Board or NASDAQ can with their antiquated and labor-intensive infrastructure. Based on these advantages, ECNs have already captured a third of the trading in NASDAQ stocks and begun to make some inroads in the highly protected trading of NYSE stocks (for a market share of 10 percent).

While ECNs have not been able to match the liquidity offered by the traditional exchanges and have suffered from their fragmentation, they are likely to expand rapidly as after-hours trading becomes more popular and more of the stock trading moves online. Comparative lack of liquidity will then become less of a problem for the ECNs. Bypassing the expensive broker operations, time-consuming order-settlement procedures and collusive trading practices by insiders found on the traditional exchanges, the ECNs are in a position to lure many investors away from the Big Board or NASDAQ. They can charge customers lower commissions, offer more information and execute trades more speedily. In the longer run ECNs promise to be the more attractive market model when compared to traditional stock exchanges, promising faster trades, lower costs, greater transparency, fewer means for brokers to exploit customers and more extensive innovation.

The Big Board and NASDAQ have already begun to see their brokerage commissions and dealer profits get squeezed by the new electronic start-ups. When in 1999 the SEC authorized ECNs to turn themselves from mere trading systems into fully fledged exchanges, a step already taken by two of the leading networks (Archipelago and Island), both the NYSE and the NASDAQ decided that the time had come to respond to this competition. Their response was not least triggered by growing engagement of their exchange members in online trading and ECNs. Both markets decided to turn themselves from member-controlled, nonprofit institutions into shareholder-controlled, for-profit organizations by going public. This step might help to secure the loyalty of their largest members by turning them into shareholders and facilitate needed organizational reforms which so far had always fallen victim to arcane membership politics. Shares issued by the exchanges could also be used as currency with which to acquire software firms that can automate the processing of orders, merge with other exchanges, set up their own ECNs for after-hours trading, or invade each other's turf of listed stocks.

But this proliferation of for-profit exchanges also poses a regulatory challenge to the SEC. Such for-profit exchanges may be less capable of self-regulation in the light of conflicts of interests and profit pressures, thus requiring greater supervisory capabilities by the SEC. Having to deal with regulatory inequality between the traditional exchanges and the new ECNs, the SEC will also have to develop a unified regulatory framework for all exchanges which befits the markets of the future. In this regulatory overhaul the SEC will need to find ways that encourage integration of different markets in order to counter liquidity-eroding market fragmentation. Eventually, say by 2015, there may be only three to four distinct stock exchanges left worldwide, each probably specializing in a specific category of stocks.[13]

Such market integration is already being fostered by two significant computer-based innovations. Soon the largest online brokers and traders are all going to use 'intelligent order routing' software which scans all the exchanges, ECNs and market-makers for the best combination of price, order size, speed and transaction costs. Moreover, some of the world's largest securities-processing firms and IT companies, grouped together in the Global Straight Through Processing Association, are currently developing a seamless electronic network, called a 'transaction-flow monitor' using 'straight-through processing' principles. This network would connect all the parties involved in a trade (investors, brokers, trading screens, clearing systems and custodial houses) to provide for instantaneous execution, processing and settlement of stock trades across the globe which, compared to the current three-day settlement cycle, would significantly lower transaction costs, settlement risk and processing errors. Here the internet promises an elegant way to integrate the myriad of incompatible accounting and processing practices and connect database systems without having to spend heavily on additional hardware for an entirely new network.

Similar developments are taking place in other securities markets as well. Take, for instance, the market for US government, corporate and municipal bonds whose daily trading volume of $350 billion is twelve times the volume of stock trading on the Big Board. The $13 trillion over-the-counter (OTC) bond market has no required reporting of bids and offers, making it difficult for institutional and individual investors to get good information about prevailing market prices. They have to call several dealers to get a sense of the price, a time-consuming and often imprecise shopping expedition. The absence of reliable price information among investors makes it easier for dealers to charge high mark-ups which secure them profits from the 'spread' between the prices they themselves paid for the bonds and the prices they charge their customers when reselling those bonds. Add to that collusive practices in the tightknit community of bond dealers aimed at restricting competition among themselves and securing their collective monopoly profits from asymmetric information access.

This opaque and clubby nature of the fixed-income market is now being transformed by technology in the direction of much greater transparency and competition. During the last couple of years, over seventy electronic trading systems have been introduced for bonds. Cantor Fitzgerald's eSpeed, for instance, has become the de facto exchange for US Treasury securities. This investment in electronic bond trading has enabled Cantor Fitzgerald to survive the tremendous blow it suffered from the 11 September attack on the World Trade Center which killed hundreds of its traders. London-based Garban and Tullet are dominant players in foreign government bonds. TradeWeb and BrokerTec serve institutional investors, while E*Trade and Discover Brokerage Direct focus on small retail investors. These e-bond trading systems give investors much better access to current market prices and allow them to trade bonds without inter-mediation by brokers, thereby eliminating the information monopoly of dealers and squeezing their spreads. Specialized internet-based trading systems (for instance TreasuryDirect or MuniAuction) have also made it possible for issuers of bonds, from the US Treasury to small municipalities, to sell their new debt instruments directly to investors rather than depending on negotiating expensive deals with underwriters serving as intermediaries.[14]

Such direct-sales practices have also rocked the market for commercial paper where large issuers (for instance Ford or General Motors) have recently begun selling new issues directly to institutional investors by using an interactive online service known as CPDirect. That system allows companies issuing commercial paper to see who is buying the paper. By contrast, traditional dealer-mediated underwriting of such paper did not provide corporate issuers with that information. Underwriters typically held onto that data and so retained their clout over issuers. CS First Boston and Merrill Lynch decided recently to offer issuers and investors access to online-trading systems for a fee rather than maintain their information monopoly as intermediaries in the commercial-paper market.

Here what we see emerge as a trend is the transformation of securities markets by electronic-trading systems. Such systems, particularly those using the internet as a ready-made infrastructure, bring buyers and sellers in direct contact with each other. The traditional need for brokers, underwriters, specialists and other market-makers is thus greatly reduced. To the extent that such intermediaries controlled prices and information about those prices for their own profit, this development is a good one. Their elimination makes markets more transparent and efficient, lowers transaction costs and removes an inherently anti-competitive power center from those markets. But intermediaries may also bring a 'human element' to bear which in the end makes the markets function better. They have specialized knowledge about the markets and know best how to make deals work. Machines are innately incapable of such knowledge. Intermediaries have a vested interest in orderly market conditions and will try to counteract imbalances between demand and supply, as is the case for instance with specialists. Not having this stabilizing force in electronic markets may make those more volatile and more susceptible to crashes when selling pressure builds up.

There are still some financial markets where the human element remains important and where the diffusion of electronic technology has been consequently slower. One example are the futures and options markets which continue to function mostly as auctions conducted by traders face-to-face in the pits of the world's leading futures exchanges (Chicago Board of Trade CBOT, Chicago Mercantile Exchange – CME, London's LIFFE). Such 'open-outcry' systems involve experienced traders who can execute trades more quickly by hand signals than computers shuffling messages to and fro. Since the pits are especially designed to bring together a large number of traders in close physical contact with each other, such intensely human markets are in their own unique way more transparent than data flowing impersonally through computer networks.[15] The $1.5 trillion-a-day foreign-exchange market is another example in which the human element dominates, here in the form of insider deals among two dozen of the world's largest transnational banks controlling that market and coordinating their activities in it. But not even these two financial markets can escape growing automation. Futures and options exchanges have opted for automation in their after-hours trading (for example CBOT's Project A experiment, LIFFE's automatic pit trading system) or when they lack the scale required for the operation of expensive open-outcry systems (such as Sidney, Hong Kong, Frankfurt, Paris). These markets have also had to face the emergence of rivals on the internet, such as the all-electronic German-Swiss exchange known as Eurex, an online commodities futures exchange called FutureCom, or an online options exchange backed by E*Trade. The currency markets also face a growing trend towards online trading which has prompted the world's leading banks to organize jointly managed trading platforms on the internet (such as FX Alliance and Currenex). These alternatives to the proprietary networks of individual banks offer lower transaction costs, allow one-stop electronic shopping for a variety of products and services (including spot transactions, currency options, forward foreign-exchange contracts, research, analytical-modeling tools), make prices available 24 hours a day and scan markets for the best possible deals.

The spreading computerization of all the major financial-market categories goes hand in hand with the increasing popularity of online trading among individual and institutional investors. In this regard, the arrival of the internet is a major catalyst for even more extensive automation of financial markets, because it hooks (increasingly electronic) markets directly to online suppliers of funds for whom the computer networks offer greater speed, more transparency and lower costs than insider networks of brokers out to profit from asymmetric information. The internet, with its access to information and facilitation of direct contact between buyers and sellers, might eventually spell the end of traditional intermediaries – not just the brokers and all sorts of market-making dealers (notably specialists and locals), but perhaps also investment banks and even mutual funds. In light of this threat it is no surprise then to see investment banks and mutual funds aggressively pursuing internet-based reorganization of their operations. As these large institutions enter the world of 'online finance' to maintain their client base and market-making relevance, the more competitive ones among them have thrived on enhanced product development. Successful online intermediaries, such as Schwab or E*Trade, have developed very attractive multi-product packages for their subscribers which combine securities trading, information access, mutual funds, credit lines and traditional banking services (that is, cash management, checking accounts) into one integrated account. The era of online financial supermarkets is dawning upon us.[16]

The movement towards online financial supermarkets is driven by start-ups, like E*Trade, or, as in the case of Schwab, by older nonbank institutions remaking themselves online. Thus the trend has the potential of bypassing traditional 'brick-and-mortar' banks altogether. Indeed, nothing has been more threatening to traditional commercial banking than the emergence of electronic information technologies. As half of the world gets hooked up to computer networks, the banks have in one swoop lost their information monopoly concerning ultimate lenders and borrowers (especially corporations) which for so long had justified their central position as intermediaries in credit relations. Corporations and other borrowers can now transmit extensive information about themselves via computers to a global audience ready to place its daily bets in the world's financial markets. It is fair to say that this fundamental change in the collection and control of financial information explains much behind the gradual replacement of bank loans by marketable securities. After having lost a lot of their primary lending business to (increasingly automated) securities markets, the banks now face a challenge on the retail front from the likes of E*Trade offering customers the full range of banking services online.

We have seen the banks respond to the threat of credit securitization by joining the trend themselves, a response made easier now in the United States with the passage of the Financial Services Modernization (Gramm-Leach-Bliley) Act of 1999. This law removed the regulatory barriers imposed on bank activity by the Glass-Steagall Act of 1933 to allow the integration of commercial banking, investment banking and insurance. In the same vein, we can expect banks to take on the challenge of computerization by integrating the new technology into their own operations. Over the last fifteen years electronic technology has penetrated and, in the process, transformed nearly all banking activities. Witness the proliferation of private automated payments services and electronic fund-transfer systems (for example the SWIFT system used by banks in the euromarket) which pose a competitive and regulatory threat to the once-secure government monopoly in this vital arena of our cash-flow economy, the payments system. Banks have also used electronic technology to offer their clients new types of services (for instance cash management or investment

advice) and to expand their links to the securities markets as service
providers (for instance credit lines or settlement assistance). In retail
banking, commercial banks have offered their customers multi-deposit
'sweep' accounts (typically combining checking accounts, savings
accounts, mutual funds, brokerage and consumer credit lines, all linked
through automated fund-transfer capability), global networks of ATMs for
fund transfers or withdrawals and computerized home banking via PCs
(and free software).

Technology-driven innovation by banks provides a strong impetus for
the emergence of cybercash. The electronification of retail banking has
introduced some of the *socio-technological foundations* of this new money
form to a large public. Specifically, we are talking here about the use of
wallet-sized debit and credit cards. Such 'plastic money' has prepared the
public for much more sophisticated 'smart cards' that will become a key
element in the activation of cybercash transactions. ATMs and POS terminals in retail outlets have familiarized people all over the world with
electronic-payments systems. Aggressive marketing by banks has
persuaded millions of bank customers gradually into conducting their
banking activities on PCs linked to each other by phone or modem. Thus
the banks are in the process of creating a new way of banking, electronic
banking, and so laying the groundwork for a new money form, cybercash.

2.5 Online Banking

The disintegration of the postwar monetary regime eroded the privileged
position of commercial banks. Threatened on the asset side by the securitization of credit, they have had to adapt to the switch from bank loans to
securities as the primary credit channel and get more heavily involved in
the organization of financial markets. Since there is no difference from the
point of view of money creation whether a bank loans out its excess
reserves or uses them to buy securities, the money-creation monopoly of
commercial banks is not directly threatened by credit securitization. That
monopoly, which during the postwar regime of paper money constituted
the decisive advantage given to banks by regulatory design, is however
under pressure from inroads on the liability side by nonbank institutions
such as mutual funds, pension funds and even investment banks. Savings
products and cash-management services offered by these institutions have
proven attractive enough to absorb a growing share of the nation's savings
at the expense of traditional bank deposits. In the wake of money's
progressive deregulation, some of these nonbank institutions have been

able to introduce products which have come close to representing money. Take, for instance, mutual-fund shares of US money-market funds which offer investors check-writing privileges for checks in excess of $500. Banks have responded to this threat by setting up their own mutual funds and taking over the management of pension funds.

In the transition to a new monetary regime, we are therefore faced with a situation where the banks and nonbank institutions invade each other's turf and so become increasingly alike. Spurred initially by innovation, this trend has now been ratified into law by the Second Banking Directive of the European Commission in 1989 and the Financial Services Modernization (Gramm-Leach-Bliley) Act passed by the US Congress after decade-long wrangling in 1999. Both landmark legislations foresee the development of *universal banks* offering the whole range of commercial banking, investment banking and insurance services. In this homogenization of financial-services firms there will be ample space for smaller, more specialized players, such as investment boutiques or hedge funds, to carve out a profitable niche in the area of their expertise. But apart from these specialists, the overall trend is clearly towards large financial institutions offering their customers a wide range of products. These financial supermarkets will allow their customers to access a variety of services at once. Key to such one-stop banking is the extensive use of computer and communication technologies which enrich the information content of different financial services and facilitate their integration (for instance automated fund transfers between different sub-accounts). We cannot discuss universal banking or financial supermarkets without also making reference to electronic banking – two sides of the same coin.

That new reality of reorganization began to preoccupy the banks a while ago. In the late 1980s and early 1990s, many of the leading US banks pushed so-called *home banking*, which would enable retail customers to conduct their essential banking business via PCs at home without ever having to visit a bank branch. Setting up their own proprietary computer networks and offering their clients free software, the banks targeted upscale households for that kind of service. But marketing efforts in this direction made only slow progress until the arrival of highly popular financial-services software, notably Intuit's Quicken and Microsoft's Money programs, prompted a rapidly growing number of people to conduct their banking on the computer. That success, however, came at a price. Banks found themselves in a situation where the delivery of their computer-based banking products came to depend on software companies and other intermediaries, such as the credit-card company Visa which operates one of the two dominant call-up services for home banking. In contrast to the monopoly rents earned from paper-based banking, the banks have to share their income from electronic banking with nonbank firms providing high-tech components that are essential for the automation of financial services.

Home banking never had a chance to show its true potential. Its life cycle was cut short by the arrival of the internet in the mid-1990s as a better alternative for electronic banking. Even though the use of the banks' own proprietary computer networks and call-up services may have given home banking a comparative advantage in terms of greater security, online banking via the internet proved in the end the more attractive medium. One advantage concerns cost. The internet provides a ready-made infrastructure for the computerization of retail banking, preempting the need for banks to build their own networks from scratch. And customers do not have to pay anything for online banking beyond internet-access charges, whereas home banking usually involved extra subscription fees. In addition, internet-based banking carries a major marketing advantage compared to home banking. With private networks for their own customers, the banks cannot increase their customer base at all. When such networks are routed through a commercial online service, such as Intuit, Microsoft, or America Online, the banks can only reach subscribers. The internet, in contrast, is an open system where banks can do their own thing and recruit new customers.

Despite these advantages, internet banking has had a slow and difficult start. Initially, in 1995–96, many bank customers expressed concern about the security of doing one's banking over the internet and also complained about the quality of service offered by banks online.[17] It has taken a few years for the banks' web sites to improve to the point where they are deemed sufficiently secure and user-friendly by a skeptical public. Even today, seven years into internet banking, only 1500 US banks, less than one in six, have fully functional sites on the web which typically allow customers to view banking records and current balances, transfer funds between accounts, pay bills online, and access credit-card, lending as well as brokerage services.

The banks' hesitation to abandon their investments in home-banking networks in favor of online banking left an opening for newcomers. Particularly noteworthy were start-ups which sought to avoid costly physical investments in branches by conducting their banking business entirely online. Several internet-only banks emerged during the late 1990s, able to offer higher deposit rates and lower loan rates as a result of operating costs that were considerably lower than those of their brick-and-mortar rivals. In the end, however, this first generation of online banks proved a failure. Security First Network Bank, the first internet-only bank, sold out to The

Royal Bank of Canada which has since narrowed its focus to so-called 'private-label' banking services offering customers access to a wide variety of mutual funds, investment advice and insurance products under contractual arrangements with the providers of such services. Tieback, America's largest internet-only bank, was acquired by E*Trade in June 1999 which six months later bought the nation's largest independent network of ATMs to move beyond a sole reliance on online banking. And Bank One abandoned its online-banking subsidiary Wingspan.com only nine months after its launch.

Why did these first forays into online banking prove so short-lived? It takes a lot of effort and time for any new bank to build trust and loyalty, and internet banks are no different in that regard. Perhaps those early online banks faced an even more daunting task than your traditional brick-and-mortar bank. Their growth potential depends on how many households are willing to move their banking activity online, and even today in the United States this number is not more than 3 percent of retail banking customers. Americans by and large still do not trust the privacy and safety protections of online banking sites. And they are often reluctant to change long-standing behavior in record-keeping brought about by the paper-less environment of electronic banking. Slow membership growth combined with thin operating margins to make the minimum capital level required by regulators difficult to reach for online banks. The resulting decline in their stock-market valuation made the capitalization task of those banks even more daunting and turned them into cheap takeover targets for anyone wishing to expand their online banking capabilities.

The failure of early online banking has not kept traditional banks from accelerating their efforts in that direction. Take, for example, Citibank. In 1998 its e-CITI unit lost $142 million, mostly due to costly advertising, research and development of internet-based financial-services products. In August 1999 America's largest bank decided to phase out Citi f/i, a retail bank and brokerage unit reachable only on the internet, which had attracted scant consumer interest. In the face of these disappointments, Citibank's management decided to reorganize its online efforts. Its comeback plans rest on a new full-service online site offering customers a wide array of investing, banking and insurance services.[18] With MyCiti.com offering already a glimpse into the future of (online) one-stop banking, other banks are not far behind. Early converts to online banking, such as the Bank of America, Wells Fargo and Chase, each have more than two million online customers. Banks in Europe, where the introduction of a single currency has created an opportunity to establish an integrated and large market for universal banking, are also aggressively pursuing online banking, as witnessed by Deutsche Bank's successful online subsidiary or the February 2000 agreement between Spain's largest bank, Banco Bilbao, and the leading telecom firm, Telefonica, for joint development of their e-commerce and internet assets in Europe as well as Latin America.

Even nonbanks see in the internet a convenient route into commercial banking, thanks not least to sharply lower set-up costs for bank sites on the web. When a small online trader known as E*Trade can transform itself within a year into a formidable commercial bank through a series of strategic acquisitions financed by stock swaps, even the largest banks will pay attention. They will worry even more when they see a leading investment bank, such as Merrill Lynch, launch its Cash Manager program (in May 2000) which gives its small business customers online information about all their accounts at Merrill and other institutions, allows them to pay bills and payroll online and automatically consolidates daily excess cash from all accounts into high-yielding Merrill investment accounts.[19] A 1996 change in the unitary thrift charter, which allowed US thrifts to branch out from home lending to other forms of consumer lending without having to open up a branch or run the entire gamut of banking services, has prompted retailers (such as Nordstrom), supermarkets (like Ukrops) and other nonfinancial companies (notably Ford) to buy thrifts as a low-cost way to strengthen their relationship with customers by offering a variety of financial services online.

These efforts demonstrate widespread interest in online banking despite early difficulties. Banks and their nonbank competitors see in the internet a cost-effective vehicle for expansion of their customer base and deepening of services. The advantages of online banking for product development have already been demonstrated by the ambitious range of financial services offered by Wingspan, E*Trade, Wells Fargo, or Citibank on their web sites. Customers too will find the convenience of online banking irresistible, once security and privacy concerns have been sufficiently allayed by a combination of regulatory measures and technological innovation. No more frustrating waiting in line on your visit to the neighborhood branch! No more time-consuming ritual of paying one's bills manually, with all those checks and envelopes to fill out, all those stamps to lick, all those visits to the post office! No more monthly wait for the banking statement in the mail! No more innumerable pieces of paper accumulating in time-less folders to account for one's spending flows and bank balances!

There remains, however, one barrier threatening the future viability of any online banking model, and that is the absence of cybercash. Without a corresponding form of electronic money, created and circulating online, we cannot consider the internet to be a fully functional vehicle for electronic banking. This problem has manifested itself already in the case of the internet-only banks discussed above. In the absence of cybercash, customers cannot withdraw cash while logged onto the internet. For the same reason putting money into an account can be a hassle online. Except for paychecks and other direct-deposit arrangements, internet-bank customers have to mail their check deposits to the post-office box of their online bank. Not having their own ATMs thus proved a major competitive disadvantage for internet-only banks whose customers had to pay fees whenever they used another bank's ATM or were forced to rely on the old-fashioned 'snail mail' for their deposits.[20] This inconvenience was enough to dissuade many households from getting involved with online banking. The absence of online money will hamper the online expansion strategies of Citibank and other traditional brick-and-mortar banks as well. Anytime you need to go off-line in order to withdraw cash or deposit checks, your banking activity gets disrupted. The banking experience on the internet is simply not complete until we can do all of our banking online without interruption. Without access to a viable cybercash system for cash with-drawals or deposits, bank customers will simply refuse to consider the banks' web sites as equivalent to their brick-and-mortar branches. Electronic banking thus requires electronic money for its sustainability.

CHAPTER 3

The Internet Revolution

That we have come to the imminent birth of cybercash is rooted not least in the logic of money's evolution. The history of money is one of its progressive dematerialization, a trend illustrated foremost when metal money gave way to paper money. The latter is now being gradually replaced by an even more immaterial form of money, existing solely as data flows between computer networks. Banks have been allowed to experiment more ambitiously with new money forms and payments systems in the aftermath of money's piecemeal deregulation. The thrust of monetary innovation has been electronic in nature, using computer and communication technologies to automate the monetary process. Responding here to the dual threat of credit securitization and computerization of finance, the banks have pushed electronic banking and in the process developed a socio-technological infrastructure for electronic money composed of ATMs, plastic cards, ACH fund transfers and electronic billing. All these components of money's automation render the payment and settlement process cheaper and more efficient than traditional paper money.

These advantages notwithstanding, electronic money still has not reached full maturity. While it has succeeded in launching highly popular computer-based payments systems (in the euromarket, for credit cards) and automating certain aspects of the dominant paper-based regime (for instance ATMs replacing human bank tellers), the new money form has yet to develop a centralizing mechanism with which to propel the ongoing structural changes in the nature of finance – securitization of credit, computerization of finance, privatization of money – toward a coherent new monetary regime. This centralizing mechanism, which during the regime of paper-based credit-money was bank loans, will be the internet for the new regime of computer-based credit-money. As traditional banks expand their internet operations, they realize that electronic banking requires a corresponding money form which can be accessed online. Nonbank institutions and even retailers wishing to offer their customers a variety of financial services find that the most promising way to meet this objective may well be via the internet. More generally, the internet has the potential of becoming a major vehicle for electronic commerce, and it is this development which may provide the most powerful impetus yet for the launch of cybercash.

Therefore this chapter looks at the internet as a locus of e-commerce to assess its capacity as an incubator of e-money. When the internet appeared in the mid-1990s as a mass phenomenon, it soon merged with the ongoing financial revolution to accelerate the pace of its technological improvement and user diffusion. Fuelled by huge sums of capital mobilized in its direction, the internet grew rapidly into a promising medium for electronic commerce, the vector of a 'New Economy' (section 3.1). The internet-related euphoria of the late 1990s has now given way to a serious high-tech crash which has devastated the dot-com sector and put into question the viability of e-commerce (section 3.2). But, far from being finished, the internet continues to hold great promise as a growth-promoting resource, provided it can be reorganized accordingly (section 3.3). The current crisis serves that purpose, forcing squeezed firms to streamline online operations and make them more revenue-oriented. The restructuring of the internet, turning it from a public good providing free access to information into a private source of profit offering restricted-access services for pay, depends not least on giving this medium a monetary sphere for online payments and credit (section 3.4).

3.1 Birth of the Internet

The origins of the internet are rooted in concerted government-sponsored efforts to promote science and technology, especially by the US military-industrial complex. In 1969 the Pentagon's Advanced Research Projects Agency (ARPA) launched a project to merge computer and telecommunication technologies into a global data-sharing and information-exchange network for scientists. This ARPANET was expanded in 1989 when scientists working at the European Center for Particles Research (CERN) created a wider and more accessible network infrastructure known as the World Wide Web. The web became ready for widespread use in 1993, when Marc Andriessen, then a student at the University of Illinois, developed a graphic interface software program called MOSAIC with funding support by the National Science Foundation. In 1994 Andriessen turned his invention into riches when he set up Netscape and introduced the Navigator browser. This tool made the internet accessible to anyone equipped with a personal computer and a telephone modem, thus reaching a mass audience. The web immediately attracted a rapidly growing number of PC users who, at the cost of a local phone call, could send e-mail messages anywhere in the world, participate in online chat clubs and access a treasure of information.

By the very nature of its design, the internet has given us a revolutionary new way to collect, organize and communicate information at the speed of light. Its origin in the late 1960s, as a government-funded effort linking computers in government agencies, university departments and research labs together, was that of a small-scale network for the circulation of data and other types of information within the scientific community. The introduction of the World Wide Web and invention of the browser opened up cheap access to the internet for the masses, turning this medium during the first half of the 1990s into a huge chat club and information exchange. Given the low cost of setting up new web sites, many firms soon realized that the internet would allow them to get in touch with a whole lot more consumers across the globe 24 hours per day, 7 days per week. Soon every major retailer and consumer goods firm with brand recognition had to have a web site to give potential customers a convenient source of enhanced product information and communication. New companies emerged, specifically set up to serve internet users (such as Yahoo!) or do business online (for instance Amazon.com). Thus the internet developed into a tool of commerce after 1996. The prospects of rapid gains through this low-cost extension of commerce fuelled a boom which provided ample funds for an extraordinarily rapid expansion of e-commerce sites, a boom that trickled down to telecom and computer firms gearing up for a major capacity expansion of the internet.

This rapid transformation of the internet into a super-hot growth sector during the second half of the 1990s cannot be separated from the aforementioned financial revolution (see section 2.3). The internet was propelled forward by rapidly rising stock-market prices through which huge sums of capital were invested in e-commerce. Wall Street had already responded favorably to massive doses of corporate restructuring and disinflation during the 1980s which had improved the long-term profitability of successfully reorganized companies. The climate for stocks turned even more positive in the mid-1990s when a combination of fiscal austerity and fast growth brought huge budget deficits under control – a turnaround which allowed interest rates to come down. Lower interest rates made stocks even more attractive. At the same time Americans became much more heavily invested in the stock market. When an accounting rule change forced US corporations to cover their underfunded pension plan commitments, a large number of them abandoned defined-benefit plans, in which they guaranteed their workforce a predetermined level of benefits upon retirement, in favor of defined-contribution plans which transferred the risks to their employees. Tax-sheltered plans of the defined-contribution kind, notably 401(k) plans, proved extremely popular with baby-boomers, who in their middle age had suddenly come to think about saving for their retirement and, in the face of continuously rising stock values, had come to regard stocks as a safe and lucrative investment. Other investment vehicles, such as mutual funds and individual retirement accounts, added to the massive influx of personal savings into the booming stock market.

When the internet emerged, it offered investors new opportunities for capital gains on their stock holdings. To the extent that this medium promised a huge number of investment opportunities and efficiency gains, it boosted already high valuations of US corporations, especially those firms standing to benefit the most from the growth of e-commerce. Market euphoria spread rapidly, fuelled in addition by America's preparations for Y2K readiness and the optimistic prognoses of investment analysts who talked up stocks, especially NASDAQ's high-tech stocks.[1] The metaphor of the 'New Economy', a highly popular term on Wall Street used to signal a technological revolution boosting productivity, incomes and the economy's growth potential, served to justify new valuation standards for high-tech stocks. Rather than looking at those investments from the point of view of traditional valuation standards rooted in past profit records and future income flows generated by physical capital, the public became convinced that the New Economy firms had to be judged differently.

Investors, whether individual or institutional, were more than ready to apply nontraditional valuation standards to the growth sectors of the New Economy. The competitive and innovation-rich nature of the internet put a premium on having good ideas and the skill pool to realize those ideas through fast-paced product development. In this race of ideas it was seen as important to be first. When you are the first one to offer a new application, you get economies of scale (that is, efficiency gains from increased volume of operations) very quickly. These produce lower unit costs and greater demand which in turn enables you to expand the range of services offered. In addition, you obtain a competitive edge from strong brand recognition when you are first. In their perennial rush to get ahead of others, internet-based producers depend heavily on new forms of productive capital, such as customer and supplier relationships, links to other sites, brand names, intellectual property rights, flexible organizational structures, entrepreneurial and technological skill pools and teamwork spirit. Attracted by the magical powers of the internet, investors were willing to value these unconventional and relatively scarce forms of productive capital at a high premium. To the extent that all these inputs are intangible in nature, they are difficult to measure. Deprived of standard measurement criteria developed by accounting and economics for physical capital, valuations of intangible capital will be more exposed to the mood swings of the investor community until it works out how to value those resources with reasonable accuracy.

In the absence of past earnings as a guide, internet firms came to be judged on the basis of optimistic forecasts of e-commerce volume growth feeding the euphoric mood of the times. It is no surprise that the notion of a New Economy gained currency foremost on Wall Street, where enthusiastic analysts pushed the concept to justify sky-high valuations of new firms without a proven track record around collectively constructed anticipations of an imminent profit explosion. The sense of speed fostered by the take-off of the internet, punctuated by stories of fabled wealth earned by 20-somethings taking their dot-com start-ups public, nourished a get-rich-quick mentality which saw the NASDAQ rise from 1500 to 5000 in just a couple of years.

In that climate investors poured huge sums into high-tech stocks. Anything related to the internet promised large capital gains in a matter of weeks. The unbelievably high valuations of internet start-ups reached in 1999 were only possible because more and more investors stopped looking at current earnings as a basis for their evaluations. Instead of imminent profits, investors preferred to look at all kinds of nonfinancial information, such as site visits, the number of 'engaged shoppers', or a dot-com firm's 'leading mind' share.[2] Underlying this focus on measures indicating potential consumer demand was the popular notion that the internet was dancing to a different drummer, propelled rapidly forward by ideas that could be worth billions tomorrow. The suspension of net income as the most important valuation standard eventually prompted investors to pay hundreds of dollars per share for companies that had so far not turned a dime of profit. Ultimately millions of rookie investors, driven to careless greed by the sweet music of imminent capital gains, jumped head-first into technology stocks and even borrowed heavily to finance their spending spree.

The bull market of the late 1990s helped to channel huge amounts of resources into the expansion of the internet. This process unfolded by means of a new funding system fed by the rapidly rising prices of high-tech stocks. During those go-go years budding internet entrepreneurs found it very easy to obtain venture capital support for their web site projects. Flush with funds, new start-ups were able to put their ideas into practice. Those firms then managed to attract young, entrepreneurial, technologically savvy workers without having to pay out a lot of cash for employee compensation. They did so by offering those employees company shares issued at a discount which could be cashed in at the presumably much higher market price once they had become vested. Tax benefits in the form of lower capital-gains taxes for payees and expensing provisions giving the employers tax deductions added to the allure of such stock options.[3] Within relatively short periods of time many of the new internet firms would go public through a string of spectacularly successful initial public offerings (IPOs), helped by the willingness of enthusiastic investors to gobble up these new shares even though their issuers had yet to earn a profit. That process would turn founders and many employees of these IPOs over night into multimillionaires when they cashed in their discounted stock options at sky-high premia. The attractive returns to venture capitalists, internet entrepreneurs and high-tech workers achieved by this sequence of stock options and IPOs was sustained by the booming NASDAQ relentlessly pushing up the stock prices of companies linked in one way or another to the internet. With high-tech stocks in the stratosphere it became easy for dot-com firms to acquire new assets or take over other firms without any cash outlays, through the simple device of stock swaps. A striking example of that practice was America Online, a pioneer launch site for access to the internet, whose market valuation of $164 billion by the end of 1999 allowed it to buy Time Warner, a company nearly five times its size in terms of revenues, in January 2000.[4]

The combination of venture-capital support, stock options, IPOs, sky-high stock-market valuations and stock swaps channeled large amounts of capital into the New Economy. It took only six years for the internet to grow into a $400 billion industry, exceeding in size the automobile industry and absorbing 4 percent of America's gross domestic product. During the boom years of the late 1990s the internet was responsible for fully one-third of US economic growth. This spectacular growth performance was fuelled by the rapid diffusion of internet usage among Americans. In late 1999 over 100 million of them were hooked up to the internet. Every second, across the globe, seven new subscribers get on the web for the first time.

While initially gripping the world as a free, open-access medium facilitating communication and the circulation of information, investors preferred to focus on a different aspect of the internet. They got most excited about the web as a locus of commerce, viewing it as a revolutionary technology bound to transform corporate organization and marketplace alike. The concentration of financial and entrepreneurial resources directed towards the internet made sure that e-commerce had the means for rapid expansion, driven forward by an explosion of ideas, applications and start-up companies.

When e-commerce began to emerge in 1996, its first wave of applications concerned *business-to-consumer* (B2C) transactions which took off with amazing speed. For instance, book selling moved rapidly online, with Amazon.com and Barnes & Noble slugging it out in the virtual marketplace. The same proved true for airline tickets, allowing airline companies to reduce ticket processing costs to $1 per ticket (compared to $8 when using a combination of ticket agents and computerized reservation systems). These early successes triggered an explosion of B2C-oriented online suppliers, as more and more firms specializing in consumer goods or services made it their primary concern to create attractive web sites and get customers to spend online. Merchant networks, a sort of electronic shopping mall, have sprung up all across the web to enjoy the fruits of co-branding, jointly organized sales-promotion schemes, centralized payment facilities and other advantages from belonging to a large network. Their rapid spread was taken as sign that B2C commerce had the potential of maturing rapidly into a viable alternative to traditional retail trade conducted in brick-and-mortar stores.

A related e-commerce segment with similarly explosive growth potential, so-called *peer-to-peer* (P2P) transactions, emerged with the phenomenal success of eBay. Specializing in online auctions, this internet company has turned millions of Americans into avid buyers and sellers of new or used goods on the internet. Our love affair with the auction model has spurred more specialized sites, such as the one organizing a market for airline tickets, as well as related market models, such as priceline.com's 'reverse auction' model of letting customers name their own price. The P2P concept seems especially appealing, since it allows buyers and sellers to find each other easily for direct exchange transactions that bypass traditional intermediaries and distribution networks. What a great outlet for the entrepreneurial ambitions in anyone of us, making it so easy to become a trader! P2P could add a lot to economic growth, because it comprises many transactions that would otherwise not have taken place. And that part of e-commerce also might improve the efficiency of resource allocation in our economy, providing an excellent outlet for matching surpluses and shortages.

While much of the early focus regarding the internet's commercial potential was on B2C transactions, investors soon got drawn to *business-to-business* (B2B) applications. Early on in the life cycle of e-commerce it became evident that many sectors could benefit from the internet as a centralized mechanism of information-gathering. Already, American truckers are making use of the internet to secure loads for return trips at a fraction of the search cost compared to when they had to call around for information where to pick up cargo. Homebuilders, a notoriously fragmented industry, employ the internet to make the search and acquisition of supplies much more efficient, in the process cutting out a whole layer of subcontractors on whom they have had to rely so far. Farmers have fallen in love with the internet where they can access valuable information about crop yields, prices and potential clients for their products with the click of a mouse. In general, the internet enables firms across the entire economy to keep better track of supplies while simplifying order-taking and a variety of other office tasks.

But B2B e-commerce has already pushed far beyond simple information-gathering and streamlining of orders. Modeled after the phenomenally successful auction site eBay, where individuals can buy or sell anything they want to, industries have developed internet-based exchanges ('e-marketplaces') where goods and services related to any aspect of that particular sector can be exchanged between buyers and sellers. These exchanges automate tasks and processes which at present consume a lot of time and effort. Searching for supplies through paper catalogues and then trying to get in touch with suppliers via phone, fax, or travel can be a difficult and expensive undertaking. Often one has to use a broker or subcontractor for a fee to get any such deal done. And any transaction requires triplicate forms to be filled out. Such middlemen and paperwork can be eliminated on the internet where buyers can specify their needs and then wait for sellers to make their bids until a deal is negotiated.[5] Apart from reducing search and transaction costs this way, the competitive bidding process of such auction-based exchanges itself reduces the cost of supplies. In addition, these e-marketplaces will offer ancillary services, such as transportation arrangements for delivery and credit checks for buyers, which make the buying process more efficient and less costly.

During the coming decade, large numbers of firms in the United States and elsewhere will move their buying of parts and components as well as their sales of excess inventories online. The advantages of internet-based markets in terms of ease, speed and cost are so overwhelming that we can expect a revolution in inventory management and sales techniques which will transform the relationships between producers and their suppliers as well as their customers. The internet allows anyone to get directly in touch with the product sought, and this is an irresistible attraction.

In retrospect, it was no surprise that e-commerce was launched with such amazing speed. Given the ease with which web sites could be set up and made fully functional, it took very little to make use of this technology provided you had the creative talent for strategy and design. Except for those skills, the start-up costs for new internet producers were quite low. So were the product development costs, creating a permissive climate for fast-paced innovation. Someone with a useful idea could implement the innovation very rapidly, encouraging constant search for the next great idea that might make billions. In this intensely competitive and innovation-driven environment it seemed critical to be first, the first one to have the idea, to implement it, to make it the industry standard. The technological race unleashed on the internet compressed time. What used to take years not so long ago in terms of product development now became a matter of months, if not weeks, when applied to the development of new internet applications.

Given the dynamic nature of e-commerce, centered at this point on merchant networks, electronic auction sites and global commodity exchanges, investors soon came to expect explosive growth in this domain of the New Economy. At the moment of take-off, in 1998, knowledgeable sources, such as the internet consulting firm Forrester, estimated that this activity would rise rapidly to a phenomenal $1.4 trillion by the end of 2003.[6] Such a thirty-fold increase in e-commerce volume within just five years implied a major transformation in the way business is organized and consumers shop. It presumed that corporations would rapidly move their supply orders and wholesale distribution to the internet (so-called B2B applications), that some goods and services such as books, airline tickets, financial services or education would get sold predominantly online, that online auctions would become a huge mass market for used or surplus products, and that the suppliers of internet technology and its infrastructure could maintain the phenomenally fast-paced expansion of this complex computer and communication network. It also presumed that consumers find buying on the internet practical, safe and convenient.

Intertwined with optimistic projections of e-commerce growth were efforts to expand the infrastructure of the internet and so accommodate the anticipated increase in online traffic. A big battle has ensued between different systems of internet delivery over who will build the most effective infrastructure for *broadband*. A digital pipeline for networks carrying large amounts of voice, data and video services, broadband technology will increase speed and volume capacity of the internet exponentially, perhaps by a factor of twenty within the next decade:

- The existing PC-based system, with computers hooked up to telephone lines, will be vastly improved. Telecommunications firms all over the world are beginning to extend their fiber-optics networks to local phone lines. Once accomplished, they will replace existing modems with high-speed digital subscriber line (DSL) technology.
- Broadband technology will also be delivered by cable-based networks offering fast internet connections, interactive television, video on demand, as well as phone services. While such cable systems can be hooked up to computers, they will also spur access to the internet via 'smart' television sets.

- Wireless technology will prove especially useful for the creation of a mobile web using cell phones as the primary access tool to the internet. Those cell phones will soon be a whole lot smarter and more convenient than today's versions. This is an area where the Europeans and Japanese have a clear comparative advantage over the Americans whose use of cell phones has been hampered so far by excessive market fragmentation. The mobility of access promised by wireless applications will be a very attractive feature and enable us to reach the internet whenever and wherever we want to.

Whether transmitted via fiber optics, cable or satellite, whether accessed by PC, interactive TV or cell phone, the internet will soon be reachable anywhere, anytime. When we log onto the internet, it will cost almost nothing and be nearly instantaneous – no matter whether we do that at home, in the car, or on the street. Once online, we will have much more powerful software and versatile portals available with which to carry out our activities. Today, not even a decade into this phenomenon, the internet has emerged as the vector of a new technological revolution, one as far-reaching as the invention of electricity at the turn of the last century.

3.2 The Dot-com Crash

During the late 1990s, continuously rising prices of high-tech stocks created euphoric conditions, as more and more investors rushed into these stocks in anticipation of large capital gains. Once shareholders became drawn to stocks because everyone else was buying, realistic valuations of stocks based on their earnings potential got crowded out by what Greenspan characterized in 1996 as 'irrational exuberance'. This kind of bull market is typically fuelled by cheap money and lots of debt. The low-interest policy pursued by the Fed in the wake of the Asian crisis in 1997–99 induced many investors to take out broker loans (and later even home-equity loans and credit-card loans) for additional stock purchases. With shares serving as collateral for those loans, rising stock prices enhanced the borrowing capacity of investors and so became a funding machine for the bull market. In addition, many firms took out a lot of debt to buy back their shares and so counter the dilution of stock ownership brought about by the extensive use of stock options as a new form of employee compensation. It is this interaction between debt and asset inflation (rising prices for financial or real estate assets) which turns a reasonably bullish stock market into a speculative bubble.

Such a bubble is, however, unsustainable. It will burst when the rosy expectations about future profits underlying those sky-high stock-market valuations turn out to have been unrealistic. As market sentiments shift and disappointed investors try to cash in their capital gains, selling waves ensue to push stock prices rapidly lower. Pressured by high levels of indebtedness in the face of declining asset values and mounting capital losses, investors rush to liquidate their assets. Greed turns into fear, even panic. Precisely such a panic began to unfold in March 2000, causing internet stocks to tumble and pulling the NASDAQ over 60 percent lower (from its all-time high of 5048 in March 2000 to barely 1800 one year later).

The most evident cause for that turn of fortune was a slowing US economy, cooled off by six consecutive interest-rate hikes from the Fed. Why did Greenspan squeeze us so hard? What prompted the Chairman of the Fed to hit the brakes was the prospect of an overheating economy trig-gering a bout of renewed inflation. He was particularly concerned with increases in spending brought about by large capital gains in the stock market. As this source of income grew amidst one of history's greatest bull markets, consumers began to feel richer and spend correspondingly more while saving less. The steady decline of America's savings rate, becoming negative in 1998 among the richest 20 percent of Americans typically holding a lot of equity shares in their portfolios, illustrated the force of this wealth effect. As this boost to aggregate demand accelerated in 1999 and early 2000, Greenspan came to view the booming stock market with rising apprehension. He worried that the spectacular capital gains in the wake of NASDAQ's meteoric rise would prompt further spending increases before supply capacity had a chance to catch up. So he decided to tighten mone-tary policy as a preemptive strike against such a scenario of an overheating economy. His interest hikes did pierce the stock-market bubble by impairing the future earnings potential of firms in the face of higher debt-servicing costs, reducing the present value of future earnings and making it more expensive to borrow for stock purchases.

As the Fed's tightening moves began to bite, the New Economy suddenly revealed itself as vulnerable. With every passing day it became clearer that the expected profit explosion among dot-com firms was far from being realized. On the contrary, most internet-based firms continued to operate in the red, even those showing rapid growth in sales revenues. Somehow, investors began to realize, the internet might not be such an easy place to make a profit. If that suspicion proved true, then the sky-high valuations of dot-com firms or their suppliers could no longer be justified. As the doubts intensified in the spring of 2000, the flight of capital out of internet stocks gained force. Within a year those stocks had lost over 90 percent of their peak value, and thousands of dot-com firms faced annihilation.

The crash of 2000–01 was inevitable. Every speculative bubble, driving itself in a self-feeding frenzy to the point of unsustainable overextension, bursts with a bang. But this particular bubble had its own unique engine, an unprecedented marriage between finance and industry bringing together high-risk investors and high-tech entrepreneurs. For the first time in the history of capitalism we had created a fast-speed industry, the internet sector, which matched the preferences of financial investors for rapid change and short payoff periods. The amount of capital mobilized in the direction of the internet allowed this new growth sector to expand with breathtaking speed, far beyond the level of sustainability based on (still relatively limited) effective demand. What Greenspan perhaps underestimated was a different kind of wealth effect, the one driving up business spending to the point where supply outpaces demand. Such a deflationary situation is actually more dangerous than the much-feared inflationary wealth effect of overheating demand. Japan's lost decade serves in this regard as a serious warning.[7]

It should be clear by now that the explosive birth of the internet ended in a classic overproduction crisis. The initial burst created simply too many dot-com firms, all experimenting with unproven business models and chasing the relatively few customers ready to conduct transactions online. Demand for paid internet services has grown much less rapidly than anticipated even just three years ago, causing the excess supply imbalance underlying the collapse of NASDAQ. The brutal shake-out now under way in the high-tech sector puts into question the future viability of the New Economy. Unfortunately, this problem may not be just cyclical (and thus temporary) in nature, but reveal itself as a structural problem of longer duration. To begin with, the internet was from the very beginning designed as an open network with practically free access, as a public good offering such enormous social benefits that you would a priori not want to exclude anyone from having access to it. Its essential benefits, as a medium of information and means of communication, were available for free and thus difficult to fit into the confines of commercial exploitation for profit. Yes, the multi-layered infrastructure of the internet proved flexible enough to direct e-commerce traffic through an encrypted high-security layer specially designed for online transactions (see Chapter 4), but that addition did not make the task of charging for services on the internet any easier. In the absence of profitable cost-plus pricing, internet-based firms tried to generate other revenue streams from advertising, sales of information about customer profiles and membership fees. But none of these alternatives generated sufficient revenues fast enough to warrant sky-high stock-market valuations.

Even under the best of circumstances it will prove intrinsically difficult for dot-com firms to earn a profit online in a sustainable fashion. The internet, as currently constituted, deprives businesses of many of the usual advantages which had previously allowed them to earn a bigger profit:

- For one, businesses lose a large degree of monopoly power when going online. In the old world of brick-and-mortar stores, barriers to entry for newcomers were quite high compared to the low start-up costs on the internet which encourage a lot more competition. Whereas in the Old Economy consumers typically chose among a handful of local suppliers for most of their goods or services, no such geographic limitation exists on the internet where consumers can easily shop anywhere. The internet turns neighborhood oligopolies into globally integrated markets where every supplier is forced to compete with the world's best.

- To the extent that the internet yields globally integrated markets, it makes it much more difficult for businesses to charge different prices in various regional market segments, depending on what the local market will bear. There will instead be a price-leveling effect of enhanced competition, forcing price uniformity towards the lowest possible level.

- In addition, businesses lose the benefit of asymmetric information when operating on the internet. Whereas before potential buyers had only limited knowledge about products and prices, specialized web sites allow any customer nowadays to compare both in an instant for the best possible deal. No longer can customer ignorance be used as a source of easy profits.

- Another change in power relations to the detriment of profit stems from the flexibility which the internet affords buyers wishing to control how they compose desired services. The net enables consumers to unbundle service packages into separate components and then pick the best combination of those among a variety of online suppliers. This ability deprives businesses of tie-ins through which they forced consumers in the real world to acquire less-desired products whenever buying most-desired goods or services, in many instances a significant source of their profits.

- The internet makes it easy for individual agents to group together, whether as buyers or suppliers, and so change the dynamic of the marketplace to their advantage. Depending on the precise constellation emerging from the centralization of bargaining power, one group of actors might squeeze the other side of the exchange transaction. This issue may arise especially in the B2B commodity exchanges where large corporations, working together, use their collective market power to impose price discounts on more fragmented and smaller suppliers forced to bid against each other for business.

In light of these online constraints on profits, investors saw their hopes for a profit explosion from e-commerce dashed and the bears chasing the bulls out of the stock market. The first phase in the life cycle of the New Economy has now ended with a bang, forcing a painful reassessment of what works and what does not work in e-commerce. The crisis of 2000–01 has cooled investor and consumer enthusiasm for the commercial viability of the internet, and this profound change in sentiment has created a much more difficult environment for all but a handful of dot-com firms. There have already been spectacular failures of once-promising e-commerce firms, such as pets.com, toys.com, Webvan, and kozmo.com. Even dot-com giants, such as Amazon.com or Yahoo!, are reeling from heavy losses and failed revenue models. All internet-based firms focusing on e-commerce have seen a massive reduction of their capitalization base thanks to collapsing stock prices, making it much more difficult to sustain ongoing operating losses for longer periods of time as is still the case with many dot-com firms. The crisis has spread to the computer industry which is suffering from a slowdown in sales amidst sharp cuts in IT investments by the business sector. Even worse hit have been the telecommunication firms, many of which took on billions in debt to build very expensive, but barely utilized fiber-optics networks or wireless data-transmission capacity for cell phones. As fast as it arose in the 1990s, the internet seems to have imploded with even greater speed in the early 2000s.

3.3 Restructuring the Internet

The initial euphoria surrounding the internet has now given way to an equally excessive reaction to the contrary. With dot-com stocks down by 90 percent, many Wall Street analysts have written off e-commerce as a passing fad. True, the crash of that sector has been devastatingly swift and brutal. More worrisome perhaps is the spread of the crisis to the telecom sector where even the largest firms have loaded up on debt to create very expensive communication networks whose revenue-creating potential is now put in question by the crisis-induced slowdown of the internet revolution. Many of those firms may not have the means to finish the huge investment projects they have launched, thus depriving the internet of the infrastructure required to prove its commercial viability. All this makes it difficult to imagine imminent recovery in that sector, adding fuel to an already deeply entrenched pessimism about the future prospects of e-commerce. If this drastic change in fortunes qualifies the dot-com craze of yesteryear as just a speculative bubble which now has burst, then our story ends here. I believe, however, that it is much too early to write off the internet as a passing phenomenon. The genie is out of the bottle, and there is no way to put it back.

Before burying the New Economy as a victim of infant mortality, let us keep in mind that technological revolutions, such as the one currently under way thanks to the internet, have typically followed a boom-bust pattern. We have seen such a pattern during Britain's Industrial Revolution in the late 18th century, also when the United States created a national market in the late 19th century through massive investments in railroads, and again with the uneven diffusion of electricity during the early 20th century. In each case the rush of capital into the opening provided by the technological revolution far outpaced the ability of society to absorb the cultural and organizational changes unfolding in its wake, thus setting up a situation where supply grew faster than demand. Schumpeter (1942) characterized technological revolutions as processes of 'creative destruction'. The destructive part comes from currently established capital structures, organizational models and modes of thinking being suddenly rendered obsolete by the new alternatives embodied in that revolution. Moreover, there is also a fair amount of destruction from learning about the new by trial and error which invites a high failure rate among the first generation of entrepreneurs making that revolution happen. The creative part comes from figuring out the new opportunities presented by the unfolding revolution, developing appropriate business models in response and carrying out those strategic changes successfully. The most intense period of creative destruction occurs during that first crisis when the speed of the revolution is slowed down while the rate of adjustment accelerates.

It is worth noting that the Chinese sign for crisis denotes both danger and opportunity. The danger of the internet crisis is that it will do irreparable damage to that innovation's progress. The fact that even the largest e-commerce firms, such as Yahoo! and Amazon.com, can be pushed to the brink of bankruptcy might frighten away investors from high-tech stocks for years to come. Once-burned venture capitalists might consider the most creative e-commerce ideas too risky even though it has become clear that the internet does not lend itself well to low-risk extensions of the traditional and demands radical new approaches to production service and marketing instead. The allure of the dot-com firms among the most talented, tech-savvy workers may have faded, yet those kinds of employees are now needed most. The implementation of broadband may stall just when the internet should be upgraded in access speed and multimedia capability to improve its prospects of commercial viability. Notwithstanding those dangers, the current crisis presents opportunity as well. Unsustainable business models, such as trying to make up for operating losses through increased volume (Amazon.com), adding little value online to a service that can be conducted in the physical world as well (Webvan, pets.com), or relying too heavily on general advertising for revenue in a medium made for customized content (Yahoo!), will give way to an intense search for more profitable strategies tailored to the unique capabilities of the internet. Survivors of the shake-out will look stronger, after having become much more careful about costs, and gained market share by the sheer elimination of some of their competitors. They will run a much tighter ship henceforth and will be more emphatic about generating revenues more quickly. The excessively low stock prices of most dot-coms will also make it that much easier for traditional firms to acquire internet capabilities and expand their online operations cheaply. To that effect, a wave of mergers and takeovers has already started.

Weighing this confluence of danger and opportunity in the current crisis of the internet, there is no question in my mind that in the end the latter outweighs the former. The technological revolution triggered by this innovation will continue to run its course, albeit more slowly than initially anticipated. There are good reasons for such guarded optimism about recovery. Throughout the downturn the number of internet users has continued to grow. More than 140 million Americans have regular access to the internet, slightly over half the US population. User growth has progressed even more rapidly elsewhere, with the number of non-US netizens rising from only 100 million at the beginning of 1998 to 240 million in mid-2001. Even more encouraging is that consumers continue to shop online, with B2C e-commerce sales growing by 67 percent alone in 2000. While e-commerce only amounted to 1 percent of total retail sales last year, it may eventually grab a 10 percent share (rather than the 15 percent share predicted during the boom). Even that lowered forecast implies a very significant role for the New Economy by the end of the decade. And large corporations continue to prepare themselves for precisely such a future. While US business spending on information technology has declined by 20 percent from its 1999 peak, most corporations with early exposure to the internet remain committed to expanding their online capabilities and getting the most out of the new technology.[8]

That commitment makes sense, considering the tremendous potential of the internet as a vector of change. A revolutionary new technology to organize and disseminate data, the internet lends support to one of the more fundamental trends of advanced capitalist societies, an insatiable need for information. The current stage in the historic evolution of capitalism is one where information becomes ever-more important in our lives. This is more than just the normal outcome of progress by the human species towards ever-greater knowledge and ever-wider exchange of what we know. Our economy itself is coming to depend increasingly on information.

Several trends in the contemporary organization of economic activity have fuelled greater reliance on information:

- For one, with competition shifting its focus from prices to products, consumers need to understand the implications of increasingly sophisticated product differentiation for their buying decisions.

- Another cause fuelling a search for more information stems from a fundamental change in the nature of our contractual commitments. In an effort to reduce risks associated with an unpredictable future, we engage with each other in an ever-greater variety of forward-money contracts (for example long-term supply contracts, pensions, insurance, financial contracts such as bonds or derivatives, even wages when predetermined by collective-bargaining agreements) which by their very nature as predetermined cash-flow commitments compel us to anticipate the future more systematically.

- In a similar vein, the intensifying linkages between finance and industry necessitate more information to help to reach sufficient consensus within a widening circle of investors about the future earnings potential of different investments.

- As the penetration of e-business increases the importance of intangible forms of productive capital (such as ideas and intellectual property rights), both corporate managers and financial investors will need a lot more information, especially qualitative data, to assist them in the difficult task of determining the value of something that is largely invisible, thus impossible to quantify numerically with precision.[9]

- In addition, knowledge-intensive services have become the growth engines of our New Economy, and these sectors (for instance financial services, health care, education) have a large information base built into their product.

- Finally, with multinational corporations transforming themselves into global production networks, their production becomes increasingly decentralized, teamwork-based and centered on mental rather than manual labor. These qualities of the contemporary production process can only be managed with a lot of information circulating within those entities.

For all these (and other) reasons, communication, regulating what people give each other in information and how they transmit it, has become a major input in our economy's organization of markets, contracts and production activities. In that context the internet has rapidly assumed a strategic role as the principal communication channel, the most efficient conduit for the transmission of information between interacting parties. Beyond using it to generate more revenues, the internet allows corporations to cut costs and improve productivity by moving more of their operations online (e-business). Instantaneous communication with suppliers will greatly improve inventory management and shorten the turnaround time when production schedules change. Moving purchases of supplies and components online, perhaps even reorganizing this activity totally through auction-like online commodity exchanges (e-marketplaces), will help to lower working capital expenditures. The filing of expense reports and calculation of daily sales tallies will now be automated, giving managers much better control over cash flow. Companies will build intranets for in-house communication to tap into employees' intellectual capital, get workers to share relevant information in collaborative projects and provide a wide variety of employee assistance and training programs. The internet can also automate interactions with customers to their mutual benefit, with more and more order-taking and purchasing as well as after-sales services conducted online. E-business pioneers, such as Dell Computers or Cisco Systems, have consistently outperformed their less-automated competitors by selling most of their products online. This has given them an extra ability to reduce delivery times, offer more customized models, outsource production more aggressively and improve coordination with their suppliers. The internet carries great potential for cumulative gains as it gradually invades every nook and cranny of corporate organization for possible cost savings.

Of course, such corporate transformation will not occur over night. On the contrary, it will be a slow and uneven process, hampered by the persistence of old thinking and other institutional barriers to change. Information-sharing among employees runs counter to the established credo among management that individual power derives from keeping information to oneself. Fears of shrinking profit margins and greater performance demands might make suppliers resist being pushed into e-marketplaces. Online customers might prove super-sensitive to prices, making it difficult for internet-based businesses to defend their profit margins in the light of more intense price competition and declining customer loyalty. But, while difficult, change will also be inevitable. Even the most hesitant managers will not be able to escape the great promise that e-business holds for cumulative cost savings. The internet is irresistible, because it provides us with three sources of efficiency gains at the same time:

1. It offers large *economies of scale*, by which economists mean efficiency gains ('economies') from the increased size of operations ('scale'). Internet-based activities typically involve high fixed costs due to the expensive infrastructure underlying that medium, while variable costs have been shrunk by automation. This cost composition in favor of mostly fixed costs, which do not rise much with growing output, means that the marginal costs of selling additional units of output online are minimal. Average costs decline quite sharply with rising volume. This explains the chase in so many segments of e-commerce over whose product variant will become the industry standard, with the winner able to reap larger economies of scale.

2. Major efficiency gains also arise online from so-called *economies of scope*, a concept applying to synergies in product development from merging different technologies together. The internet itself is a manifestation of such scope economies, born out of a highly original fusion of computer and communication technologies. It is also an excellent carrier of new scope economies, because it accelerates the diffusion of

new ideas and facilitates interconnection between hitherto separate products or technologies.

3. Finally, the internet provides a strong impetus for *network economies*. Representing the most sophisticated and extensive network for human interaction ever created, the internet proves that the value of a network to its individual members rises dramatically as the network manages to expand. Large networks are inherently more beneficial than small networks. This phenomenon is known as Metcalfe's Law, named after 3Com founder and ethernet inventor Robert Metcalfe, according to which the usefulness of a network equals the square of the number of its users. If you can double its size, you make a network exponentially more valuable. Corporations chasing these network economies enter into alliances with other firms and reorganize internally into semi-autonomous teams cooperating with each other.

The internet raises the enticing prospect of cumulative cost savings, precisely because it offers scale, scope and network economies all at once. These different sources of efficiency gains are interdependent and thus mutually enhancing. But they are by no means easily achieved. Many dot-com experiments have faltered because they never managed to reach sufficient volume in time for scale economies to kick in. Scope economies have been limited so far by the unresolved question of how far to push online when most of the operating costs still occur in the physical world (of human labor, machines, offices and warehouses) and when in addition many customers still prefer conducting a variety of transactions off-line. Network economies can also work in reverse at the beginning of a project's life cycle, making its launch quite difficult. New merchant networks, for instance, have had a hard time signing up enough merchants when the customer base was still small, yet could not attract enough customers while the list of merchants remained skimpy. Most importantly, network economies are intrinsically difficult to harness. When companies want to construct an online network, they enter into alliances with other firms which, if not their outright competitors, at least have conflicting interests over the distribution of jointly created revenues. The standard model on the internet is thus one best described as *coopetition*, a combination of cooperation and competition. The tension embodied in this duality may prevent or undermine network economies. Take, for instance, electronic banking. The banks know that their most potent source of online expansion is electronic billing, yet have not been able to agree with utilities and internet service providers (ISPs) on whose web site the bills should appear. Online commodity exchanges grouping together competitors, such as America's 'Big Three' automakers in Covisint, find participants hesitant to cooperate for fear of giving away potential competitive weapons, such as their supply network. Coopetition only works when collective gains are strong enough to warrant cooperation and when competition is regulated by shared norms that can be enforced.

All these barriers to success will get easier to handle, once broadband and third-generation wireless technologies become widely available. That process might take a few years, with heavily indebted telecom firms forced to rewire the entire globe with unproven technologies at great initial expense. But the stakes are too enormous and the already-sunk costs too high for this leap into the unknown not to unleash a collective search for ways to use all that new capacity coming on stream. Luckily the upgrade itself will make that task easier. Once delivered through broadband to computers or spreading to smart cell phones on the mobile web, the internet will be accessible anywhere, anytime. It will offer instant access and operate with much greater speed. It will incorporate dramatically enhanced multimedia capabilities and other improvements which will make tomorrow's web sites a lot more user-friendly, more entertaining and safer. The enhanced capacity of the internet will provide interactive communication, video clips, captivating data presentation and other 'hooks' to attract potential customers and then win their loyalty. As these improvements come on stream, we will see a reacceleration of efforts to make the internet work for business. E-commerce will expand along different vectors, each embodying a distinct type of online activity. This process will be decidedly uneven, as some activities and sectors will prove more prone to online automation than others.

B2B applications will grow rapidly to an estimated global volume of $6 trillion by 2004 (according to the latest forecasts of internet specialists Forrester Research and Gartner), motivated by corporate efforts to use the internet as a cost-cutting and productivity-enhancing tool. A survey by Forrester of 1000 large American and Canadian corporations in early 2001 showed 65 percent of them as having either already implemented e-business strategies or begun to put such plans into action. Underlying all these initiatives is the notion of harnessing the internet's power to generate and transmit information for the purpose of better coordination of production-related activities – both internally between teams of employees and externally in alliances with other firms. Companies will certainly establish tight online relations with their suppliers and shift a lot of their purchases to e-marketplaces. Many firms will use intranet networks to tap in-house knowledge and skills of their workforce, foster teamwork and offer employee assistance programs. They will also try to reach their customers online, get them to buy services or goods there and seek the development of long-term relations with their better clients while weeding out those not considered cost-effective. All these steps towards the online automation of any business aspect involving communication of information sets the stage for a much more radical extension of e-business into manufacturing processes itself, which will come about when machines can communicate with each other directly – one of the future growth areas of the internet moving us beyond the World Wide Web.

Yet another tremendous growth area for the internet bypassing the web involves P2P technology, such as MP3 software popularized by Napster to download music for free. This technology lets PCs communicate directly on the net without third-party intermediaries, such as ISPs, operating as access ramps. Start-ups in this segment of e-commerce have tried so far to make a buck by selling P2P software that allow PC users to access each other's computer files, exchange data and collaborate on projects. But they have not yet worked out how to charge users beyond that initial software sale. Still, P2P has a lot of potential, as was seen by the music industry's virulent reaction to the threat posed by Napster and the proliferation of even more elusive MP3 offsprings after a court injunction took out that company. One only has to look at the success of eBay to understand the power of creating spontaneous or well-organized direct-communication networks between PC users wishing to get in touch with each other for a variety of reasons. Political campaigns can be launched that way quite effectively, and so can informal exchanges for the circulation of information or trading of goods and services. With P2P we see an aspect of e-commerce emerging which may in the not-so-distant future involve millions of people organizing new ways of interaction and new channels for transaction. Such spontaneous network creation may be greatly facilitated by additional technologies currently being developed on the internet, specifically the wireless ('mobile') net transmitting information via cell phones and instant messaging which makes it easier for people to communicate with each other over the internet.

B2C applications, by contrast, have a more uncertain future than either the B2B or P2P segments of e-commerce. So far online consumers have in large measure proven fickle, hypersensitive to prices and inclined to use web sites of target firms more to gather information in preparation for the eventual shopping trip to a real-live store, mall, or broker. This difficult environment is further complicated by the frequent failure of B2C firms to secure more than one revenue source (for instance Yahoo!, whose revenues depend on up to 90 percent advertising sales) or charge high enough prices to make a profit on each transaction. Dot-com firms trying to operate exclusively online have found themselves especially vulnerable in the current crisis, in particular those among them which had opted for a very aggressive expansion of products offered (for instance pets.com, Amazon.com and E*Trade). This has prompted some lessons to be heeded. One concerns the need to develop hybrid structures where your firm operates both online and off-line in a balanced and supplementary fashion. The other lesson applies to the potential advantages of focusing one's product development more narrowly on specialized market niches rather than trying to be all things for everyone. In the end B2C enterprises will have to ask themselves some tough questions about the relative importance of the internet in the overall picture of their operation. What are the real-world resource demands, including those in manufacturing or distribution, going to be in order to maintain a cost-effective web site for customer sales and service? What kind of revenue sources can the firm expect to generate online and how can these streams of income be diversified so as not to depend just on one or two inflows?

In trying to answer these questions, we can expect very different responses depending on the industry of the respondent. Some of the early B2C successes will run up against supply bottlenecks beyond their control. The crisis of airline and road transportation systems naturally puts a dent on the viability of online travel sites, while online energy exchanges are ultimately constrained by inadequate power generation and transmission capacity in the United States and elsewhere. Manufacturers must still be able to produce a high-quality product at an affordable price, no matter how glitzy their web site. Similarly, online retailers have found that the logistics of their distribution are a more important determinant of their competitiveness and profitability than customer traffic on their web sites. The most promising prospects for e-commerce lie with information-rich services which can be produced on the internet themselves. AOL's acquisition of Time Warner, aimed at offering its customers an integrated package of multimedia entertainment, shows the internet's potential in the production of online services for a mass audience. In the same vein one can imagine online education to make the acquisition of knowledge available to many who would otherwise have neither the time nor the means for more traditional schooling. Health care services, a very labor-intensive and paperwork-oriented sector, is an area where internet-based automation of information-processing, data storage and interactive communication could dramatically improve the quality and cost-effectiveness of service delivery. Those improvements will have to be weighed against the loss of the human element when turning teaching or healing from a direct interaction between people into a cyberspace relation. Just as in e-business, these public services of education and health will have to find their proper online–off-line balance.

So far, however, the most important push for online automation of information-rich services, has been in the area of financial services (see also sections 2.4 and 2.5). A start-up, such as E*Trade, has completely transformed the retail brokerage business by offering no-frills online stock trades at rock-bottom prices, giving its customers access to thousands of different mutual funds, opening participation in IPOs to the public, providing new types of information (such as online chats with corporate managers and investment analysts), and moving into commercial banking when it first bought an online bank and then a large network of ATMs to be installed in all kinds of retail outlets. The banks have realized that they now face direct competition from other (nonbank) institutions which are using the internet to transform themselves into financial supermarkets. After a slow start, large US and European banks have become much more aggressive in offering attractive web sites and a variety of online services which the internet allows to connect into one package (such as combining online banking services with online brokerage services, as FleetBoston did recently). The banks with the most ambitious internet programs, such as the Bank of America, Citigroup and Wells Fargo, have each been able to sign up more than 2 million online customers. As in the case of education and health services, this sector too will have to overcome major technological and institutional barriers before online automation can succeed. A good example is the battle between banks, utilities and ISPs over electronic billing, generally considered to be the 'killer application' with which to move a lot of households to online banking. That battle, still unresolved, has slowed down progress in the online expansion of financial services.

The drama of online banking has broader implications for the post-crisis role of the New Economy. It is from there, in that battle to create financial supermarkets for one-stop banking on the net, that we will get a crucial element in the restructuring of the internet – the introduction of cybercash possibly fuelling the growth of e-commerce along all its unique vectors. Cybercash can play this key role by making it easier for e-commerce firms to charge reasonable prices for services delivered online and have buyers pay those prices. So far the greatest problem for e-commerce has been the lack of e-profits, the inability to sell online services at a price above cost. This will have to change if e-commerce is to become a viable and vibrant part of our 21st century economy. Simply put, the internet will have to prove itself as a fountain of profit, and this involves charging users adequately for services provided on the net. The presence of cybercash, organized as an integral part of online shopping protocols, will make that process of charging and getting paid reasonable prices quite a bit easier to implement.

The dot-com crash of 2000–01 reflects not least the fact that the internet, in its original design, was not meant for e-commerce. Initially, the internet emerged as a free digital bazaar for the exchange of ideas and information, vastly expanding our access to knowledge and ability to communicate with each other at low cost. User fees of $20 per month for private access, supplemented by a public sphere of free-access facilities in public libraries, schools, churches and at work, made the internet widely affordable. Access ramps to the web, ISPs, have extended that afford-ability by offering their basic log-on service for free and relying instead on advertising for revenue. But the original promise of online advertising, namely that it could finance the expansion of the net, has failed to become a reality. In retrospect, that failure was not surprising. After all, the internet was first conceived as a public good offering such tremendous social bene-fits (notably productivity gains, better communication, the fostering of entrepreneurship in the population and faster circulation of new ideas) that you would not want a priori to exclude anyone. The original model of basically free internet access and reliance on advertising revenues expressed precisely this priority, tempered by the online equivalent of bill-boards on highways. Of course, that same public-good aspect of the internet also allowed surfers to ignore the banner ads at will, rendering them basically ineffective.

Its e-commerce dimension will require the internet to become more profitable than that, and this will come about when net users are made to pay for online services above cost. We are talking here about transforming the internet more and more from a public good into a profit center for private enterprise (meaning the net as a 'private commodity'). This change centers on the *commodification of information*, that is, on making people pay for a valuable information-based service which they cannot access so cheaply or easily by alternative means. Much of the internet will probably escape this commodification and remain free, notably widely available information (news, weather reports, stock quotes and so forth), price and product information for easy comparison shopping, search engines whose marginal costs of additional searches are miniscule and e-shopping which cannot afford surcharges if it wants to compete with catalog sales or brick-and-mortar stores. Other services, offering greater value added, will however become subject to subscriptions or user fees. Such once-free services subject to commodification include internet access ramps, espec-ially when those begin to offer high-speed broadband access and better technical support, highly valued analyses of information (for example investment advice, stock-market prognoses and economic forecasts, list of best doctors in a given city), net-based entertainment such as videos on demand or music downloads and specialized services for upscale customers joining online clubs for a membership fee.

The ability of the internet to turn itself into a source of private gain from e-commerce depends not only on the willingness of its users to pay for online services, but also on their ability to do so easily and rapidly when prompted. In other words, more and more online products will be sold if buyers can access online money conveniently for automatic payments. The existing online-payment system, heavily dominated by credit cards, fails in that regard for several reasons. Credit cards, for instance, are useless for very small transactions ranging from a few cents to a handful of dollars. Yet precisely such micropayments make a big difference in the commodi- fication of information where most transactions involve small sums. Nor do credit cards work very well in the world of P2P, where most part- icipants lack the merchant status required for access to credit-card payment services, or in B2B commerce where the sums involved are simply too large. And in B2C commerce, the one segment where they are practical, credit cards are expensive. Consumers pay super-high interest rates on unpaid balances, and merchants pay fairly substantial user fees (ranging from 1.5 percent to 6.5 percent of the transaction value) to the credit-card issuers. Given these limitations, credit cards are an inadequate means of online payment. Up to now their dominance on the net has been due to the absence of better alternatives. Yet as long as credit cards remain so dominant in online transactions, e-commerce will be hampered in its development. A better alternative for online payments is urgently needed.

3.4 The Internet as Payment Sphere

We have now, at the beginning of the internet's restructuring from a public good into a private commodity, arrived at the point where we can see the outlines of such an alternative emerge. Currently there are several experi- ments under way to introduce online monies which are created and circ- ulated on the internet in the course of e-commerce transactions. This new type of electronic money, termed here 'cybercash', comes in different vari- ants, depending on the type of e-commerce it is supposed to serve. Some experiments, such as those involving the design of e-checks, aim to estab- lish a general cybercash system that can be used anywhere online. But much of the monetary innovation pertaining to cybercash now has a narrower focus on specific e-commerce applications. For instance, e-mail money (involving online money transfers between parties via e-mail) has already proven very attractive for P2P transactions. Smart cards might one day help to revolutionize B2C transactions. That same segment of e-commerce has also seen efforts in the direction of coupon money as the dominant form of cybercash used in electronic shopping malls. Online money for B2B transactions will perhaps develop more slowly, since businesses already use highly automated fund-transfer mechanisms (wire transfers, ACH transfers) for transactions with each other. But even here we can see the first efforts to create genuine cybercash variants tailored to e-marketplaces or to typical e-business transactions, such as supply-chain management.

While these various cybercash variants have had a difficult time getting off the ground, a subject we shall explore in much greater detail in the next three chapters, some of them have progressed quite a bit in both design and scale. Such progress justifies thinking about their potential impact on the post-crisis evolution of e-commerce. To the extent that the future success of the internet as an engine of economic growth depends on its restructuring from an open-access medium of communication into a restricted-access supplier of paid services, online money would surely help that transformation along while at the same time also completing the transition to electronic money. In the process debit and credit cards will be replaced by smart cards which can be inserted into the access tools of the internet. Electronic fund transfers will move beyond wholesale (B2B) transactions to retail (B2C and P2P) transactions and so become the primary mechanism for moving money around. Net-based payments systems, using digital cash, will become part of sophisticated online shopping protocols which in turn will facilitate the rapid growth of e-commerce. Banking will increasingly move online, as will the trading of securities in financial markets. The internet might evolve gradually into the primary locus of money creation and credit extension, whereby it pushes its impact on our economy beyond commerce to production and finance. We have arrived at the threshold of a new era in which online money reshapes the modus operandi of our 21st-century economy.

PART II

The Complexities of Cybercash

CHAPTER 4

Money as Software

The era of cybercash is about to begin. We have come to this threshold from two different directions. One has been the irresistible spread of computer and communication technologies in banking which has habituated us to the use of plastic cards, automated teller machines, point-of-sale terminals, electronic fund transfers and access devices such as personal computers and cell phones – the components of a socio-technological infrastructure for cybercash. The other direction is the internet whose most dynamic application, e-commerce, demands an online-payments system for its full development.

E-commerce today still suffers from some transient problems limiting its volume, such as a lack of familiarity with this new medium or a limited selection of products offered online. The dot-com crash, following a period of overinvestment that seems typical for the birth phase of revolutionary technologies, is a challenge which only the fittest e-business models will survive. But that shake-out will also help to streamline the internet and in the process revive the still-considerable growth potential for e-commerce. The internet enables businesses to automate many operations and create a worldwide, 24-hour/day presence at low cost. At the same time it empowers customers to e-shop across the globe, greatly increasing their choice of products and their information about prices. These advantages of e-commerce will remain, the current crisis notwithstanding. Of course, we now know that the sensational e-commerce forecasts driving the dot-com bubble of 1998–2000 will not come to pass. The bursting of that bubble in 2000–01 followed the collective realization of stock-market investors that the internet, as currently constituted, was actually a difficult place to make a profit in. While first-generation dot-com firms tried all kinds of revenue-generation models, from banner ads and sale of consumer-profiling data to subscriptions and licensing fees, nothing in the end proves as profitable as selling services online at cost-plus prices to as large a number of customers as possible. And for this to happen on a mass scale, you need to have anchored among the public a culture of online payments. Unless internet users find it natural to pay for services online with an automatic click of the mouse or push of a button, e-commerce will not be able to realize its full potential as the marketplace of tomorrow, the mainstay of our 21st-century economy.

Central to the challenge of reviving the internet as a locus of commerce is thus the question of how best to pay for such purchases online. The predicted explosion of e-commerce has failed to materialize not least because of the limitations of existing money forms when used for online payments. Sending cash is slow, poses security problems and involves considerable conversion costs in cross-border transactions. Paying with a check, while far safer than sending cash, is equally time-consuming and limited to domestic transactions. Bank wires are another option, but they are cumbersome and quite expensive. In light of these disadvantages, it is not surprising that credit cards have become the preferred choice for e-commerce payments. But credit cards also have their limitations. Not every potential internet customer owns a credit card. Many consumers, especially the young in America as well as large percentages of Europeans or Asians, are willing to spend online, but lack a credit-card account. Moreover, credit cards do not work for peer-to-peer or business-to-business transactions. Nor are they available for small-denomination payments (so-called 'micropayments') which are likely to dominate much of business-to-consumer commerce. They are also quite expensive as debt, unless outstanding debt balances are paid off right away. Merchants do not like to pay the considerable processing charges for credit-card transactions. They also worry about online fraud and disputes.

In light of these drawbacks, something better is needed than cash, checks, bank wires or credit cards to pay for transactions on the internet. Never has the need for a simple, safe and secure online-payments mechanism been greater. The urgency of that situation is beginning to be realized by those in the industry who specialize in the provision of electronic-payments services. However, their intensifying efforts to develop precisely such an online-payments mechanism raise a number of questions about the very nature of cybercash. These are taken up in this chapter. After first discussing the unique properties of cybercash as a software product (section 4.1), we take a closer look at the challenges posed by this invisible money form to our concerns with privacy protection (section 4.2) and safety (section 4.3). Unless these issues are resolved satisfactorily, the public will not trust cybercash sufficiently to permit its widespread use.

Another issue, which arises inevitably when money becomes software, is that of its control. This question goes beyond asking ourselves how to regulate the supply of money when new liquidity can be created on computers by pushing a button. Even more interesting is the possibility that the very nature of online money may bring nonbank firms into the monetary process and thus destroy the monopoly enjoyed by banks with regard to money creation (section 4.4). Finally, money as software will have unique technology-derived capabilities and thus be able to do things that no other money form could do (section 4.5).

4.1 The Properties of Cybercash

Neither the gradual habituation by the public with the tools of electronic banking (for instance credit and debit cards, computerized transaction terminals, online banking) nor the emergence of the internet as a locus of commerce will automatically bring about the dominance of cybercash. These developments are necessary, but not sufficient conditions for the successful spread of the new money form. Given the aforementioned embeddedness of existing money forms and payments habits, reinforced by daily practices of repetition, the public does not easily abandon what it has become used to as money. New money forms can only succeed if they are clearly advantageous to users as well as issuers. They have to be attractive enough for a hesitant public to try them and, upon trying, prefer them over existing money forms.

Which beneficial features will allow cybercash to attract a large pool of users? This question preoccupied computer specialists a decade ago when the idea of digital money first began to circulate. Okamoto and Ohta (1991) listed six qualities which cybercash has to possess in order to compete effectively with cash and checks:

1 *Security:* The modalities of cybercash transactions must guarantee a high degree of security in the sense of not being easily counterfeited. Neither party to the transaction, nor anyone else, should be able to alter or reproduce the electronic tokens transferred from buyer to seller. The public must be convinced that cybercash is unforgeable.

2 *Anonymity:* People and businesses will use cybercash if they see it as an untraceable money form, much like cash. Users will want to have at least the option of remaining anonymous in relation to the payment,

perhaps even to the point of being completely invisible with regard to the mere existence of a payment on their behalf.

3. *Portability:* Cybercash should not depend on any physical location so that it can be transferred freely through computer networks as well as other storage devices or alternative delivery systems which do not depend on computers (such as PalmPilot or cell phones). In other words, it should not be confined to a unique, proprietary computer network restricting its circulation.

4. *Indefinite preservability:* Cybercash should not expire. Assuming that its issuer will not debase it or go out of business, such electronic money will have to maintain its value over time so that it can be stored ('saved') somewhere safely and retrieved for use later. Of course, as is the case with other forms of money, cybercash may be destroyed under the rules governing its issue – either when the credit part of such electronic credit-money has been repaid in full or by a conscious decision of the issuer.

5. *General acceptability:* Money works as such only if it is generally accepted and, based on this social acceptance, can be transferred to others who know in advance that they in turn will be able to spend it in that form. The more widely accepted by others, the greater is its use. This condition surely also holds for cybercash. In the case of cybercash, such acceptance should extend to peer-to-peer (P2P) payments so that neither party has to attain registered merchant status as is the case with today's credit-card payments. If I go out to dinner with a friend and pay for him, he should be able to send me his share of the expense in digital cash.

6. *Off-line capability:* It would be useful for cybercash to have unrestricted availability so that it can be spent anytime and anywhere, without either party to the transaction having to be hooked to a computer for authentication and processing.

Once actual cybercash experiments got under way on the internet in the mid-1990s, additional properties for this new money form gained in importance. Matonis (1995), for instance, added three new characteristics to the ones listed above:

1. *Divisibility:* Electronic money should be divisible into small units and allow for reasonable portions of change to be made. Towards this objective most cybercash designers have aimed at allowing for electronic-

money units as small as $0.01. In this effort they have been fully aware that such fungibility would give cybercash a competitive edge over credit cards which generally cannot be used for small-denomination transactions. A very large number of daily small-value purchases (for example newspapers, mass transit, movie tickets) will move online, once cybercash can be used for such micropayments.

3. *User-friendly protocol:* It should be easy for both spender and receiver to conduct a cybercash transaction. Simplicity of use is key to cybercash gaining wide acceptance, especially among new internet subscribers who lack the experience and confidence to cope with complicated protocols.

4 *Unit-of-value freedom:* Free-market protagonists, such as Matonis, regard cybercash as better than traditional government-issued or -regulated money, because it is determined by market forces and thus nonpolitical in nature. Whether this presumed freedom from state interference makes cybercash truly a better money form remains to be seen and is, in my opinion, doubtful. Be that as it may, there is no question that cybercash is a private money form capable of escaping government regulation quite effectively. Whether or not we agree with the free-market advocates of cybercash, we cannot deny the potential of its disassociation from government control.

It is difficult to argue that any of the cybercash experiments currently under way satisfy each of these criteria unambiguously (see Chapter 5 for more of this). Yet it is equally obvious that many such experiments strive towards endowing their variant of cybercash with most, if not all, of these characteristics. In that sense the nine properties of cybercash outlined here serve as a benchmark on the basis of which one can assess and compare the different cybercash versions in development.

4.2 Privacy Concerns

Money only works effectively if it is trusted by the public. The public trust underlying money's general acceptability was previously anchored in the money form itself, as in the case of metal money, or was based on confidence in third parties backing the currency, as in the case of paper money. In the case of cybercash, which is nothing but a software product and thus the first fully dematerialized form of money we have had to face, the focus of the public's trust shifts from the money form per se or third-party intermediaries to the technology supporting the transfer of invisible funds. People will only feel comfortable with cybercash, if they believe that the computer and communication systems used for such electronic money work properly. Since electronic money itself is immaterial and thus exists beyond our physical senses, the public needs to trust its infrastructure beyond the shadow of a doubt. If online-payment systems cannot guarantee any monetary commitments with predictable automaticity, the public will prefer to stick with old payment forms even though they may have to be routed off-line.

One of the more persistent challenges in this regard is the issue of regulating the information collected about e-shoppers by businesses in the wake of e-commerce. Americans clearly worry about the degree to which their privacy might be compromised on the internet. Various polls, such as a *Business Week*/Harris poll undertaken in February 1998, a 1999 study by the Boston Consulting Group and a 1999 survey by the American Association of Retired Persons, clearly illustrate that large majorities of Americans do not trust their privacy to be protected on the internet. This mistrust apparently prevents many households from going online or shopping online. Public fears are particularly acute with regard to the use of credit cards and the protection of financial information, which bodes ill for the future of cybercash.[1]

Those fears about one's online privacy are well grounded. The internet has proven an absolutely amazing tool for information collection. It contains a variety of powerful and highly efficient data-gathering technologies. So-called cookies, for instance, record your web site visits. Such data can be connected with personal information you provided during site registrations to construct a highly detailed profile of your interests, preferences and habits. Other examples of intrusive data-gathering technology include Intel's attempt to give each personal computer a traceable identity by encoding a unique serial number on every new Pentium III microprocessor, Microsoft's electronic marker which allows identification of the source of any Word document created and so-called 'web bugs' which gather information about site visits by unsuspecting web surfers. Such data collection and identification is not confined to computers, but extends to the mobile net. Sprint cell phones offering wireless web connections, for instance, transmit a user's phone number to whatever site he or she has accessed.

E-commerce companies, most of whom have found it difficult to create revenue streams and thus have come under tremendous pressure from the stock market, have a great interest in collecting all this information about you. They can turn this knowledge into two sources of revenue. One consists of constructing customized ads or sales pitches which speak to your interests and taste preferences. Such targeting has a much better chance of encouraging cybersales than general banner ads which most internet users tend to ignore. Alternatively, they can sell this information to other interested parties, including web-based firms specializing in cyber-tracking as their main business (such as DoubleClick or Broadcast.com). Since the virtual nature of the internet makes it impossible for consumers to know what information has been collected about them and how it will be used, they have reason to worry about this surreptitious activity. To the extent that this worry impedes the willingness of people to shop online, the issue of privacy protection has become a key challenge for the New Economy. It is a particularly urgent issue for cybercash, since the public worries most about the (ab)use of personal financial information in unauthorized hands (see note 1). If people are so afraid of dealing with an online trader or an internet bank, imagine how they will feel transacting online in cybercash which may provide a lot of information about their buying habits and financial status.

Recognizing the need for more effective privacy protection, industry has recently intensified efforts in that direction. Whereas only 43 percent of the top 100 web sites had displayed privacy policies in early 1998, more than 90 percent did so two years later. Such privacy policies inform consumers as to what is being done with the information collected about them. Some companies may also give site visitors an option to restrict the use of such information and/or allow consumers to view and correct information collected about them. There are several independent agencies on the web, such as TRUSTe, eTrust, the Better Business Bureau and BetterWeb, which evaluate the privacy policies of companies and give those meeting certain standards a seal of approval. Some of these rating agencies also conduct audits which examine all aspects of a firm's performance with regard to safeguarding consumer privacy and suggest improvements. Privacy consulting has become a big business, with a growing number and variety of firms (such as IBM or Pricewaterhouse Coopers) helping companies to set up more effective policies.

However, these self-regulation efforts are often seriously flawed. Privacy policies, while now much more common, are frequently hard to find. They tend to be located on the bottom of a site and announced in small print.[2] Once you find them and click on, you are more likely than not confused by highly ambiguous wording and inconsistent statements. For instance, the common privacy-policy statement 'We may use the information you give or we collect about your online behavior to enhance your experience' means de facto that the site could be sharing that information with all kinds of marketers. All too often companies do not follow their own privacy policy, as many internet users have become aware of recently in the wake of several scandals widely reported in the media.[3] Even companies with a strong commitment to a tough privacy policy often find it difficult to protect privacy as intended. Most companies operating on the web engage in a myriad of partnerships with other operators whose sites they are all connected to. Each company then is responsible for the privacy policies of its partners without being able to control them. Finally, even the seal of approval of an online-privacy watchdog, such as eTrust, does not mean much, since it may be outdated and generally lacks ongoing enforcement.

A recent study of the Federal Trade Commission (FTC) concluded that only 20 percent of e-commerce sites met its privacy-protection standards regarding the posting of privacy policies, the accessibility of such policies for web users, the freedom of consumers to limit use of their personal data and the secure handling of such information (see Simpson, 2000a). In light of that rather sobering picture it is no surprise that consumers do not have much confidence in the privacy-protection efforts of online sites. In the aforementioned 1998 *Business Week*/Harris poll only 9 percent of the subjects fully trusted a company to follow its own privacy policy while 33 percent did not trust any company to do so at all.

For self-regulation to work, companies must adopt credible policies and then adhere to them strictly, not an easy feat considering that any company violating industry-wide rules might thereby gain a competitive advantage over others. It would also help to place enforcement powers in the hands of 'trusted third parties' acting as privacy watchdogs (for instance eTrust) by endowing them with special audit powers. Abused consumers or organizations representing them, such as the Electronic Privacy Information Center, should have redress in the courts through amendments in federal tort laws which would add a privacy right to action. Finally, consumers need access to new state-of-the-art technology which allows them to see information collected about them or block information-gathering devices more effectively.[4]

In the meantime, growing public disaffection with the hitherto inadequate self-regulation approach has prompted the government to take a more active role in regulating the confidentiality of personal data on the web. Several states, among them New York, California, Maryland and Virginia, have legislation pending which would regulate various aspects of corporate privacy-protection efforts. But, given the transcendental nature of the internet and the difficulty of complying with regulations that differ from state to state, it makes much more sense to implement uniform regulations on the federal level. A first step in that direction occurred in

July 2000 when the FTC approved a new plan by the Network Advertising Initiative (NAI), a consortium of the largest internet advertising companies which together control 90 percent of the market, to regulate the secret gathering of information used to profile web customers. This plan would allow consumers to opt out of the collection of anonymous data on the internet for the purpose of profiling, to prevent web sites from merging previously collected anonymous data with personally identifying information and to give permission for the collection of such personal information at the time and place it is gathered on the internet. Companies adhering to the NAI standards would also commit themselves to give consumers 'reasonable access' to personally identifiable information collected about them and to make 'reasonable efforts' to protect the data they collect.[5] Some members of Congress, such as Senators Pat Leahy (D – Vermont) or Fritz Hollings (D – South Carolina), want to go further than that and force web sites to get explicit customer approval before collecting and sharing personal information. During the presidential election campaign of 2000 this opt-in approach had the support of Al Gore whereas George W. Bush favored the weaker opt-out approach of the NAI and FTC.

While Congress has yet to pass comprehensive privacy-protection legislation, it is already clear that American e-commerce sites will have to get accustomed to a modicum of government regulation in that area. For instance, US companies face much tougher privacy-protection standards when dealing with consumers in the European Union (EU). The EU's Data Protection Directive of 1998 does not allow internet companies operating there to sell or share any data without prior customer approval. An agreement between the US and the EU, concluded in March 2000 after several years of difficult negotiations, allows US e-commerce sites to operate in Europe, provided they abide by the stricter EU privacy-protection rules for disclosing consumer information. In return, those American companies playing by EU rules would obtain 'safe harbor' from prosecution or litigation by EU governments.[6] This deal, however, does not cover financial services, because the EU rejected US privacy-protection rules governing financial institutions even though those had been strengthened in the Financial Services Modernization Act (FSMA) of 1999. Freed by that law to merge commercial banking, investment banking and insurance into full-service financial supermarkets, US financial institutions have successfully resisted applying the tougher FSMA rules to the sharing of information among affiliates, whereas the EU gives its consumers more control over the in-house flow of personal data about their financial condition.[7] Since cybercash is intimately tied to financial services, failure to provide strong and internationally recognized financial privacy protection will slow down the evolution of this new money form in the United States.

4.3 Safety Concerns

Another issue most relevant to the success or failure of cybercash is that of safety. Many people fear that anything to do with money routed through the internet, such as their payments or bank accounts, renders them vulnerable to criminal activity by unauthorized parties out to gain access to their cash. Such fears are, of course, nourished by the virtual nature of the medium where you do not see the money physically represented and therefore feel that you do not have any control over it. But these concerns with safety also have a material basis in fact. Cyberhackers, who invade unprotected computers or web sites, have made for spectacular headlines in recent years. Frightening stories about viruses disrupting e-mail, denial-of-service attacks paralyzing popular web sites, digital identity theft, online theft of credit-card information and even successful penetration of electronic banking networks for diversion of funds (as happened to Citibank in 1995) abound to make the public insecure about safety on the internet.[8] Unless addressed in convincing fashion, the safety issue promises to be an insurmountable barrier to the widespread acceptance of cybercash.

The solution to this challenge lies ultimately with *cryptology* (from the Greek *kryptós lógos* which means 'hidden word'), the science of coding messages and scrambling those codes so that they cannot be deciphered by third parties. Initially the purview of specialists in the military, cryptology has now been turned into a civilian technology of mass application on the internet. Data flows in and out of web sites can be secured by cryptographic methods, in particular *encryption software* which makes it possible for information to be recoded ('scrambled') in such a way that no unauthorized third party could ever conceivably reconstruct the original text or number sequence from the code. As a result of this technology, credit-card numbers, contracts, signatures and any information pertinent to commerce can now be sent over the internet in unreadable code rather than in their original form. The future of cybercash thus depends not least on the quality of encryption software and proper arrangements to scramble and rescramble messages.

Modern cryptographic methods embodied in encryption software use so-called 'keys' which allow qualifying parties to decipher the code and reconstruct the original message. The first technological standard, so-called 'symmetric cryptography', worked with only a single key for decoding any given message which must be known to both seller and buyer. That single-key method leaves the recipient sure that the message could have been coded only by the sender while the latter knows that only the recipient will be able to decipher the message.[9] But any single-key encryption technology has the distinct disadvantage that the key has to be exchanged between the two parties involved in the transaction. If you want to have safe communication with 100 parties, you have to exchange 100 keys. When applied to cybercash every buyer and seller would have to exchange keys with each other. This is a hopelessly cumbersome undertaking, especially as we cannot transfer keys over any communication network since no unauthorized third party must ever gain access to the key.

The solution to this problem has been the development of asymmetric (or 'public key') cryptography which uses two different keys. The message can be coded by both keys, but can only be decoded by one of the keys. This mechanism enables a party to make copies of one key for anyone, the 'public' key, while keeping the other ('private') key a secret. Anyone can then code a message while only one party is able to decode those messages, a design perfectly suited for the typical marketplace situation of many buyers transferring purchase-related messages or payments to a single seller.

Today's cryptography has evolved far beyond the simple steps of encryption and decryption of messages for secure communication to a variety of other applications. These more sophisticated uses are important for the development of cybercash whose virtual nature poses certain problems, most notably the seller's verification of the buyer's payment capacity, the safeguarding of anonymity and, above all, the assurance of security both in terms of preventing counterfeiting and protecting funds against raids by criminals. Standard encryption software nowadays permits, for instance, electronic identification to verify someone's identity as well as authentication which determines whether a person or entity is authorized for whatever is in question (such as accessing an internet account) without necessarily identifying that person or entity. Cryptography can also be used to prove that we know certain information without revealing the information itself or to share a secret in such a way that a subset of the shares can reconstruct the secret. Finally, cryptographic methods for remote access provide a higher level of security than passwords, which can be forgotten, eavesdropped, stolen or guessed.

The most important extension of cryptographic technology concerns the linking of electronic documents to particular individuals. In June 2000 the US Congress passed a law endowing a digital signature, which binds a document to the possessor of a particular key, with the same legal status as a written signature – surely a key step in the evolution of electronic commerce. A digital signature is an encrypted block of data bits which is created with a private key and which can then be verified with a public key as really coming from a claimed sender. The new law on digital signatures is bound to give a huge boost to e-commerce in services requiring a written contract, such as legal services, accounting or home repairs. Likely to benefit the most, however, are financial-services institutions whom this law freed from requirements of keeping paper records, issuing paper disclosures, or obtaining written signatures when opening a brokerage account or extending a home loan. Now, with these off-line impediments replaced by digital signatures and electronic record-keeping, financial institutions can move a much greater range of activities online and bring together insurance, securities, mortgages and other financial instruments on one computer screen.

Digital signatures can also be used to certify that a public key belongs to a particular sender. Such certification is done by trusted agents vouching for unknown agents, such as users. These agents, known as certification authorities (CAs), may be at the root of a centralized key infrastructure where they provide the one a priori trustworthy key in a hierarchy of trusted keys. Such a structure allows you to trust one key, because it was signed by another key you trust. In more decentralized systems the CAs bind together parties, who each rely on their own trusted roots (for instance a party's own key and any key signed by it), into a web of keys that each side can trust. This so-called 'web of trust' concept is crucial for the development of cybercash where certification authorities might take on the role of the 'trusted third party' played by the banks in payments systems based on paper money.

Digital signatures may prove to be crucial in e-commerce inasmuch as they aid firms in the crucial task of making consumers pay for online services. Their recent legalization will greatly change the way we conduct business on the internet. Rather than marking identity on the internet through identification of specific PCs, as is the case now with the cookies, we will endow net users themselves with an identity. Once such digital signatures are fully incorporated into the security architecture of the internet, it is only a question of time before every internet user is expected to have one and use it when registering with web sites. That change from PC identity to user identity makes all the difference. As long as web users could not be reliably identified as so-and-so and thus remain anonymous if they wanted to, it was difficult to privatize access to information on condition of payment. Now, however, you can demand a digital signature as a prerequisite for access and have such a step trigger an automatic payment obligation, thereby forcing people to pay if they want to obtain specific online information or service. Of course, you will want to bundle that access restriction with highly attractive additional features that kick in automatically upon providing the requested digital signature, such as strong encryption safety, handy payment options and other conveniences of online shopping.

All these applications of encryption software can be combined to build elaborate schemes and protocols for online payments with credit cards or in cybercash. In this regard the architects of the internet have constructed a multi-layered system which allows higher level application protocols requiring more powerful data protection to be plugged into the layer below – a very practical design which saves space and time. At the bottom of this pyramid-like structure is the 'transmission control protocol/ internet protocol (TCP/IP) which governs the routing of data over the internet and supports other protocols for different application tasks running on top of it. The next layer is the 'secure sockets layer' (SSL), a connection-based protocol first developed by RSA (in collaboration with Netscape) and today incorporated in all browsers, which is used typically between server and client to secure their connection by encrypting data transferred over the connection with a private key. The activation of SSL requires a digital certificate, issued by a certification authority and accepted by your browser from a list of trusted CAs (such as VeriSign or GTE CyberTrust), which facilitates the public-key exchange necessary for enabling a SSL connection. Whenever enacted, SSL allows authentication of both server and client to each other to confirm their respective identities. The SSL in turn supports higher level applications for specific internet-based tasks, including those that require more sophisticated encryption technology for greater security. One such application, for instance, is the 'secure electronic transaction' (SET) format, adopted by Visa and MasterCard in February 1996 as a uniform standard, which facilitated the take-off of e-commerce via credit-card payments. SET includes, among other services, protocols for purchasing goods and services electronically, obtaining authorization of payment and requesting 'credentials' (that is, certificates) binding public keys to identities. The format uses the DES standard for bulk data encryption (see note 9) and RSA, the leader in asymmetric cryptography, for signatures and public-key encryption of keys and bank card numbers.

This elegant security infrastructure of the internet is not, however, without significant flaws. For one, the elaborate protocols for enhanced security still take up a lot of time and space, thus making your computer much less efficient.[10] Encryption technology will thus have to become a lot more time- and space-saving if we want to avoid slowing internet traffic to a crawl. But the development of more sophisticated and better performing encryption methods has been greatly complicated by US government classification of this technology as a weapon, which subjected it to the restrictions of the Arms Export Control Act. Apart from imposing the mandatory submission of information about this technology for review, the registration of software developers as arms dealers and stringent licensing requirements, the US government also argued that top-of the-line encryption technology should not be exported lest it falls into the hands of hostile governments, criminals and terrorist organizations thus able to plan their misdeeds in secret. US exports were limited to encryption devices with electronic key lengths of 40 bits, a rather ridiculous limit considering such codes have already proven to be breakable with powerful supercomputers in a short period of time and that the current frontier of the technology is 128-bit keys. Because of these restrictions, until recently most browsers carried only 40-bit encryption software which was too weak for online banking transactions, let alone cybercash. That barrier was finally removed in January 2000 when the US government relaxed its export restrictions for encryption software in response to ferocious lobbying by the software industry and civil liberties organizations.[11] The change in policy will make it much easier for browsers to incorporate 'strong' (128-bit) encryption software and so lay the ground for accelerated developments in online banking and cybercash technologies.

When designing their secure-communication protocols, potential issuers of cybercash will be well advised to come up with better solutions than the SET protocol used for credit-card payments on the internet. That system is not as safe as it should be. The underlying cryptography used in the SET format is too easy to decode and too difficult to upgrade. Since hackers could eventually break the industry's standard encryption code if they tried hard enough, the introduction of SET has not calmed consumer fears about using credit cards in e-commerce. Americans have been willing to put up with these fears, because their losses from credit-card fraud are limited by law to $50 per occurrence and they have the right to block any potentially erroneous charge on their statement until the credit-card company has investigated the complaint. Major banks and credit-card companies have even gone further than that and promised zero losses for online transactions. Such protection does not apply to cash advances or direct deductions from checking accounts, the typical payments schemes of cybercash. That is why the designers of cybercash will have to come up with an equivalent degree of safety protection if they want to compete effectively against credit cards.[12]

A possible solution is C-SET (chip-secured electronic transaction) which a consortium of 200 French banks introduced in March 1997 to secure online payments. Instead of relying solely on software and certificates stored on a user's hard drive, as in case of the US standard, C-SET adds a hardware component outside the user's computer in the form a numeric pad that an online buyer must use to key in a personal identification number (PIN) as part of every purchase. Another possible approach to internet security focusing on hardware rather than relying on encryption software is the idea of shielding machines themselves from cyberhackers who usually commit their misdeeds by invading user software. In May 2000 IBM announced a very interesting idea in that direction, namely the development of a truly secure storage location within its computers which would serve as a sort of a digital vault. This project, a joint venture with encryption software specialists Atmel and Gemplus, would allow personal computers to store critical information behind a hardware 'firewall' which hackers would not be able to penetrate.

While hardware devices may provide useful protection against hackers, in the end internet safety will be improved more effectively through software upgrades. In June 2001 the US Commerce Department's National Institute of Standards and Technology (NIST) approved a new 'advanced encryption standard' (AES), the Rijndael algorithm developed by Belgian cryptographers Rijmen and Daemen.[13] Designed to protect sensitive information with 128-bit, 192-bit and even 256-bit keys, AES will replace the NIST's aging 56-bit keys 'data encryption standard' (DES), but not the stronger Triple DES. This new standard provides foolproof protection against any type of attack by cyberhackers and thus constitutes a major advance in internet safety. Its adoption will make it much easier for cybercash issuers to resolve the safety question and so help to build public trust in digital money.

Because of its much lower memory requirements, AES is especially equipped for restricted memory devices such as smart cards. But its spread will boost cybercash experiments more generally. It is quite conceivable that in the next few years we will see the development of a new AES-based high-security layer on top of the general-access protocol TCP/IP and the secure-communication protocol SSL which can only be accessed by those willing and able to pay. This restricted-access layer would be exclusively reserved for services that are being paid for. Such a construct would offer an elegant solution to the restructuring of the internet into a source of profit for e-commerce. You could combine public-good and private-service dimensions of the internet as separate, coexisting spheres in much the same way we have already connected open communication within the TCP/IP layer and private communication within the SSL layer. Of course, since payment-related exchanges on the internet require a high degree of security and privacy, such an AES-based e-commerce layer would offer additional security features beyond the current SSL architecture.

Whether or not routed through a special high-security layer, the encryption of payments will eventually come to be embedded in a broader *shopping protocol* which will regulate and standardize all the different aspects of a cybercash transaction. Buying online consists of more than just payment. It usually involves a three-step process of interaction. That process starts with negotiating the terms of a contractual engagement between merchant and client, including agreeing on a mutually acceptable payment form, then proceeds to the actual payment and concludes with the fulfillment steps of order confirmation, delivery, warranties and after-sales service. Each of these three steps – negotiation, payment and fulfillment – can be integrated into a common framework, which would seamlessly connect the different protocols designed for them. Such an integrated shopping protocol would allow online sellers to focus just on the selling and delivery part and outsource all the other aspects of a transaction to a central processor or to several firms, each undertaking a specific task according to the protocol.

Since 1998 we have seen significant efforts in this direction. Several major projects are under way to create feasible shopping protocols, such as the 'joint electronic payments initiative' (JEPI) developed by the World Wide Web Consortium and CommerceNet, the 'open trading protocols' (OTP) initiative launched by AT&T in cooperation with Master-Card/Mondex, Hewlett-Packard and Open Market, or American Express's 'open buying on the internet' (OBI) protocol aimed at the B2B sector. The presence of considerable network economies will encourage standardization, allowing e-merchants to provide their services as 'plug-ins' to just one, perhaps two and certainly not more than three shopping protocols. Which of the ongoing experiments ultimately emerges as the industry standard will depend not least on the respective quality of its security infrastructure, giving those firms currently developing alternative shopping protocols a powerful incentive to come up with new and better security solutions. I suspect that the integrative approach underlying shopping protocols may yield synergies that will make the whole more secure than each of its parts, especially if those were kept separate.

In this context it is worth noting that Microsoft's new Windows XP, introduced in October 2001, bundles online shopping services into an integrated platform and charges for access to that platform. This latest version of its core product, combining pay-for-access restriction and a platform architecture for connected services, is designed to extend Microsoft's dominance beyond operating software for PCs to the internet. Using new computing standards which help sites to share information and communicate with each other so that they can be seamlessly linked on people's computer desktops, Microsoft has designed a multi-functional launch pad for the internet. Windows XP offers its users, among other things, instant messaging (Windows Messenger) and a digital music and video player (Windows Media Player), two of the hottest online services right now. The most far-reaching innovation embedded in Windows XP, however, is Passport, a universal log-on and registration card which gives users a personal ID, stores their credit-card information and passwords and serves as the gateway for a variety of new online shopping and notification services known as .Net MyServices.[14] Passport represents the kind of restricted-access barrier that we had identified earlier, when discussing digitial signatures or a possible AES-based high-security layer for online payments, as crucial to the future success of e-commerce. By making Passport account-holders pay a few dollars a month for access, Microsoft hopes to collect more revenue from recurrent subscription fees rather than from one-time sales of software or licensing agreements.

Digital signatures, the new advanced encryption standard, Microsoft's Passport and other innovations mentioned here illustrate that the infra-structure of the internet is progressing rapidly. As cybercash evolves, we are bound to develop better ways to protect privacy and ensure safety online. Technological and regulatory solutions exist to deal with these twin challenges so that the public can gain the necessary trust in the new medium of cybercash. Only then, if and when these solutions are in place, can we hope to turn cybercash from an intriguing experiment into a mass application.

4.4 The Control of Cybercash

Cybercash, by its very nature, also raises complex challenges concerning its control. The question of money's control is central to its stability and its ability to function as a public good. In the case of cybercash the control question is complicated by two factors. One concerns the modalities of its issue. How easy will it be to create new digital money when such a process can be achieved in a second with the simple device of point and click? Money creation on the internet promises to be a whole lot faster and more fluid than was the case when banks created paper money by accumulating excess reserves and turning those into loans. Central banks will find it much harder to regulate the issue of cybercash which, after all, in its circulation transcends national boundaries and real time. That challenge is complicated by yet another factor, namely the prospect that the creation of cybercash moves beyond banks to nonbank agents endowed with that capability. It is possible that the emergence of cybercash will end the banks' monopoly over money creation and bring other players into the monetary process. How will central banks deal with that proliferation of money issuers?

The utterly spaceless and timeless nature of cybercash renders this virtual money form inherently more difficult to control than metal or paper money. Being able to move beyond physical boundaries at the speed of light, capital flows denominated in a specific cybercash unit pose an amazing challenge to anyone trying to keep track of them. Yet such cybercash flows must be taken account of in a timely and diligent fashion if its issuer is to have a chance of managing the money under its command in a responsible manner worthy of the public's trust (see Chapter 6 for more on this). Most issuers will try to keep close track of online money flows and redemption patterns, both of which occur almost instantaneously. And they will try to provide clearing and exchange systems which can accommodate online transactions at high volumes and in real-time immediacy. Luckily, the internet's data-processing capacity and cybercash's information content are most likely to become so advanced over the next decade that these tasks should be manageable.

While issuers of cybercash may have the technological capacity to keep track of their supply, it is not so evident that they will also have the discipline to manage that supply responsibly. To the extent that they stand to gain from the creation of additional supplies of digital money, they will try to encourage greater public demand for their particular variant of cybercash. There will be a strong marketing component guiding the creation of cybercash by competing money issuers. Those agents will be tempted to encourage greater use of their cybercash variant and then meet that additional demand with new supplies.[15] The temptation of accommodating ever-larger demands for money as a source of income gains generates serious risks of overissuance. This danger will be especially pronounced if issuers can create new cybercash to finance their own purchases of goods and services. There is a reason why banks are not allowed to do that, namely the need to safeguard money's public-good quality by ensuring equal access to everyone in the marketplace. No bank, other than the central bank representing the monetary authority of the state, can write checks against itself or create new money to pay for its own purchases. Instead it creates nothing but tokens (an empty book of checks) which are transferred via a loan to users in whose hands they become money (when the loan gets spent). This transfer mechanism explains why money is issued as a simultaneous asset and liability. For cybercash to be considered true and fully functioning money, it will ultimately have to follow the same modalities of issue (as tokens), transfer (through a loan) and meta-morphosis (into money) when users spend the tokens. Alternatively, cyber-cash issuers can create new digital tokens, booked as liabilities, by increasing reserve assets which, besides government-issued currency, can take a variety of forms and may include anything that can be easily mone-tized (for instance bonds).

The dual asset–liability nature of money also means that reductions in money supply are a bit more complicated than simply destroying digital tokens, which, from a technological point of view, should be as easy as deleting a computer file. Such reductions in the supply of cybercash involve the simultaneous elimination of assets and liabilities which may come about when loans are repaid or in the wake of selling off reserve assets (open-market sales). Since money destruction involves a shrinkage of the issuer's balance sheets, it will not be undertaken lightly. Issuers of cybercash will try to preserve their monetary base and keep their money supply growing steadily.

We shall see in Chapters 6 and 8 how the unique demand and supply features of cybercash operate in the aggregate, comprising the totality of different digital-money variants circulating online, and what the implic-ations of such macro-level behavior are for monetary policy. Here we are turning our attention to a different concern relating to the control of cybercash, namely the possibility that the provision of digital money will involve nonbank institutions as well and so undermine the monopoly of money creation enjoyed by the banking sector for centuries. Banks, of course, will most likely continue to occupy a dominant position in that regard. Given their long-standing expertise in managing cash, they more than anyone else are trusted by the public in matters of money. As we shall see in the next chapter when discussing specific variants of digital money, the banks have been involved in most of the major cybercash experiments so far. They also control a key route in the proliferation of cybercash, namely online banking, which will help to spread the use of electronic money on both wholesale (B2B) and retail (B2C, P2P) levels. Those strengths will allow the banks to play a key role in shaping this monetary innovation.

But the banks will certainly not be alone in the creation of cybercash. While they could handle the issue of paper money tokens on their own, with a little help from the central bank running the payments system of check clearing and reserve transfers for them, they are not in the same position with regard to cybercash. That particular money type requires a high-tech infrastructure which goes beyond the in-house capabilities of your typical bank. Hence the banks will need assistance from other actors specializing in the technology of cybercash. Having moved to the internet, such assistance will be provided by the suppliers of that medium's infrastructure – telecom firms, computer software firms, internet service providers. The development of any type of cybercash will require the banks to enter into joint ventures with these high-tech firms. Depending on their relative bargaining strength based on the importance of their expertise, some of these firms will be able to exact a fairly significant technological rent for their participation. Even if banks play the dominant role in the creation of cybercash, they will have to share the income generated from that activity with high-tech partners.

Since cybercash has the typical New Economy features of large set-up costs, mostly fixed costs as operating expenses, and near-zero marginal costs, the stakes of this game will be very high. Such a cost structure benefits those operating at high volume where, once start-up costs have been amortized and fixed costs have been covered, every additional user represents pure profit. But whenever a more competitive alternative emerges and depresses demand for the existing systems, operating losses can mount very rapidly among the losers. The key to the success of any joint cybercash venture is to generate lots of income and find equitable ways to share those gains among partners. Such income generation depends not only on user volume, but on the ability to exploit the plethora of income sources associated with the issue of cybercash – user fees, licensing fees, interest income on loans or investment of unused customer balances, capital gains on open-market operations and so on (see our discussion of digital seigniorage in section 6.2 for more on this).

The income-creation potential of cybercash will motivate the nonbank partners in those joint ventures to refine and expand their area of expertise, perhaps even to the point of trying to gain direct control over the actual issue of such money. The prospect of making a lot of money from the creation of money will certainly attract other players to try their hand on cybercash:

■ Credit-card companies, for instance, constitute potentially serious competition in this regard. They have the advantage of an early lead in the area of online payments. They already operate sophisticated payment systems for electronic fund transfers. And they are most likely to control the issue of smart cards which might be a key component in some of the major cybercash variants about to emerge.

■ Computer software firms and ISPs could also threaten the bank monopoly, especially those among them in control of a key aspect of any cybercash-based payment system – be it the user base, the access ramp to the system, or the software which that electronic money is made of. Take, for instance, Microsoft's aggressive online strategy to turn itself into the dominant internet access platform. When the software giant introduced its new operating system Windows XP in October 2001, it also announced plans for a new package of web services, known as .Net MyServices, which will be made available to subscribers for a fixed base charge plus additional user fees. These services include e-mail, instant messaging, personal calendars, travel services, bank statements and electronic billing (see section 4.3 above). The strategy of offering an integrated multi-application platform in the hope of becoming the principal toll collector for most online transactions puts Microsoft in a strong position to add online-payment facilities and so get involved in the issue of cybercash. Currently dominant ISPs will have to respond to Microsoft's challenge. AOL wants to use its huge information and entertainment platform as a springboard for a major foray into e-commerce. Yahoo! and Sun Microsystems also seem attracted to the idea of facilitating e-commerce through the provision of online-payment systems and intend to play a major role in the development of cybercash technology.

■ Deregulation, especially the European Commission's Second Banking Directive of 1989 and the Financial Services Modernization Act of 1999 in the US, has made it possible for financial institutions other than banks to enter the hitherto protected area of money creation and for such institutions to be owned by nonfinancial enterprises. Investment banks, consumer-credit companies, thrifts, credit unions or brokerage houses may find that the fastest way to turn themselves into fully fledged banks is via the internet *à la* E*Trade. In the process they will want to get their hands on the lucrative business of money creation and do much of that online.

■ Finally, we can expect cybercash initiatives also coming from e-commerce firms organizing online shopping malls or merchant networks, such as Mallpark (www.mallpark.com) or nouveaumall.com.

These online intermediaries have extensive contact with consumers as well as merchants and are thus in a good position to organize the payment system connecting both. If they manage to issue a popular cybercash variant, they can utilize money issuance as a marketing tool with which to set themselves apart from competitors and build brand loyalty among both merchants and consumers.

The implication of having such a large variety of different cybercash issuers are quite far-reaching, not least for the central banks in charge of the nation's payments system. These institutions have the authority, expertise and means to control the money creation process of banks, but lack such powers vis-à-vis nonbank participants in the monetary process. Central banks can, of course, decide by regulatory fiat, as has been done by the European Central Bank (ECB), that they wish to confine the actual issue of cybercash to commercial banks.[16] But such a restriction hampers innovation, endows banks with a monopoly profit that a free-market environment would certainly spread more evenly and may not even work in the context of a truly global money form which transcends national boundaries in its circulation. Subjects of the EU may simply switch to less regulated cybercash alternatives issued outside the jurisdiction of the ECB. Central banks will need to develop a collaborative approach to the regulation of online banking and cybercash, including the question how to deal with nonbank issuers of electronic money (see Chapters 6 and 8 for more).

4.5 High-tech Money

Cybercash is ultimately nothing but an encrypted series of 0s and 1s flowing with the speed of light through a globally connected network of computers. Because digital money is composed of computer software, it can be programmed to do things that paper money was never able to. While it is difficult to predict the evolution of cybercash's high-tech capabilities at this early point in its life cycle, we can already detect trends worth pondering.

For instance, it is quite conceivable that the creation of cybercash itself will be characterized by a much higher degree of spontaneity, since from a technical point of view digital coins can be brought into existence, their virtual existence, with the push of a button or the click of a mouse. This facility makes it possible for cybercash to be created spontaneously, at the point of sale, to finance a transaction. Let us remember that modern money is after all credit-money, tied in its creation to the extension of loans.

Instead of having new money injected into the economy through banks giving borrowers empty checks to write in subsequent purchases, as has been the case with our paper-based system of bank money up to now, why not have new money being created electronically as loans to online buyers so that their intended purchases can be directly financed and thus become reality? Were such an electronic credit-money ever to materialize on the internet, cybercash would rapidly move beyond a financing tool to becoming a key marketing tool with which e-commerce companies could entice greater sales volume from willing buyers. At the same time, such purchase-related money boosts at the same time spontaneous consumption, a crucial socio-psychological phenomenon in advanced capitalism which began to take root a couple of generations ago with the appearance of shopping malls and credit cards and which since then has fuelled ever-more demanding social consumption norms. Our consumption-driven society will be moved to much higher levels when reasonably credit-worthy online shoppers can browse the web and get immediate financing for whatever they see worthy of buying.

The spontaneity of cybercash extends beyond its creation to its circulation. We will be able to zap money around the world at the speed of light with our cell phone, personal digital assistant, television or computer. Such zapping will surely include paying machines, such as the laundromat, the parking meter, vending machines, public transport, toll booths and so forth. It will be very easy to send funds to family and friends or receive funds from them. Much improved location technology will be used by merchants to entice e-shoppers with online coupons when they are approachably near. Of course, the zapping quality of cybercash also means that such money moves fast and knows no physical boundaries. This complicates any government's job a great deal, whether in terms of tax collection, money laundering, or effective monetary policy (see Chapter 8 for more).

Yet another technological specificity of cybercash is its ability to carry with it much greater flows of information generated in the wake of transactions paid for in this digital money form. Such information can be in and of itself useful, for example for profiling customers, which is why satisfactory privacy-protection standards will one day have to be put in place in the interest of public trust. The information-intense environment of cybercash will also spur new payment arrangements which will radically alter the way we buy and sell. I am thinking here of how useful cybercash could be in auctions, for example when wanting to make contingent bids (for instance advance bids with a price ceiling). I can also imagine how practical all that information-enhanced capability of cybercash will be when organizing large-volume online commodity exchanges where different firms dealing with each other as buyers and sellers could cancel out their mutual debts and pay only the net balances. Such netting, the principal function of clearing-houses, is inherently easier with computer power and can be made that much more efficient with a money form whose information-processing capabilities match those of the computers organizing the electronic marketplace of tomorrow. More generally, information-rich cybercash will revolutionize the ways we conduct our banking and manage our finances. Bills will be presented and paid electronically. At the heart of online banking, cybercash will enable customers to move funds around more easily, keep better track of their cash flows, pursue investment opportunities more aggressively with their excess cash and learn more about the nuts and bolts of finance.

We will certainly be able to determine a priori when a certain online payment should be carried out. This timing capacity of cybercash will have many useful applications. For instance, your typical e-commerce transaction may involve putting the sum of cybercash required into an online escrow account, allowing the seller to verify that the funds are there, and releasing those funds once the product has been delivered to the buyer's satisfaction.[17] To the extent that cybercash gets issued as a loan, it would be helpful for the lender issuing that money to secure proper servicing of that debt by means of pre-programmed funds which will be automatically transferred in specified intervals. To the extent that the internet accelerates outsourcing of production-related activities and revolutionizes supply-chain management, trade credit in the form of payment delays will multiply with the growing interaction between businesses. Being able to program the timing of payments in advance makes cybercash a very convenient money form for that kind of inter-business credit, so convenient in fact that businesses might extend trade credit to consumers by allowing them to pay later or in installments over a specified period of time. Given our growing reliance on all kinds of forward-money contracts, the ability to program the timing of cybercash flows in advance will prove a very handy feature.

Apart from its timing, all kinds of other cybercash features can be programmed into its software. We can foresee such 'smart' money to be earmarked for special purposes, specifying not only when, but also where and for what it can be spent. Such earmarking capability would surely prove a useful tool for all kinds of situations. For instance, parents wishing to control the not-so-healthy consumption impulses of their kids away from home could transfer some cybercash to their offspring in college with the proviso that he or she can spend this money only in bookstore X or restaurant Y. One can also easily foresee firms routinely authorizing cyber-cash for their on-the-road sales representatives that can only be tapped for overnight stays at a particular hotel chain or some other specific purpose. Earmarking of money may also have a huge impact on our credit system, not least by allowing the creditor to dock a certain portion of the debtor's future income automatically for debt-servicing. We can therefore expect cybercash to give rise to a highly automated system of installment-credit plans which will transform both our system of consumer credit as well as trade credit between businesses.

High-tech cybercash is likely to serve not just as a payment mechanism, but also as a marketing tool used by its issuers. Competing with each other for market share, the different issuers of cybercash will try to endow their variant with attractive features and so generate greater user demand. Much of that competition and product differentiation among cybercash issuers will be technological in nature, setting one's version apart from the rest of the pack. Such efforts may yield enormous rewards. Imagine the kind of brand recognition you get when millions of netizens are pricing online goods and services in your money unit. If anyone using a particular cyber-cash variant has to go through the web site of its issuer, that company automatically gains a large captive audience for the promotion of its products. The provision of electronic-payment facilities may then be bundled with other services offered by the issuer to any user of its money unit. Benefits derived from the issue of online money may therefore go beyond concrete income streams and become much more broadly conceptualized in terms of making the issuer widely known and trusted by the public (see section 6.2 for more on this).

The high-tech capabilities of cybercash will surely take on many mani-festations, as competition among its issuers drives them to continuous innovation and refinement of their electronic-money product. It is now time to get a taste of what the future may hold in store with respect to online-payments technology by taking a closer look at specific cybercash experiments already under way.

CHAPTER 5

Three Generations of Cybercash

While we are still some years away from a universal electronic-payments system that is widely used for e-commerce on the internet, it behoves us to take a closer look at ongoing cybercash experiments. Even in this embryonic stage we can get a glimpse of a future in which cybercash will have become a dominant money form.[1]

When looking more closely at these efforts to develop online-payment systems, one is struck by the variety of designs for electronic money and their complexity. There are many different types of cybercash being developed. Such heterogeneity, so different from the highly standardized metal and paper monies, begs the question of how to classify these various cybercash systems. One way to do this is to distinguish between hardware-based and software-based cybercash systems. This approach is the one commonly shared by central banks (notably the European Central Bank or the Fed) and international organizations (the Bank for International Settlements). However, in my opinion, it is too broad a categorization inasmuch as it fails to take account of the clear distinctions between the subsets within those two categories. A similar problem of excessively broad categorization exists with yet another distinction commonly applied to cybercash, namely whether such money operates purely online or carries with it the ability for off-line use as well.

A more nuanced approach to the classification of cybercash may help us to understand this phenomenon better. To begin with, it is useful to adopt a case-study approach which takes a closer look at each major experiment in this area in order to identify its specificity as well as its communality with other alternatives. Moreover, we need to appreciate that different segments of e-commerce will each develop their own specific type of cybercash, widely used there but with limited application elsewhere. We can expect to have cybercash systems which are much more applicable to B2B transactions while others are better fit for B2C or P2P transactions. Finally, if we look at those experiments in chronological sequence to get a sense of the product's life cycle, we can distinguish three generations of cybercash. The first proved the technological feasibility of this new money form, but failed commercially (section 5.1). The second generation built a strong marketing component into its infrastructure and focused on specific segments of e-commerce – either as e-mail money for P2P transactions (section 5.2) or as coupon money in B2C commerce (section 5.3). The latest experiments focus on the construction of highly sophisticated online-payment platforms for the creation and transfer of digital tokens that can be used in a large variety of situations. This emerging third generation of cybercash, while still at the very beginning, points to the most dynamic area of product development over the coming decade (section 5.4).

5.1 The Birth of Cybercash

The earliest experiments with cybercash in the mid-1990s were conducted by some of the most talented and innovative software designers who had started out as scientists and turned entrepreneurs when e-commerce emerged as both a technological challenge and a commercial opportunity. This pattern, in the mode of Marc Andriessen who first invented the MOSAIC software program and then founded Netscape, made perfect sense at the time when cybercash had yet to prove its technological feasibility.

5.1.1 NetCheque

One such early e-money pioneer was Clifford Neuman who had developed the security and authentication software called Kerberos as well as the discovery and retrieval software protocol known as Prospero. With financial support from the Pentagon's ARPA and under the auspices of the University of Southern California's Information Sciences Institute, in the early 1990s Neuman launched a project to develop a software program for the creation and exchange of electronic financial instruments which could be used to pay for goods and services over the internet.

Neuman's idea was disarmingly simple, namely to extend the traditional check-clearing system at the heart of our current monetary regime to the internet by setting up an online mechanism for fund transfers using checks. Rapid advances in digital-imaging technology had made it possible for such checks to be produced and processed electronically. His *e-check* product, called NetCheque, was designed to work in much the same way as a conventional paper check. A payor would issue an electronic document bearing pretty much the same information as a paper check, sign it electronically, have that signature authenticated by a third computer, and then sent on to the payee who endorses the document with a signature. Once authenticated, that endorsement transforms the instrument into an order to a bank computer for fund transfer. Properly signed and endorsed NetCheque instruments could be electronically exchanged between banks through electronic clearing-houses to settle accounts. That electronic-check system had two interesting extensions. One concerned accounting scrver software to allow organizations, such as e-commerce firms or ISPs, to set up their own in-house online 'banks' which would pay bills, receive payments and make electronic fund transfers. Such software made it easy for anyone to open up accounts with customers for purchases, settle those accounts and move funds to other firms or banks. The second extension concerned a software package, called NetCash, for the creation of anonymous electronic currency backed by fund transfers routed through the NetCheque system.

Neuman's NetCheque did not catch on commercially, even though it had been copyrighted by his university and made available to the public. Price was not an issue in that failure, since USC charged only commercial users and kept its user fee low. The system failed, because it relied on conventional symmetric cryptography which around that time, in 1995, was being replaced by more secure public-key encryption software. While obviously introduced before its time, with e-commerce not yet born, NetCheque deserves attention as the first integrated design for cybercash mimicking the existing system of paper-based bank money. This early electronic-check system showed the potential of cybercash to bring nonbanks into the business of banking (through the aforementioned accounting-server software).

5.1.2 'Smart' Cards (Gemplus vs. Mondex)

Another online extension of an already existing payments system in the direction of cybercash centered on 'plastic money'. The public's growing infatuation with plastic cards – first credit cards, then debit cards – as a vehicle for retail purchases has set the stage for the introduction of so-called *smart cards*. These cards resemble the other types of plastic money, except that they have an electronic microchip embedded in a small gold plate in front of the card rather than a magnetic strip in the back like a conventional credit or debit card. That chip stores electronic data and programs which are protected by advanced security features. Such smart cards have to be inserted into a reader whereby they make contact with electrical connectors that transfer data to and from the chip. Therefore all kinds of payments processors, such as PCs, wireless hand-held devices, TVs, POS terminals or ATMs, have to be either equipped with or hooked to such readers – a costly proposition which up to now has constrained the commercial usefulness of smart cards.

The development of smart-card technology first took off in Europe. The French in particular managed to take a leadership role not least because of the active encouragement of their government. France's leading public-sector enterprises introduced smart-card schemes early on which habituated the large majority of that country's citizens to this new technology, as in the case of France Telecom launching the first stored-value chipcard application known as telecarte or the health insurance card issued by the government's social security agency. The so-called carte bancaire, which most French citizens use today in lieu of traditional credit cards, is like a smart debit card tied to a checking account. But these accounts have an overdraft facility which makes these cards also function like credit cards, subject to settlement of outstanding debit balances at the end of each month. These immensely popular bank cards are issued by a consortium of France's leading commercial banks. In Gemplus (www.gemplus.com), a software company founded in 1988, France also possesses one of the world's two leading developers of smart-card technology with worldwide demand for its many software applications. Gemplus specializes in all aspects of smart-card technology, especially security protection, e-commerce and wireless applications.

Gemplus's most serious competitor is Mondex (www.mondex.com), a British software company launched in 1993 by two UK banks (National Westminster, Midland) to develop a digital-cash system based on smart cards which can be filled up with cash and used for transactions via Mondex-enabled phones, computers and personal digital assistants. The great advantage of this Mondex Electronic Cash system was that it did not need any central clearing authority because of the ability of its chips to authenticate, authorize and transfer payments (including even direct card-to-card transfers). Elimination of any central clearing authority promised to make digital-cash systems much cheaper, despite the high start-up costs involved in enabling access devices with Mondex compatibility.

It should not surprise us that smart-card experiments have so far caught on more in Europe than in the United States. Especially in the smaller European countries, such as Holland, Denmark and Norway, there are only a couple of banks controlling the entire domestic market which renders the coordination problem associated with launching local smart-card experiments much less burdensome. Such experiments have also worked well there, because individual households in those countries are much less wedded to traditional plastic money and thus much more willing to try out something new in the form of cash-storing smart cards. Given the relatively high telecommunication costs and incidences of credit-card fraud in Europe, people there have been attracted by the dual promise of lower costs and added security offered by smart cards.[2] Finally, as we have seen already in the case of France, smart cards enjoy the active support of European governments. Public-sector enterprises, notably national health insurance systems, public universities, postal services and phone companies, have successfully pushed for widespread use of such cards by their clients. Early on, the European Union, in its so-called CAFE (1992–1995) and SEMPER (1995–98) projects, took the first steps towards an EU-wide standard for smart cards. Having such a uniform standard is bound to help European banks with their cross-border integration of banking services, spurred on by the introduction of the euro.

No comparable government support has been forthcoming in the United States. Moreover, there are thousands of American banks which makes it much more difficult to coordinate bank-sponsored launches of smart-card projects. This coordination role therefore passed early on to Visa and MasterCard which possessed the centralized payments systems to facilitate the widespread use of smart cards through their respective credit-card networks. Yet, at that point, neither company was very aggressive about pushing the use of smart cards in the United States for fear that such a shift in consumer preferences would undermine their market for credit cards, which both deemed more profitable because of the exorbitantly high interest charges on unpaid balances. The initial reluctance of Visa and MasterCard hampered key local smart-card experiments in the United States, the first one in 1996 during the Olympic Games in Atlanta and the second on Manhattan's Upper West Side in 1997 where Citibank and Chase tried to get people and merchants in the neighborhood to use Mondex Electronic Cash cards. Neither of these two trials managed to attract much public interest. So far smart cards have found only a marginal presence in the gigantic US market, mostly for limited-purpose use in closed systems such as transportation, laundries or phones. We shall see in section 5.4 that this situation is about to change.

5.1.3 DigiCash

A third type of cybercash developed early on, besides Neuman's e-checks and the smart cards of Gemplus or Mondex, were the *digital coins* designed by David Chaum, a pioneer in the development of cybercash who used to teach computer science in California before turning himself into an entrepreneur to exploit some of his ideas commercially. The unique mix of Chaum's academic background in cryptography and his entrepreneurial proclivities, as the founder of DigiCash, was fused by a strongly populist focus on consumer privacy, access and convenience of use.[3] Chaum's goal for his company was to develop an integrated online-payment platform using digital coins which matched hard cash in terms of convenience, safety and anonymity. Once accepted as the functional equivalent of cash for the internet, his digital coins could be marketed as even better than cash inasmuch as they could not be stolen or lost.

When DigiCash introduced its eCash system in 1994, it was the first company to have designed a fully fledged cybercash system using public-key cryptography and digital signatures for protection. These features have become standard since then. Apart from these innovations, DigiCash also incorporated one of Chaum's most interesting design ideas, so-called blind-signature technology. This special encryption technology, allowing for blind customer signatures that can be verified without identifying the signer, enables banks to issue eCash currency which contains no information linking the money to the payor. Chaum's invention thus created a form of cybercash which was potentially as anonymous as physical cash where bills never identify who is spending them. In an effort to address one of the most persistent consumer fears about losing their digitial cash whenever their computer crashed, eCash software also offered a recoverability feature which enabled customers to recover their money in the event of a hard disk crash. Chaum's design contained yet another innovative feature, namely bidirectionality which allowed customers to receive eCash from other users and thereby established the possibility of peer-to-peer payments early on.

DigiCash primarily targeted banks as buyers of its eCash software package which would then offer their consumer and business clients the option to open up eCash accounts. Those institutions could customize the service, brand it as they choose, and either provide it solely to their customers or link it to other services. Banks could integrate their eCash software package into their existing infrastructure, thus keeping their start-up costs down. Standard interfaces into the account applications of banks made the sign-up and funding processes of new eCash accounts easy and cheap. The software also managed the authorization, clearing and settlement process with the merchant and the consumer, designed to anchor the central position of the host bank in any triangle of eCash transfers. If consumers agreed that they preferred to keep their eCash accounts hosted by their bank or their favorite portal on the internet, they would not even have to download the eCash software. This option had the additional advantage of allowing consumers to access eCash from any computer or mobile device anywhere in the world.

Whether they downloaded the software or not, consumers could fund eCash accounts online or off-line with money from various sources. For example, they could transfer funds between different bank accounts, use credit-card payments, write paper checks, or even receive eCash deposits from other users. They would then simply connect to their bank's web site and download digital coins from their eCash account directly onto their PC's hard disk. Once the eCash account was funded, it could be used immediately for money transfers to anyone equipped to receive such digital coins. At that point, account-holders could withdraw eCash currency with a simple click of the mouse. There would be no need to enter any PINs or fill out any forms at the time of the transaction, no need to remember any card numbers or keep any records. Not only did that render eCash transactions fast and simple, but it also enhanced safety and privacy – two key concerns of Chaum. Finally, in yet another safety feature guaranteeing the validity of its digital coins, DigiCash allowed banks, bank customers and merchants to verify through a simple online request that any eCash issued by a particular bank was neither counterfeit nor a duplicate, thus authentic.

With such sophisticated and user-friendly software in place, DigiCash was ready by 1995 to enter into deals with banks for pilot programs that would test the viability of its eCash system. But progress on that front was disheartingly slow. While the company managed to sign up a few banks to launch its product, notably the innovative Deutsche Bank 24 (an internet bank launched by Germany's largest bank), Bank Austria and Norway's leader Den norske Bank, it was difficult to convince merchants and consumers that eCash was worth a try. Neither side wanted to partake in this payment option without an adequate number of the other side having signed up already to do business with. Beset by cash-flow problems and frustrated by the slow response to his product, Chaum decided in November 1998 to fold DigiCash. Eventually he sold his patents to a couple of software designers who had made a name for themselves at e-commerce specialist i2 and who wanted to continue the eCash experiment. Their new company, set up in August 1999, was appropriately called eCash Technologies (www.ecash.net).

DigiCash existed long enough to put together a sophisticated and efficient online-payment platform which it had managed to test with six banks and a hundred merchants in Europe, Japan, Australia and the United States. Customers had been able to use eCash to pay for a wide range of goods and services, including database searches, stock quotes, news, entertainment, software and mail-order products. Transactions totaling $32 million had scored a 100 percent success rate, with no security breaches reported. When eCash Technologies took over DigiCash's patents and trademarks in August 1999, the product had proven its technological feasibility and commercial potential. In that sense DigiCash's end was less an outright business failure than a situation, so typical of promising start-ups, where the charismatic founder of the firm steps aside in favor of more experienced and structured management better equipped to take the new firm into adolescence. Chaum's successors have been able to do so (see section 5.4).

5.1.4 CyberCash

Another interesting experiment in digital coins was launched by Cyber-Cash (www.cybercash.com). That start-up made its mark in 1995 when it introduced the first commercial electronic wallet as a software product replacing 'electronic purse' hardware. This innovation, which turned the hard disk of your PC into an ATM, formed the basis for the introduction of CyberCoins in 1996. The new software package allowed consumers to download an empty electronic wallet and fill it up with anywhere between $20 and $100 from their bank account before taking a shopping trip into cyberspace. Those digital coins could then be spent on any site equipped to accept CyberCash payments. When CyberCash launched its digital coins, it had agreements with six US banks, including First Union which at the time was the nation's sixth-largest bank, to offer electronic wallets to their customers. At the same time it had signed up some 30 web-hosting companies to offer CyberCash to their client sites for transactions with their customers. The profits from this money issue for CyberCash would come from transaction fees paid by banks which would in turn charge their merchants slightly more to get a profit themselves. Given the economies of scale inherent in software-based technology, CyberCash expected to lower those transaction fees steadily with rising volume and still generate profits.

The problem faced by CyberCash in its digital-coin experiment was the slow expansion potential of such bank-mediated payment platforms. You have to find banks willing to deal with electronic wallets, then get merchants used to the idea of digital coins and finally convince consumers both to download wallets from their bank and use them for payments with digital coins. This tripartite demand structure makes for slow growth, especially if merchants hesitate to participate when the consumer base is still low and vice versa. Soon CyberCash, realizing that its expansion plans could not rely too much on digital coins, began to push other online payment-processing services and software products more aggressively. It continued to develop its electronic-wallet technology, but moved from its CyberCoin client-side wallet technology to a server-side service known as InstaBuy. This strategic shift in digital-wallet technology placed the wallet with the vendor and so bypassed consumer resistance to downloading and operating the wallets themselves. That shift away from consumers also narrowed the focus of the digital wallet to automation of online purchasing rather than spending CyberCoins.

This first generation of cybercash experiments, all taking place between 1994 and 1996, proved the technological feasibility of online-payments systems. They put in place the key design ideas for cybercash – electronic checks, smart cards and digital coins (see Table 5.1). In that sense they signaled the birth of this new money form. But none of these first-generation experiments managed to reach sufficiently widespread use to qualify as a commercial success. Some of their problems were of a technological nature, as in the case of Neuman's outdated encryption software or the considerable spending on hardware required to operate smart cards.

Table 5.1 Summary of first-generation cybercash experiments, 1994–96

Name	Category	Type	Creation	Features
NetCheque	E-check	Software, online	Checking accounts	Symmetric cryptography
Gemplus	Smart card	Hardware, on-, off-line	Stored value	Reader
Mondex	Smart card	Hardware, on-, off-line	Stored value	Reader
DigiCash	Digital coins	Software, online	Stored value (multiple funding)	Anonymous, recoverable, bidirectional
CyberCash	Digital coins	Software online	Checking accounts	Electronic wallet

Even more constraining were the difficulties involved in marketing these products. The diffusion of smart cards, for instance, has suffered in the United States from the reluctance of credit-card issuers to endorse a potential competitor for their lucrative credit cards. And in the case of digital coins it proved difficult to break into the long-established triangular relationship between banks, their retail customers and merchants with a radical new innovation. All these experiments struggled in vain with the brutal reality of reverse network externalities where merchants refuse to sign up for the new payment service unless they see enough consumers willing to use it and consumers hesitate to use it if they do not see many merchants accepting it. This barrier proved especially formidable, because e-commerce – the logical place to use cybercash – had just started at that point. And right from the start, when B2C transactions still prevailed, a large share of e-commerce came to use credit cards as means of payment thanks to the collaboration between Visa and MasterCard to develop a joint standard for online transactions using their cards. Having a ready-made infrastructure in place and able to muster huge marketing resources, these two firms made it difficult for early cybercash alternatives to launch and reach critical mass.

5.2 E-mail Money

When e-commerce began to take off and fuel the dot-com bubble in 1997–98, new cybercash experiments emerged to profit from that boom. Even though these second-generation experiments differed in significant ways from each other, they had three things in common to set them apart from the earlier wave of experiments in 1994–96. For one, they all focused more narrowly on areas where they might have an edge over credit cards. Moreover, each of these experiments was designed so as not to rely on banks for their diffusion. Freed from dependence on banks, these later experiments could all search for innovative marketing solutions to the problem of reverse network externalities.

One key innovation emerging out of that second phase of cybercash experiments has been the use of e-mail for the mobilization of fund transfers. Online payments via e-mail utilize an existing infrastructure and popular service, thus rendering their start-up costs more manageable. Such *e-mail money* might prove especially attractive for those who hesitate to use their credit cards on the internet. From the point of view of safety e-mail is advantageous, because you need to provide personal financial information (name, address, Social Security number, bank account details) only once, at the beginning when registering with the service, rather than providing such sensitive information each time you transfer funds. Moreover, the intermediary arranging for the fund transfer can store that information outside the internet and thus beyond the reach of hackers. This information does not have to be shown to the other side of the transaction, whether buyer or seller. Capable of satisfying the security and privacy concerns of many internet users, online payments via e-mail are likely to be especially popular among individuals engaging in P2P transactions. This form of low-tech cybercash can expect widespread use for such mundane transactions, as sending your kid in college some cash, splitting the costs of lunch among friends, giving a loved one a present, donating to charities and conducting all kinds of daily micropayment transactions (such as buying flowers, groceries, movie tickets, magazines).

While generally offered to consumers for free, such money transfers via e-mail can be an attractive source of income for service providers to the extent that participating merchants can be charged a fixed or per-transaction fee for access to this service. Given lower transaction costs, such a fee could be quite competitive compared to credit-card transactions and thus attract a large number of participating merchants. E-mail money contains another advantageous feature which concerns the way demand for this service may spread. If any designated recipient of funds is not yet registered with that particular payment service, he or she will have to do so and supply an account number. Since few would refuse receipt of a payment, most can be expected to sign up for the service when informed that they have been targeted to receive funds. In this way e-mail money has the potential to spread much like a virus. The greater the number of participants already in the system, the more potent such 'viral marketing' will be in reaching new customers. The negative network externalities faced by start-ups, where small numbers of merchants and consumers hold each other back from use, are thereby possibly overcome more easily.

5.2.1 PayPal

Because of these advantages, recently there has been growing interest in setting up fund-transfer systems activated by e-mail.[4] Perhaps the most interesting variant of e-mail money to date is PayPal, introduced by Silicon Valley start-up Confinity in November 1999. When you open an account with PayPal, you provide your name, address, e-mail address and credit-card or bank-account information, depending on how you want funds transferred in and out of your account. There are three different ways to fund the account. One is from your credit card which will be auto-matically charged whenever an e-mail transaction is authorized. Another way is to transfer funds electronically from your bank account, and the third is to send a check into your account. There are no minimum balances to keep in your PayPal account. Nor is there any minimum transaction amount, making this service interesting for consumers wishing to make micropayments. Whenever you want to pay someone out of your PayPal account, you provide all the relevant information on a standardized online form, including the recipient's name and e-mail address, the amount to be sent and the choice of payment mode.

If the recipient does not yet have an account, PayPal will automatically create one, send the recipient e-mail notification under the enticing subject heading 'You've got cash!', provide with this message a link to the new account and then register the new customer. Any recipient is instantly credited with the funds in his/her account for use right away rather than having to wait for clearing of any electronic fund transfers via automated clearing-houses which may take up to a week. The recipient may withdraw those funds as credit to a credit-card account, through direct deposit to the payee's bank account involving an electronic fund transfer, or have a personal check sent by PayPal through 'snail mail'. Each of these payment methods could take up to a week to clear. Alternatively, the recipients could also keep funds in their PayPal accounts for later use when they themselves want to spend some money for purchases. The hope is that most customers, who grow to like PayPal's service, will chose that last option which gives them access to funds more rapidly than any of the fund-withdrawal options.

The ability of customers to keep funds in their accounts for later use distinguishes PayPal in a fundamental way from the other e-mail transfer mechanisms mentioned above (in note 4). Their design does not preserve cash in the accounts of payees, but transfers them instead to the recipient's credit-card or bank accounts. In contrast, by allowing payees to keep their funds and reuse them to pay for purchases later, PayPal creates an autonomous circuit of money flows which operates parallel to the banking system. Such autonomy makes PayPal money more like a true form of cybercash, capable of circulating beyond the traditional bank-based route. This difference in design means that PayPal can act more like a bank itself. Rather than relying for income on transaction fees or membership subscription fees like its competitors, PayPal can offer its service free of charge and make money instead much like any bank, by reinvesting unused balances parked in accounts for interest income. While it does not offer its customers any interest on unused balances in their accounts, it invests those zero-interest balances in an escrow account at Merrill Lynch for a return of about 1.25 percent. Confinity expected that such an interest float would allow it to earn a profit even after covering all the credit-card charges it had to absorb.

Unlike other payment mechanisms on the internet, PayPal does not require any proprietary software. Instead it simply hooks onto the existing network of e-mail and web clients. In order to convince potential users that its low-cost infrastructure option is as safe as fancier systems using their own software, Confinity put a lot of emphasis on security and privacy protection. It stacked its board of directors and top management with encryption specialists. For security reasons it decided to restrict the amount of any transaction to a $200 maximum and allow larger transfers only with preauthorization. Confinity also kept the amount of account information provided by users to a minimum and personal financial information strictly private. Transfers are routed through a secure server protected behind state-of-the-art firewalls.[5]

The idea of PayPal, with its promise of mass appeal, attracted a lot of venture capitalists from the very beginning as well as funding support from Deutsche Bank, Nokia and Goldman Sachs. These funds enabled Confinity to launch its e-mail payment service on an ambitious scale. Its thin profit margin from the interest float, kept down by the need for guaranteed liquidity provided by a low-yield escrow account, put pressure on Confinity to sign a lot of members quickly, the challenge of any business operating on razor-thin margins. Only at high volume did it have a chance to collect sufficiently large unused balances at any time to make a profit. The company thus decided to add to its competitive advantages of free service, immediate fund availability and strong fraud protection another incitement, namely a sign-up bonus of $10 and a referral bonus of the same amount when getting someone else to register. Confinity's push for rapid membership growth succeeded. Just three months after its launch, in February 2000, PayPal had attracted 190,000 customers, signing up 9000 new accounts every day. The potential to turn this service into a mass product was there right from the beginning. Apart from settling accounts among family or friends (such as sharing a restaurant bill), PayPal's most promising area for expansion was person-to-person payments arising from auctions. PayPal has been the preferred payment method in online auctions organized by eBay despite the latter's purchase in early 1999 of Billpoint.com, a software specialist for P2P payments, in order to offer customers its own e-mail payment service.

In March 2000 Confinity merged with X.com, one of its competitors. Since then X.com has expanded PayPal services to include $100,000 in fraud protection per account (giving its accounts a degree of protection akin to the federal deposit insurance for bank accounts), increased maximum spending ceilings of up to $1000 and enhanced service packages for P2P accounts with features that are more commonly found in B2B accounts (such as electronic billing or batch payments). These refinements have enabled PayPal to compete head on with Billpoint for market share in the auction market. Six months later, in October 2000, PayPal had nearly four million customers of which 300,000 were business accounts. Being the preferred payment method in more than half of the auctions conducted on eBay, at that point PayPal completed about 130,000 transactions each day averaging $50 for a daily volume of $6 million. Today PayPal has about ten million customers in 36 countries.

While holding its own against Billpoint, PayPal nevertheless has had trouble generating a profit.[6] Its service offered individuals, who lack merchant status to accept credit-card payments on their own, a way to send and receive money through the web for free. Thus, making it much easier for people to pay each other, PayPal took off precisely in that P2P market niche as a payment service for eBay and other internet auction markets. This, however, saddled PayPal with very heavy credit-card processing costs, since a large number of its customers turned out to be fledgling online entrepreneurs who would receive lots of payments with credit cards. That payment mode also limits the company's revenue-generating capacity by not leaving any funds in its accounts for the float. An interest float of some $50 million with paltry money-market returns of less than 2 percent is not enough for a company with over 400 employees. Struggling to find the right balance between maintaining the critical mass of customers and how to earn adequate income from fund transfers, PayPal decided that it could no longer afford to offer its service for free to those high-volume, high-cost customers receiving a lot of credit-card payments from their buyers. In June 2000 PayPal introduced business and premier accounts whose enhanced service features were combined with the introduction of transaction fees. Both types of accounts require recipients of credit-card payments to pay 1.9 percent plus 25 cents for each transaction. In October 2000 PayPal extended that charge to all customers receiving more than $500 in credit-card payments in a six-month period, irrespective of their account category. When you suddenly announce a fee structure for your biggest customers after enticing them with heavy advertising of your free service, it weakens your customer base. It matters little that banks and credit-card companies charge higher fees for the processing of transactions – broken promises tend to anger customers.[7]

PayPal has proved that e-mail provides a convenient, safe and efficient payments solution for P2P transactions and auctions. Its rapid growth has provided strong momentum for the take-off of cybercash. Its innovations – the simple platform design without proprietary software, the emphasis on keeping balances in one's account for later use and its use of sign-up as well as referral bonuses – show the potential of such cybercash applications to move beyond being mere extensions of traditional bank money to becoming an autonomous money form. While not chartered as a bank, PayPal increasingly acts like one, as evidenced by its current plans to offer its customers a money-market account and issue its own credit cards.[8]

5.3 Coupon Money

While PayPal established the viability of e-mail money for P2P transactions, another category of cybercash experiments arising in the late 1990s focused on the B2C segment of e-commerce. Building on the popularity of frequent-flier miles and coupons among Americans, a number of internet start-ups had the idea of designing their own online currencies for use as a marketing tool to attract more customers to sites and entice them to shop there. Certain types of cybercash emerged which could be spent as coupons on products within a network of participating e-tailers.

One such application of coupon money concerned the liquification of frequent-flier miles. While many of us love to get these rewards, we do not have the chance to use them very often. A lot of these rewards end up unused, frozen money whose purchasing power is locked up. The consulting agency Frequent Flyer Services, as reported in *The Economist* (2000), estimated in early 2000 that there were currently 3 trillion unused air miles locked in the accounts of airline customers. With airlines selling those miles usually for between one and three cents, we are talking here between $30 billion to $90 billion in spending power if those miles could be used online to buy gifts, luggage, electronics and all kinds of other in-flight goods typically offered by the airlines. In 1999 a former Northwest Airlines executive had the smart idea to launch MilePoint.com which converts frequent-flier miles into a currency that can be used online. In May 2000 the largest US airline, American Airlines, announced that the 38 million members in its frequent-flier program would henceforth not only be able to accumulate frequent-flier miles by buying goods and services on AOL, but also spend them there. There is no question that this move, a very popular way to make cybercash resonate with an increasingly large number of Americans collecting such reward points, will eventually force other airlines to follow suit with a similar service for online shopping. Here it is the frequent-flier miles themselves which are endowed with spending power to represent cybercash, and I can imagine that all kinds of store coupons, loyalty points and other types of rewards will eventually incorporate this quality of electronic liquidity.

5.3.1 GiftCertificates.com

Another application of coupon money operates like gift certificates, except that you can now obtain such virtual certificates from hundreds of different retailers centrally by visiting just one site without ever having to go to a store. A web service known as GiftCertificates.com, for instance, allows its customers to use their credit cards for purchases of gift certificates from over 700 different merchants (including premier retailers, hotels, spas, internet retailers and travel service companies) over the net. You can send a certificate of your choice to anyone to whom you wish to make a present, and the recipient can redeem that certificate either in the issuer's store or on its web site. Alternatively, the certificate can also be exchanged by the recipient into another one more to his or her liking. So-called SuperCertificates can be e-mailed as a gift to friends or family members who can then exchange them for gift certificates of their choice. Besides offering a large selection of gift certificates for any type of consumer taste and preference, GiftCertificates.com offers a whole infrastructure of gift-giving services, including a service reminding account-holders when to give gifts to whom, gift cards, gift wrap, shipping and handling options for rapid delivery, as well as reward points whenever you purchase a gift certificate.[9]

5.3.2 Online Money for Teenagers

In 1999 several start-ups, including Cybermoola, RocketCash and iCanBuy.com, introduced coupon-money schemes aimed at teenagers. That demographic group tends to be very familiar with the internet and likes to shop, but very often lacks access to credit cards. Coupon money overcomes this problem by offering an alternative payment mechanism with which to turn these youngsters early on into life-long e-shoppers. The dot-coms mentioned above organized online shopping malls geared towards the tastes of American teenagers. Prospective consumers opened up accounts there which could be loaded up with the site's virtual currency through money orders, checks sent through the mail, even cash payments in qualifying stores. Most of the time, however, funds were transferred into those accounts by parents of customers who used their credit cards for that purpose. Gift certificates purchased by family members or friends could also be used to fill up customer accounts with spendable cash. In addition, each of these services offered promotional cash bonuses or gift certificates issued by participating merchants as a way to get customers to surf and shop on their site. An interesting variant of such teenager-oriented coupon money was DoughNET (www.doughnet.com) which offered its young customers a bank account, complete with federal deposit insurance and 5 percent interest on unused balances, as well as ample advice on budgeting, smart shopping and responsible saving. DoughNET's concern with the social responsibility of teenagers in matters of money was further demonstrated by the fact that it allowed customers to donate money to all kinds of civic causes and awarded them with extra cash for any donation.

The sites offering coupon money for teenagers initially proved quite popular, as evidenced by the 350,000 youngsters using iCanBuy.com by mid-2000. They provided a handy way for parents to reward their adolescent kids, most of whom love to surf on the net but lack a credit card to pay for online purchases. The less obvious appeal for parents was the ability to use these coupon-money accounts as a means of controlling the shopping habits of their consumer-oriented kids. Consequently, these services initially saw fairly strong membership growth and typically managed to sign up between fifty and hundred different e-tailers, each of whom was paying the service a modest fee for providing a direct link to its customers. But most of these sites did not survive the internet crash of 2000–01. Cybermoola, iCanBuy.com and DoughNET all had to shut down when initial venture-capital support was withdrawn. Having to build an expensive infrastructure from scratch, none of these start-ups managed to reach profitability soon enough to satisfy impatient investors who in mid-2000 suddenly turned pessimistic about the prospects of e-commerce. Perhaps these dot-coms would have fared better if they had forged a link with an established ISP or bank rather than go it alone. Today only RocketCash continues to operate in that category.

5.3.3 Flooz.com

The idea of issuing gift certificates as spendable coupons took a major step forward with the appearance of Flooz.com in December 1998. Flooz, an Arab word for money, served as an online gift currency which users could purchase with credit cards or money orders and send via e-mail to benefi-ciaries (complete with electronic gift-card message). Recipients could then spend that money on any one of 75 exclusive online sites accepting flooz (including Barnes & Noble, J. Crew, Dean & Deluca, Godiva Chocolatier, Martha Stewart and Tower Records). Participating merchants could also issue bonus flooz for promotional purposes as a way to reward consumer shopping. In addition to individual users of its service, Flooz.com targeted corporations wishing to give gift certificates to their sales reps when reaching targets, to their employees in recognition for performance, to their best clients as reward for loyalty, to customers in sales incentives schemes, as a way to make donations, or in connection with special events. In March 2000 Flooz.com set up a special web site targeting its corporate customers for that purpose.

While it lasted, this Silicon Valley start-up proved to be a very innov-ative outfit. Its advertising campaigns introduced a variety of new marketing strategies to deepen brand recognition. Its user-friendly site was one of the first to include a customer care center offering live help. Also unusual was Flooz.com's highly selective process of signing up e-tailers to its network, which had the double advantage of giving participating merchants a benefit from positive co-branding and boosting the start-up's reputation as a desirable intermediary. Like PayPal, Flooz.com relied on the viral-marketing technique of spreading the use of its currency via e-mail which would prompt recipients of such gift money to open up accounts with the company. Flooz.com's infrastructure centered on a soft-ware application program interface (API) which participating merchants had to download on their web servers. This API provided for encrypted communication within the Flooz network, allowed merchants to verify account details of the buyer and gave customers the option of replenishing their accounts automatically.[10]

Flooz were automatically convertible into dollars on a one-to-one basis. Since all flooz balances were fully backed by equivalent sums of dollars, the circulation of flooz did not constitute independent cybercash capable of adding to the nation's money supply. Nor did this online currency replace traditional payment methods to any degree. Still, by maintaining the appearance of a different money form, issued in the wake of making gifts and used solely for purchases within a particular network of online merchants, users got the sense of a unique and distinct form of cybercash. In another major innovation Flooz.com entered into partnerships with four major online-rewards companies (beenz, FreeRide, MyPoints, and Netcen-tives) to establish convertibility for the first time between otherwise incompatible variants of cybercash. For instance, 200 beenz could be converted into one flooz. Since such conversion was unidirectional, allowing the swap of its partners' loyalty points or reward monies into flooz but not vice versa, Flooz.com hoped to boost the supply of its currency with these arrangements.

Flooz.com benefited early on from solid investor support, raising $43.5 million in 1999 and 2000 for the launch of its payment service. Its revenue model relied on fees paid by participating merchants. All other aspects of its service were offered for free to attract the largest possible number of users. Flooz.com took off almost immediately. Within six months of its launch, by February 2000, about 450,000 people had sent or received flooz and $5 million worth of flooz certificates were in circulation. Yet in the end Flooz.com became another victim of the dot-com crash of 2000–01. Like many other small e-commerce start-ups pioneering new services on the internet, Flooz.com faced the challenge of having to spend heavily on setting up an infrastructure and gaining brand recognition before securing an adequate revenue stream. By running major losses in the early stages of its life cycle, its managers never had effective cost controls in place to withstand much higher cash-burn rates once the internet crash slowed down revenue growth. The knock-out punch for the company came in June 2001 amidst reports that a Russian gang had charged $300,000 of flooz currency to stolen credit cards over a period of three months. Once the credit-card processor realized that such fraud was under way, it refused to pass revenues from genuine credit-card sales onto Flooz.com until it held enough reserves to cover possible fraudulent orders. This caused Flooz.com's already-shaky cash flow to break down, since it still had to pay all those retailers who were accepting flooz as payment for online purchases. On 8 August 2001 the company shut down its site without prior notice, thereby rendering the flooz in customer accounts worthless. Three weeks later Flooz.com filed for Chapter 7 bankruptcy.[11]

5.3.4 Beenz.com

Another spectacular failure of a once-promising start-up pitching a novel payment system in the form of coupon money to web shoppers was the British start-up Beenz.com. Introduced in March 1999 with dual headquarters in London and New York, this company had the ambition of creating a global web currency which could challenge the dominance of credit-card companies in online payments for B2C commerce. While flooz had to be purchased outright in the form of gift certificates, Beenz.com saw its currency as something that had to be earned. In effect, Beenz.com treated the online consumer like an e-worker who deserved to be paid for the 'work' of engaging in e-commerce. Consumers could earn beenz as a reward for surfing the net, visiting e-commerce sites, setting up accounts with e-tailers, or shopping online for goods and services.[12] They could then spend their beenz worldwide at any of 300 leading e-tailers accepting this online currency (including Barnes & Noble, Eddie Bauer, Martha Stewart, Garden.com, Hammacher Schlemmer, Dell, Sharper Image, Borders and Wine.com).

Participating merchants could give away beenz as promotional incentives to reward consumers for specific actions in the hope of generating more sales, perhaps even a longer term relationship. They could purchase this coupon money at a rate of 100 beenz to a dollar while merchants accepting beenz for payment could exchange them at Beenz.com at a rate of 200 beenz to a dollar. The difference between the two exchange rates, between the selling price of beenz and its reconversion rate, constituted Beenz.com's source of income gains from the issue of online currency.

During the two-and-a-half years of its existence Beenz.com managed to build a formidable presence on a global scale. Supported by over $80 million in venture-capital funds raised in four rounds of financing, Beenz.com set up ten operational sites in North America, Europe and East Asia as well as joint ventures with local companies in six additional countries. While these sites contained many local e-tailers, consumers from anywhere in the world could buy from any of the 300 retailers accepting beenz, thus making this currency truly global in nature and offering its participating merchants a worldwide market without borders. Each of the 16 local sites converted beenz in the respective national currency at rates which would give beenz the same value everywhere in cyberspace. In some of its joint ventures Beenz.com actually paid its partners in beenz for services rendered, a very interesting innovation that goes to the heart of money's contradictory dual role as a public good and a private commodity (see section 1.4).

Cooperation with three leaders in infrastructure technology – Oracle, Sun Microsystems and Exodus – enabled Beenz.com to be an innovative leader in the technology used for the creation of a universal online currency. One of the start-up's goals was to make its currency available through a wide range of access devices – from cell phones and interactive television to personal digital assistants. Another goal was to create a user-friendly service which provided direct consumer assistance, up-to-date account information and e-mail messages about promotional deals. Particularly clever was the company's emphasis on anchoring its e-currency among its customers with an iconic representation of beenz, with its own currency symbol (a 'b' with two dashes as in the symbols for the yen or the euro) and ubiquitous red-beans signs which can be clicked to earn or spend beenz.

As the company put into place its ambitious plans for a global online currency, it was hit hard by the dot-com crash. Beenz.com was particularly vulnerable to the bursting of the e-commerce bubble after March 2000, since many of its partners were themselves dot-com start-ups squeezed hard by the crisis in their sector. It also had spent heavily on expansion as one would expect from a company which, in wanting to introduce an online-payment service on a global scale, had entered into more than twenty cooperation agreements with other internet firms and set up sites all over the world. In December 2000 the company had to retrench, closing some of its sites and laying off 10 percent of its 265-strong workforce. These steps were accompanied by a switch in business strategy, thanks to the introduction in October 2000 of a new technology known as beenz-Codes. The company decided to use this technology for a new reward program and make it the major engine of its growth. BeenzCodes were unique codes issued to consumers off-line at point of sale, in direct mailings and inside product packages which could be redeemed online for prizes. In effect, with this program, consumers could earn beenz in exchange for providing a tracking code supplied by manufacturers interested in gathering information on consumers and their shopping preferences. Beenz.com hoped that this RewardzCodes program would prove attractive for manufacturers and retailers. In another audacious move Beenz.com entered into a collaboration with Mondex to develop a beenz-enabled smart card, the so-called 'beenz rewardzcard', which account-holders could use to pay in beenz at over 18 million locations where MasterCard was accepted.

Neither product extension managed to generate sufficient revenues fast enough to compensate for the rapid decline of Beenz.com's main business of selling its monetary units to e-tailers in its network. After several rounds of layoffs in the first half of 2001 and a last-minute change in top management, the company simply ran out of cash. Unable to receive additional venture-capital funds or find a buyer, Beenz.com closed its site in August 2001 – within days of the collapse of Flooz.com.[13] The simultaneous demise of the two major independent online-currency systems for B2C commerce dealt a serious blow to the once-euphoric dreams about alternative payment platforms crowding out the credit-card duopoly on the internet.

As with all failures, there are valuable lessons to be learned from the collapse of Flooz.com and Beenz.com:

■ It costs a lot to build the infrastructure of a global online currency. Start-ups will find it difficult to bridge the cash-flow gap between the initial burst in spending on infrastructure investments and more gradual revenue creation. They will therefore be vulnerable to failure, especially if they depend on impatient venture capital and rely on just one revenue source. Apart from the infrastructure costs, it also takes a lot of time and effort to build brand recognition sufficiently to tempt a hesitant public into experimenting with a new money form. For these reasons, more established and better capitalized firms will have an edge over newcomers in the business of online money.

■ Flooz.com and Beenz.com must be lauded for their ingenious designs of online-payment platforms which may serve as models for future endeavors. Both have certainly shown how innovation-rich cybercash can be. Their basic idea, generating a distinct online currency issued as a gift or reward in the context of promotional incentives to encourage e-shopping, is a good one, good enough to be tried again. People like to get paid in coupons, as the popularity of frequent-flier miles and other off-line reward schemes attests. Online coupons, however, will take a bit longer to reach the same degree of popularity, because they are embedded in a medium of commerce that is still in the earliest stages of its development and not yet sufficiently anchored among the public at large. This limitation, which proved fatal for Flooz.com and Beenz.com, is part of the broader problem of having to rely on the fickle B2C segment of e-commerce which has had a hard time competing with traditional off-line transactions in retail stores or through mail-order catalogues. PayPal succeeded, while flooz or beenz did not, because it managed to establish itself in the P2P segment of e-commerce which represents pure value added without an off-line equivalent (see Table 5.2).

■ When you try to establish a cybercash system for B2C transactions, you compete head on with the credit-card networks, notably Visa and MasterCard, which managed early on to grab the lion's share of online payments by consumers to businesses. As a matter of fact, the major impetus for PayPal's e-mail money or the coupon-money schemes of GiftCertificates.com, Flooz.com and Beenz.com was precisely to estab-lish viable payment alternatives to credit cards. Yet none of those experiments managed to escape the dominance of the two large credit-card networks. PayPal was saddled with unexpectedly large credit-card charges, when its service became especially popular among individuals-turned-entrepreneurs whose customers often paid with credit cards.

Table 5.2 Summary of second-generation cybercash experiments, 1997–2000

Name	Category	Type	Creation	Features
PayPal	E-mail money	No software, online	Multiple funding	Reusable balances
GiftCertificates.com	Coupon money	No software, on-, off-line	Credit cards	Merchant network
RocketCash	Coupon money	No software, online	Stored value (multiple funding)	Merchant network, earmarking
Flooz	Coupon money	Software, online	Multiple funding	Merchant network, convertibility
Beenz	Coupon money	Software, online	Autonomous creation	Merchant network, convertibility

Flooz.com was brought down by credit-card fraud, and Beenz.com, in a desperate attempt to salvage its operation, bet its future on a deal with Mondex, a subsidiary of MasterCard since 1996. Thus the first round in the battle over B2C payments has clearly gone to the credit-card companies.

Although ultimately they failed within a couple of years, nevertheless Flooz.com and Beenz.com posed enough of a threat to force the credit-card companies to react. Visa, MasterCard, American Express and Discover Card have tried hard to neutralize the challenge of alternative online currencies. These credit-card networks have offered guarantees against fraud and easy online approval of card applications. They have also tried to address the privacy and security concerns of people, who are afraid to place their credit-card information on the internet, by offering disposable credit-card numbers which are used only once. Responding directly to Cybermoola and RocketCash targeting the teen market, Visa introduced its Buxx Card which has a pre-loaded value and is designed to appeal to teenagers. Credit-card companies are all trying to gain or maintain a dominant position in other market niches as well, intensifying their efforts in the B2B zone while experimenting with stored-value products, micropayments and bio-security cards which allow users to authorize the use of electronic information through the spoken word or the touch of a hand.[14]

5.4 The Maturing of Cybercash

In the last couple of years first-generation design ideas for cybercash have been advanced greatly by much larger players. Because of their greater size, these monetary innovators are able to overcome the scale barriers which had so plagued the start-ups of the second generation.

5.4.1 Smart Cards

As the major credit-card networks decided to make the online use of their credit cards more user-friendly, they finally also began to take a more active interest in the development of smart cards. Much of the impetus in that direction has come from American Express, forced to market its cards on its own without support of banks. In 1999 an antitrust suit initiated by that company with the backing of the US government against Visa and MasterCard charged both, among other alleged antitrust violations, with colluding to slow the spread of smart-card use in the United States.[15] That same year American Express also launched a successful experiment with a smart card known as Blue. Within 14 months of its launch Blue had attracted 2.2 million users in the United States, proving that sophisticated American shoppers are willing to forego their credit and debit cards in favor of something more practical and better adapted to the New Economy of retailing. This success, coupled with public-relations pressure from their antitrust suit, has prompted both Visa and MasterCard to accelerate their efforts with smart-card technology:

- In May 2000 Visa entered into a technology partnership with Gemplus to develop a portable framework integrating all the necessary security features, personalization commands and data formats for a new generation of highly sophisticated smart cards known as Open Platform cards. Over the coming year Visa is planning to issue seven million of its new smart cards through four banks belonging to its network.

- In turn MasterCard has teamed up with Gemplus's principal rival Mondex, having acquired a controlling majority interest in the smart-card software specialist in 1996. Even though its Electronic Cash system has failed so far to catch on in the United States, Mondex has managed to test this product across the globe by entering into franchise agreements with banks and retailers in over 80 countries. It has also adapted its smart cards for multi-purpose use in special environments, such as university campuses, corporate headquarters and clients of phone companies as well as postal services. The company, participating actively in a consortium of smart-card technology suppliers known as MAOSCO, has played a leading role in developing a multi-application operating system for smart cards known as MULTOS as well as open e-commerce trading protocols. MasterCard is finally planning to use its investment in Mondex for a launch into the smart-card business.

While the three major credit-card networks now seem more committed to the issue of smart cards in the United States, this payment technology is still beset by barriers. As long as it entails a significant hardware invest-ment, in this case specially fitted readers which need to be connected to cash registers at retailers or computers at home, the spread of smart-card technology will be seriously hampered by large set-up costs. Moreover, at this point smart cards have very limited applications in the US, serving primarily as stored-value cards for specific payment uses (on university campuses, for laundry machines) or to give consumers loyalty coupons and discounts. The use of smart cards as a vehicle for electronic cash, their most obvious 'killer' application, depends on removing these two barriers.

In this regard there is a lot of progress under way. For one, new tech-nology will remove the expensive hardware requirement by allowing smart cards to communicate without any physical contact via antennae. Furthermore, the new smart cards being offered now (Amex's Blue, Visa's Open Platform) are endowed with Sun Microsystem's Java Card tech-nology which makes different smart-card standards compatible with each other and allows multiple applications to be run on a single card. Java-enabled smart cards, of which there were 10 million new cards issued worldwide in 2000 (a five-fold rise over 1999), offer users customized application configurations which meet their specific needs at low cost. Finally, the use of smart cards will also spread more rapidly because of major improvements in digital-wallet technology. An essential component of any smart-card infrastructure, digital wallets simplify e-commerce by allowing consumers to fill out the relevant billing and shipping inform-ation only once and then zap it to any wallet-enabled merchant with a simple click of the mouse. Some of these wallets also contain a verifi-cation and processing service for vendors (for example Qpass's Power-Wallet). The internet's biggest players have moved digital-wallet technology from the client-side model storing software on a user's personal computer to server-side wallets which consumers can access on the web with the proper user name and password (such as Sun's Java Wallet, Microsoft's Passport). Server-side wallets have the dual advantage of being under the control of merchants or ISPs and at the same time more easily accessed by consumers who no longer have to download software. Since the wallet's payment automation becomes more valuable with growing use, this technology is especially fit for micropayments.[16]

The rapid pace of technological improvements in microprocessor technology leads one to anticipate that smart cards will eventually become very smart indeed. Today we have smart cards with considerable data-processing powers and fully developed encryption/decryption capacity for a high degree of safety and privacy. But these cards will become a lot more sophisticated in the next few years, capable of downloading funds, storing them, transferring them across a wide variety of applications and processing the relevant information generated by such transfers. They will provide authentication, account verification and other advanced safety features while allowing users to program a variety of payment specifications (for automatic billing, netting provisions, dated payment installments and so forth).[17] Endowed with these capabilities of convenience and processing power, smart cards are in a position to replace both traditional credit and debit cards. In the process they are likely to emerge as a key ingredient of any large-scale cybercash system, both as a widely used payment tool with which to carry out cybercash transactions and as a bridge between online and off-line commerce (where they can be hooked into POS terminals at retail outlets or ATMs).

5.4.2 Electronic Checks

While the product development of smart cards has matured to the point of mass use, another first-generation experiment in cybercash has continued to progress at the same time. We are talking here about e-checks. Since the early days of Neuman's NetCheque, a number of firms have designed better e-check alternatives using asymmetric public-key encryption software for security, intermediary payments services for financial-data verification and automated clearing-houses for the transfer of funds.[18] The Financial Services Technology Consortium (www.fstc.com), a consortium of financial institutions (the Bank of America and Fleet Bank), government agencies (the US Treasury and the Federal Reserve Bank of Boston) and computer as well as telecommunications firms engaged in the internet infrastructure (Sun Microsystems, RDM, IBM), has launched the Electronic Check Project (www.eCheck.org). Designed to become the industry standard, eChecks can be used with existing checking accounts and can be initiated from a variety of hardware platforms and software applications.

For that purpose the FSTC has developed an open architecture using its 'financial services markup language' (FSML), with state-of-the-art security features for authentication, public-key cryptography, digital signatures, certificate authorities and duplicate detection. Just in terms of safety eChecks promise to be far more effective than e-check systems using an intermediary. They will also be more user-friendly, not least because they cut out the intermediary and use standardized, easy-to-use electronic forms. It should be noted that the FSTC's eChecks system is the only electronic-check system so far approved by the US Treasury which uses this payment option for its own checks. In October 1999 the FSTC entered into a cooperation agreement with CommerceNet, a worldwide consortium of 500 e-commerce developers and end-users, to take over management of its eChecks system. This deal assures the FSTC a potentially large user base for its electronic-check system with which to facilitate its successful commercial launch.

5.4.3 Citibank's c2it

Repeating the pattern of earlier cybercash experiments being copied and refined by larger operators seeking to establish an industry standard, Citibank has decided to take up PayPal's successful idea of e-mail money. In July 2000 America's largest bank launched a P2P payments service called c2it which enables individuals to send cash via e-mail to anyone with an e-mail address. Customers set up a c2it account for cash transfers funded out of credit-card, checking, saving, or money-market accounts. Accounts funded through credit cards can also be used for international transfers to over 30 countries, giving c2it from the very beginning a strong global presence which Citibank intends to deepen. Transaction fees consist of a minimum charge of $0.50 plus 1 percent of the transfer value, up to a maximum of 2.2 percent of the transaction. Cross-border transfers cost between $10 and $15. These fees are lower than credit-card or wire-transfer charges. The fact that fund recipients do not have to pay anything might interest merchants who pay a quite bit each time they get paid by credit cards.

Citibank's entry into the online-payment business for P2P transactions targets millions of users who can thereby be brought in touch with the bank's other online services. Its c2it service is available to users holding accounts at other US financial institutions who might eventually be persuaded to switch all of their banking to Citi. In addition, the viral-marketing aspect of e-mail money, where recipients not yet having a c2it account are bound to enroll in that service to get the cash, promises to help fuel user growth. Finally, Citibank also expects to take market share away from PayPal, Billpoint, and other independents because of its brand advantage as the largest US bank and so subject to regulatory supervision, protected by deposit insurance and deserving of public trust. Using the infrastructure of its credit-card business for transfers of e-mail money, Citibank offers its c2it clients the same customer service (including 24/7 telephone contact for assistance), technology and fraud protection as the 60 million holders of its credit cards.

Searching a very large user base to boost economies of scale, Citibank has aggressively pursued partnerships with major internet players to co-brand its c2it payment service. The first step was an alliance with America Online, concluded in July 2000, which brought Citi's c2it service to the nearly 30 million subscribers of AOL and Compuserve under the brand name AOL Quick Cash. In May 2001 Citibank entered into an agreement with Microsoft which allows c2it to be used by the tens of millions users of Microsoft's internet services under the brand name of MSN. Embedded in the MSN platform, this payment service can be automatically accessed from any MSN base, whether MSN Auctions, eShop, the Hotmail e-mail service, or other relevant e-commerce applications. At the same time Citi also concluded a deal with AuctionWatch to connect c2it to the online auction services offered by the latter.[19] These partnerships will give Citibank a large user base for its c2it service and so ensure its leadership position in online-payments systems.

5.4.4 eCash's Monneta

While smart cards, e-checks, and e-mail money are now poised for take-off thanks to the entry of major players, a fourth method for online fund transfers in the form of digital coins is still trying to find a niche in the payments space of the internet. The idea behind these digital coins is to provide software which transforms money available for transfers in existing off-line networks (checking accounts, credit-card systems) into digital markers that can be transferred from buyer to seller on the internet for reconversion into 'real' money by the latter. The ultimate goal of digital-coin systems is to build a universal online-payments system which can be used anytime, anywhere, by anyone (with the right tools) for fund transfers.

While CyberCash has abandoned its early CyberCoin experiment, eCash Technologies has managed to build on the foundations laid by Chaum in the mid-1990s (see section 5.1 above). After taking over his eCash experiment from DigiCash in August 1999, the new company rapidly expanded the scope of its pilot programs, extending them to eight banks, over 300 merchants, and more than 30,000 accounts by February 2000. Especially important was the testing of eCash P2P in conjunction with Deutsche Bank 24, opening up the platform to a wide variety of peer-to-peer transactions and thus dramatically enhancing its user application potential. As in earlier tests, the highly advanced safety standards of eCash continued to prove fail-safe. In the meantime eCash Technologies adapted its system to Europe's WAP (wireless applications protocol) standard for smart cell phones able to connect to the mobile web.

Throughout 2000, Chaum's successors developed a variety of payments options which they then integrated into one multi-application software package known as Monneta. This co-branded product suite included 'debit' payments deducted from one's checking account, a 'prepaid' option based on storing value in one's eCash account for immediate spending, a special P2P feature transferring funds between consumer eCash accounts via e-mail, access to cell phones for mobile web transactions, a B2C application linking consumer and merchant accounts, as well as a B2B application for transactions between businesses. Those payment options were complemented by two merchant-specific payment methods, namely electronic gift certificates and customer-loyalty points, with which to reward consumers for repeat purchases. In 2001, eCash Technologies was working on a multi-currency eCash software product for cross-border transactions.

Even though eCash Technologies introduced a multi-application online-payment platform whose innovative features with regard to security, privacy, flexibility and convenience of use set a benchmark standard for any other cybercash system to follow, its growth strategy needed revision. Entirely bank-centered, eCash Technologies interacted only indirectly with merchants or consumers and depended on banks with considerable online capacities for its growth. But the company did not succeed in establishing a significant presence in the United States, its home market, through a partnership with a leading bank, as it had managed to do in Germany with the help of Deutsche Bank. In February 2002 eCash Technologies was acquired by the software firm InfoSpace. While Monneta may not survive as a stand-alone product, its basic design idea will be folded into an even broader electronic-payments platform that can be directly marketed to merchants. InfoSpace has the capital and technological know-how to launch such a product. Irrespective of what happens to its patents in the hands of InfoSpace, eCash Technologies has proved that the technology exists today for a fully integrated, global, safe and fast cybercash system whose digital coins are as anonymous as hard cash.

5.4.5 Oakington's Amadigi

Another interesting experiment in digital-coin technology has been undertaken by Oakington (www.oakington.com) during the past couple of years. This British software firm has developed a standard software platform which other organizations so inclined can use to issue their own currency for online transactions. Its Amadigi platform allows for pre-authenticated rights of ownership of digital tokens to be transferred securely online. Such tokens can represent any kind of value agreed to between two interacting parties, thus giving online businesses maximum flexibility in designing their own tailor-made payment mechanism. Oakington's online-currency platform provides for automatic payment of taxes, a feature especially useful for businesses collecting sales taxes. It also comes with 'time escrow' whereby a transaction is only settled once the product purchased online has been delivered, thus addressing a major concern of many online shoppers. Finally, its Amadigi platform technology includes earmarking capabilities whereby any type of money issued through Amadigi can be given specific-use features, such as restricting its use to anyone over 18 years old. Oakington's Amadigi platform, just as eCash Technologies' Monneta platform, demonstrates that some software firms driving the third-generation experiments in cybercash are putting the emphasis on integrated multi-application platforms for online fund transfers using actual digital money, a qualitatively different type of electronic money than the smart cards and e-mail transfers discussed above.

5.4.6 B2B Money

The latest round of experimentation with cybercash has also begun to focus on B2B transactions, potentially the largest segment of e-commerce. A good example is the joint venture launched in June 2000 between B2B e-commerce giant Ariba, internet-security specialist VeriSign and American Express to deliver the first card payment processing utility for online B2B transactions which will dramatically simplify authorization, settlement and reconciliation processes. In December 2000 CyberCash launched an updated version of its industry-leading payment-processing software CyberCash B2B which, besides handling credit-card payments for online purchases of supplies that do not require an extensive reporting and approval process, also processes purchasing card payments for transactions requiring more back-end accounting and reporting as well as electronic fund transfers (EFT) typically used in larger transactions. Its EFT service is especially promising, given that the electronic payments between businesses are expected to grow from 14 percent of all payments in 1999 to 61 percent in 2009. This new CyberCash B2B service is now being built into the leading B2B platforms (such as Microsoft's CashRegister, Oracle's e-Business Suite and IBM's WebSphere Commerce Suite). CyberCash has also entered into a partnership with YourAccounts.Com, the e-commerce subsidiary of Output Technology Solutions, to integrate its CyberCash EFT with the latter's web-based electronic bill payment and presentment program known as anywhere.B2B to offer an integrated package tailored to Fortune 500 companies.

The development of cybercash systems for B2B extends to e-marketplaces, in particular mega-exchanges organized as auctions. An early manifestation of this trend can be seen in the case of online barter exchanges which have been set up recently by such firms as BarterTrust, BigVine and LassoBucks. These allow businesses to unload their excess inventories in exchange for something they find more useful. Since those barter markets require value comparisons between otherwise incommensurable products carrying many different characteristics, actors in such markets find that they are better off having an objective measure of value on the basis of which they can compare valuations. Thus these markets inevitably tend to create their own currencies. A good example is Ubarter.com (www.ubarter.com) where sellers get Ubarter dollars in return which they can use to buy excess goods which other companies post on the site. Since these private currencies in the service of barter markets need to establish trust among all market participants, their issuers will have to put into place credible and generally accepted monetary governance structures, as BigVine has tried with its effort to patent its money-issue mechanism for its Trade Dollars (T$).

One of the more interesting applications of cybercash in barter exchanges was developed by Mojo Nation (www.mojonation.net), a Silicon Valley start-up which in 2000 introduced a radical new technology to improve content distribution on the internet. Even though broadband and other communication technologies are being introduced to handle a lot more traffic on the web, dial-up and other low-bandwidth connections to the internet still make up 80 percent of the system. In other words, we have an information superhighway with very narrow access and exit ramps. These create traffic bottlenecks, especially when trying to move large content files to user terminals. Mojo Nation technology avoided overloading these narrow ramps by breaking down a large file into thousands of small fragments and scattering those among participating network peers who at the moment had unused traffic capacity to rent out. Once these fragments had been moved by volunteering peers to their final destination, they were automatically put together to recompose the original file sent out. In return for offering their service of transportation, these peers earned an online currency called mojo which they could reconvert into dollars or spend when they themselves rent excess capacity from other peers. For that purpose Mojo Nation built into its data-transmission software a micropayments system coupled with very sophisticated accounting software to keep track of all the mojos accumulated by participating network peers. Here we have a very innovative application of online barter exchange using its own currency as a unit of account.[20]

Thanks to their site-specific currencies, online barter exchanges have been able to revive an age-old institution of social interaction, cashless trade, with a third-millennium version of a medium of exchange and price standard. In the process they may turn all kinds of hitherto market-excluded goods into marketable commodities, a net addition to economic activity and source of growth. The market-making intermediaries, such as BigVine, UBarter.com and Mojo Nation, earn real-dollar transaction fees ranging between 3 and 4 percent of the value traded from purchasers as well as sellers while issuing the quasi-dollars fuelling this income stream free of cost. They can thus gain income from the issue of money even though their trading dollars are cybercash only in the limited sense of being spendable solely on the issuer's site. The already amazing scope of offerings on those sites, however, makes that limitation tolerable. They comprise a very large variety of product categories, including all kinds of services extending even to labor services of highly skilled specialists.

When looking at the ensemble of third-generation experiments in cybercash (see Table 5.3), we can see a definite maturing in the life cycle of this new money form. During 2000–01 some of the earliest applications dating from the mid-1990s overcame their initial commercial failures. Finally attracting the attention of the largest players, they have been given a second chance and grown into much more sophisticated instruments for online fund transfers. We have seen this happen with the sudden push of smart cards by credit-card companies, with the refinements of digital-wallet technology by Sun Microsystems and Microsoft, with e-checks benefiting from the support of the Financial Services Technology Consortium, with Citibank's launching its c2it service for mass use and with the takeover of Chaum's digital coins by eCash Technologies. Integrated multi-application platforms generating their own digital tokens, such as eCash's Monneta and Oakington's Amadigi, represent the cutting edge of online-payment technology for two reasons. For one, they are especially well suited to expand into broader shopping protocols which regulate the

Table 5.3 Summary of third-generation cybercash experiments, 2000–02

Name	Category	Type	Creation	Features
Amex's Blue	Smart card	Hardware, software, on-, off-line	Stored value	Reader, Java-enabled
Visa's Open Platform	Smart card	Hardware, software, on-, off-line	Stored value	Reader, Java-enabled
eChecks	E-check	Hardware, software, online	Checking accounts	No intermediary
Citi's c2it	E-mail money	No software, online	Multiple funding	Alliances with ISPs
Monneta	Digital coin, multi-type platform	Software, online	Multiple funding	Anonymous, recoverable, bi-directional
Amadigi	Digital token, multi-type platform	Software, online	Autonomous creation	No intermediary, earmarking

negotiation, payment and fulfillment steps of any online transaction. And they go beyond the other payment technologies discussed above (smart cards, e-mail) inasmuch as they move us from the automation of online mechanisms transferring off-line funds to actual cybercash generated online (digital tokens).

Third-generation experiments in cybercash have also reinforced the heterogeneity of this emerging money form. It has become clear that the different segments of e-commerce each tend to develop their own unique variants of cybercash tailored to the immediate needs of their respective participants. A good example is the e-mail money offered by PayPal and Citibank which has already gained a significant foothold in P2P transactions. The B2B segment also creates its own cybercash versions, as evidenced by American Express's cooperation with Ariba and VeriSign, the CyberCash B2B service, or mojos. B2C transactions represent the most difficult challenge, not least because they have been captured by the credit-card companies. Successful cybercash variants in that segment will have to exploit the flaws of credit cards and offer a more attractive alternative. Smart cards and e-checks may become very popular. Both are, after all, online extensions of off-line payment mechanisms which are already deeply anchored in the public. And both lend themselves to easy integration with online banking services. Notwithstanding the premature demise of flooz and beenz, coupon money still has great potential as a payment vehicle for B2C transactions. This kind of incentive-based online gift currency can be used as a marketing device with which to encourage higher volumes of online shopping. The Monneta platform of eCash Technologies and Oakington's Amadigi represent multi-application cybercash systems which cut across the different segments of e-commerce and can be used for all kinds of online transactions.

CHAPTER 6

Managing Online Money

Cybercash has had a difficult birth. Its developers have faced one formidable challenge after another. Privacy and security concerns have made it harder to convince a skeptical public that it can trust a virtual money form flowing invisibly through computer networks. Right from the start credit-card companies managed to establish a commanding lead in B2C transactions which left less room for online-payment alternatives in that segment of e-commerce. A first generation of experiments proved the technical feasibility of key cybercash designs (e-checks, smart cards, digital coins), but was unable to make a decisive dent in the dominance of credit cards. Then e-commerce, the principal force driving the development of online-payment systems, was hit by the bursting of the dot-com bubble on Wall Street. The sudden deterioration in the financial condition of internet-based firms undermined the commercial viability of a second generation of cybercash experiments. Their large set-up costs necessitated significant revenue creation which failed to materialize in the wake of the crisis hitting the internet sector. A third wave of monetary innovation is now under way, building on the proven design ideas of the first experiments and digesting key lessons from the failures of the second round. While still struggling amidst unfavorable market conditions, these latest experiments may generate the critical mass for a successful launch of cybercash – seven years after its first appearance.

The current dot-com crisis notwithstanding, there are reasons to be optimistic about the long-term prospects of cybercash. Use of this new money form is driven by several powerful forces which are not likely to abate. Most notable among these are the accelerating spread of electronic fund-transfer technology, the diffusion of online banking, the computerization of financial markets, e-business strategies of automation aimed at cutting costs and generating operational efficiency gains, the proliferation of e-marketplaces to streamline supply-chain management, online consumer purchases in electronic shopping malls, micropayments for information access or routine services and a host of peer-to-peer transactions which cannot be conducted with credit cards. Each of these activities stands to gain from the availability of online-payments systems which allow the parties involved to transfer funds without having to go off-line for that purpose. It behoves us therefore to look beyond the current troubles of the internet sector and take a longer view with regard to the future prospects of cybercash. In so doing we will inevitably arrive at new questions concerning the management of online money as it moves from its birth to adolescence and eventual maturity.

Trying to address some of those questions, this chapter starts with a discussion of the life cycle of cybercash in an attempt to project forward how and through which channels cybercash may establish itself as a dominant form of money over the next couple of decades (section 6.1). As cybercash matures, it will offer its issuers a variety of benefits whose distribution will be subject to the complex rules of coopetition within the alliances of online firms comprising the various cybercash systems (section 6.2). The internal regulation of any given cybercash variant, complicated further by the propensity of private issuers to create excess supplies, will have to take account of the unique risks associated with this essentially privatized money form (section 6.3). Given the inherently unstable nature of self-regulation, cybercash will need external stabilizers for support. Facing a heterogeneous money form appearing in many variations, such stabilizers must contain central-control mechanisms which manage the organizational complexity of this new monetary regime. Those mechanisms have to ensure a systemic coherence and robustness of the electronic-money regime in the face of possible technological mishaps, cyberterrorism, incidences of financial crisis, and our economic system's propensity to monetary instability (section 6.4).

6.1 The Life Cycle of Cybercash

When making prognoses about the evolution of a major innovation around which a whole segment of the economy is organized, it is useful to apply Raymond Vernon's concept of *product cycles*.[1] Like humans, products also go through a certain life cycle of birth, rapid growth, maturity and stagnation. Each of these stages in a product's life cycle has its own unique characteristics. With regard to cybercash, we are now moving from the birth phase, a period of intense innovation, trial-and-error experimentation and diversity, to the rapid-growth phase of adolescence. In this stage of its life cycle, cybercash can be expected to gain widespread acceptance and standardize its use, leading to a few large-volume survivors of the post-birth shake-out which are ready for mass use. As the money form matures, it will take its rightful place at the center of a new monetary regime around which exchange, production and credit will all be reorganized into a qualitatively different capitalist economic system (see Chapter 7). Such a far-reaching development will take time, probably more than a decade. By 2020, however, we should have concluded this maturing-into-adulthood phase in the life cycle of cybercash.

While 2020 seems very far away, especially when measured in the compressed time concept of the internet, we can already identify some of the forces which will get us there. In the fast-growth phase of its adolescence, unfolding over the next decade or so, cybercash will spread along two vectors of diffusion. One growth engine is the completion of money's automation which began two decades ago with ATMs in retail banking and ACHs in wholesale banking. Today that process has advanced enough to move every component of the traditional payments system online. Having put the infrastructure for electronic money in place to fund economic activity on the internet, the banks will push such killer applications of online banking as EBPP technology (see section 1.1) which one day soon may be used by millions of households and businesses to process and pay their bills over the internet. E-checks or smart cards will allow online cash deposits or withdrawals which will make online banking a lot more attractive than it is today. These two bank-dominated forms of cybercash will also foster the growth of online trading of securities and currencies which will become increasingly popular as the computerization of financial markets proceeds (see section 2.4). Just as deregulation (through the FSMA of 1999) allows for the formation of universal banks offering the full gamut of financial services, so technology will facilitate the integration of these services into centralized full-service accounts through which bank customers, small and large, manage all their banking-, investment- and insurance-related needs. Cybercash will play a crucial role in that integration, since it has the high-tech capabilities to manage the informational and transactional complexity of such multi-purpose 'sweep' accounts offered by tomorrow's financial supermarkets.

The other engine fuelling the growth of cybercash over the next decade is e-commerce whose continued expansion depends not least on offering transacting parties a convenient and safe method to pay each other online. The inherent flexibility of cybercash designs will bring forth different variants of digital money which will spread through a variety of channels in our internet-based economy. B2B-based cybercash, endowed with trade-credit, overdraft and netting facilities, will help push cost-cutting and productivity-enhancing e-business strategies to a whole new level by allowing firms to deepen their relationships with their customers, employees, suppliers and partners. Such cybercash will also benefit e-marketplaces by facilitating auctions, streamlining transactions and simplifying fund transfers between a multitude of parties. In B2C commerce cybercash will have to compete with credit cards by offering users comparable degrees of security, fraud protection and reward points while promising greater anonymity and lower transactions costs. Micro-payments for routine services purchased online will thrive with the intro-duction of cybercash, as will P2P transactions between individuals.

These growth vectors of cybercash – the automation of the monetary process, online banking, online trading in securities and currencies, e-business, e-marketplaces, consumer shopping on the internet, micropay-ments and peer-to-peer transfers – will gradually propel the new money form into a dominant position within our payments system. Driven by different engines, cybercash will come in many variations. The contours of the major cybercash variants, which have survived birth and early child-hood to grow into adulthood, can already be discerned quite clearly:

■ Electronic checks have come a long way since the days of Neuman's NetCheque experiment and are now being readied for widespread use by an alliance of government agencies, leading money-center banks and software developers grouped together in the Financial Services Tech-nology Consortium. They will in all likelihood play a major role in any future regime of electronic money, considering that they are the last step in adapting our traditional check-based payments system to the internet. Electronic checks will complement other moves to bring the monetary process online, in particular software allowing online merchants to automate the entire check-collection process, as already offered by ACH DataSoft (www.achdatasoft.com) or the Electronic Funds Clearing-house (www.efunds.com).[2] Thus integrated into a fully computerized payments system operating online, e-checks will find a wide variety of applications. Their advantage, as the internet extension of a long-established mode of payment, is their ubiquitous use across all possible segments of the cybercash-based economy – from large-volume B2B transactions to micropayments by consumers or P2P transfers among peers. E-checks will be heavily promoted by banks, since this will be the type of electronic money over which they are most likely to retain monopoly control. In that case we are not too far away from the day when e-checks will be issued in acts of credit extension by banks trying to transform their zero-yield cash reserves into interest-yielding loan assets, just like paper checks are today. At that point banks will be in a position to create new e-money and pump liquidity into the internet in support of economic activities organized there.

■ Now that the major credit-card networks have committed themselves to the development of smart cards, this latest version of plastic money has a good chance to become the second major pillar of cybercash. In a few years from now smart cards will be easily connected to any access medium for the internet, function even without contact via antennae, and be activated thanks to biometric technology with the touch of a finger or the authentication of your iris. The potent microprocessor embedded in a smart card will allow programming of other payment-related features, such as collection of coupons, receipt and use of gift certificates, or automatic switching to alternative money forms (currencies, online coupon money). Smart cards can be used as stored-value devices which card-holders can fill up with existing funds taken out of their bank accounts. More likely is that smart cards will contain an overdraft facility, as already the case with France's carte bancaire, and so become the vehicle for the creation of new money on the internet. While banks will continue to control the issue of smart cards, certain nonbank institutions will try to get involved in their distribution as well. Computer software firms may offer smart cards in software format (for example Sun's Java Card). Merchants may want to issue their own branded smart cards, much like gasoline suppliers or department stores do today with credit cards, in order to deepen customer loyalty and boost online sales. Smart cards will have a variety of practical applications across all segments of e-commerce, notably B2C transactions in lieu of credit or debit cards and P2P transfers where plastic money could not be used until now.

■ PayPal's brilliant idea of using e-mail as a vehicle for fund transfers online has caught on sufficiently to prompt Yahoo!, eBay and Citibank to launch their own systems of e-mail money. The simplicity of this fund-transfer mechanism opens many avenues for its use, especially between individuals wishing to move funds to each other. One can easily imagine e-mail money transfers to be just as practical in flows of funds between friends or within a family as they would be between two individuals who do not know each other well (as in online auctions). It will surely prove a highly popular method for paying one's monthly bills as well. The spread of this cybercash variant relies on a viral-marketing strategy which induces fund recipients to open up accounts and users in general to accumulate funds in those accounts. This form of cybercash thus has a sort of self-feeding quality of network expansion. And to the extent that users are willing to build up funds in their accounts for later use rather than reconvert those into off-line cash, e-mail money will evolve into a self-sustained form of cybercash which no longer relies on the intermediation services of banks. While e-checks and smart cards are both online extensions of traditional private bank money, e-mail money moves us into the realm of electronic money no longer controlled by banks. PayPal, the originator of this monetary innovation, in effect became like a bank when it began to reinvest unused balances building up in user accounts. Citibank's alliance with AOL and Microsoft to promote its c2it marks an attempt by America's leading bank to ensure a modicum of bank control over this evolving online-transfer technology.[3]

■ If e-mail money constitutes a first step towards a new kind of electronic money circulating outside the banking system, digital coins take us one step further in that direction. Even though eCash's Monneta platform still accords banks a central role in eCash-based transactions between online buyers and sellers, its multi-use design can be easily adapted to include cybercash variants beyond the reach of banks. Oakington's Amadigi platform points the way here. This software allows any company, not just a bank, to issue digital tokens which are, in effect, money. Once the tokens agreed to have been transferred securely by the payor, the payee owns the rights to the value that they represent and can spend them again. Provided the two parties in a transaction have agreed, Amadigi's tokens can be used to represent anything containing potential exchange value. Besides traditional cash, tokens might represent loyalty points, frequent-flier miles, telephone minutes, software licenses, or equity shares. The more these alternatives to traditional cash are used and become trusted, the greater their interchangeability and the more they start to act like cash. Ownership rights to these tokens are pre-authenticated by separate parties which avoids the scalability problems associated with complex centralized databases and offers an alternative to the typical account verification by banks. Using messaging protocols for communication and online registers to store the records of digital tokens, Amadigi adds two more features designed to remove the need for banks as third-party intermediaries. Digital coins thus constitute the potentially most innovative and autonomous form of cybercash yet.

Besides e-checks, smart cards, e-mail money and digital coins we have seen other experiments which might advance the progress of internet-based money. Take, for instance, the various forms of coupon money which formed the core of the second-generation cybercash experiments between 1998 and 2000. Even though most of the early coupon-money variants ultimately went bankrupt in the dot-com crash of 2000–01 (for example Cybermoola, DoughNET, Flooz and Beenz), this type of cyber-cash application may very well have a second chance. The idea behind it, offering online shoppers additional purchasing power as an incentive with which to encourage consumption-oriented behavior, is simply too tempting not to be tried again. The success of supermarket coupons, frequent-flier miles and loyalty points demonstrates that most people like to be recompensed for good behavior and respond eagerly to behavioral incentive schemes encouraging them to shop some more. The next time around, however, such coupon money will in all likelihood not be launched by start-ups. The double hurdle of high set-up costs and reverse network externalities requires bigger players. It is quite conceivable that coupon money will reappear as the central component of sophisticated online shopping protocols offered by the internet's major access platforms, such as Yahoo!, AOL and Microsoft. What better marketing tool than providing subscribers with your own money which they will forever asso-ciate with your company? Imagine how deeply brand recognition will be anchored when consumers price products and pay for them in Yahoos or MSN dollars! The circulatory dynamic of this consumer-oriented B2C variant of cybercash, which users earn by satisfying certain behavioral thresholds related to consumption, promises to spread its use like a virus. What we have here is a new form of credit-money transferred to users as gifts or rewards to which one can get quite easily habituated, if not addicted. Merchants, too, will want to join the coupon-money networks, provided these have reached sufficient scale to attract a significant number of new and repeat customers.

When businesses engage with each other via the internet, they will want to have an integrated online-transaction system which includes an auto-mated system of payments. Such B2B money will be tailored to the specific conditions of transactions between businesses. It will have to accommodate the need for trade credit (delayed payment) through arrangements of automatic income deductions at predetermined dates. It will have to facilitate the collection of indirect taxes, such as value-added taxes or sales taxes. Most importantly, it will have to provide netting facil-ities which cancel out matching credits and debits between members of a multi-firm alliance. The latter service drastically reduces the actual amount of cash needed to settle a large volume of payment obligations, so that a relatively small sum of cybercash can support much larger (gross) volumes of transactions between businesses.[4] Ongoing efforts by American Express (in cooperation with VeriSign and Ariba) and CyberCash, albeit still in the embryonic stage of product development, indicate that sufficient interest already exists in developing uniquely B2B-based forms of online money. These may eventually extend to e-marketplaces, such as online barter exchanges (for example Mojo Nation, BigVine, BarterTrust), which need to have their own money as a unit of account to value transactions and keep track of them. While the birth of B2B commerce has spurred much small-scale and niche-oriented monetary innovation, that segment may see its true growth potential come to fruition over the next decade with the establishment of larger scale, multi-functional cybercash systems offering a variety of user applications to satisfy the diverse needs of e-business and e-marketplaces.

6.2 Digital Seigniorage

Going back to our earlier discussion of money's contradictory dual nature as a public good and a private commodity (see section 1.5), one of money's key aspects is the ability to provide its issuers with a variety of benefits. The gains associated with the issue of money have been termed *seigniorage*. In its original medieval meaning seigniorage referred to government revenue accruing from the difference between the face value of coins and the costs of their mintage. More recently, with the establishment of central bank notes as a principal form of government-issued currency, seigniorage accrues to the state's monetary authorities in the wake of open-market operations. When the central bank buys government securities (ostensibly to increase the money supply), it acquires an interest-yielding bond while at the same time issuing zero-interest bank reserves or central bank notes as liabilities. This difference is pocketed by the central bank as a gain which it transfers regularly to the Treasury. A more indirect form of seigniorage accrues to the government from inflation, fuelled typically by rapid growth in the money supply, which operates as a hidden tax to increase government revenues.

The issuer of the vehicle currency acting as an international medium of exchange, today primarily the United States with its dollar, earns a third type of seigniorage from the global circulation of its currency. Technically speaking, such international seigniorage is earned when the country issuing the vehicle currency supplies the rest of the world with liquidity through capital exports, acquiring in the process income-yielding assets which are matched by zero-interest or low-interest liabilities (its currency held as a reserve by foreigners). More broadly defined, global seigniorage points to the fact that the issuer of world money is the only country freed from any normal external constraint by having to run chronic balance-of-payments deficits. These deficits, which supply the rest of the world with the international medium of exchange, are automatically financed by foreigners willing to hold its currency as a reserve, akin to an interest-free loan of indefinite maturity.[5]

While governments have always enjoyed the benefits of money issue, which extend beyond actual income gains to legitimation of authority and exercise of power, our modern monetary system is dominated by seigniorage accruing to private, profit-seeking entities – the commercial banks. When those institutions create new money in the wake of credit extension, they profit from turning zero-yielding reserves into interest-earning loan assets (see section 1.4). This has traditionally been the major source of income for banks, prompting them recurrently to extend too much credit and create too much money. Such credit overextension is at the heart of financial crises and monetary instability which is why the business of bank lending has come to be regulated by the government via monetary policy and bank supervision.

Compared to the interest income earned by banks when issuing new paper money, electronic money potentially provides its issuers with a much greater range of income-enhancing benefits. This is especially true for the creation of cybercash on the internet. Benefits from this kind of online money creation, characterized here as *digital seigniorage*, can come in many forms, as evident from PayPal's reinvestment of unused balances in an escrow account or Beenz.com's profit from charging merchants twice as much when offering them new beenz than paying them for reconversion of beenz into dollars. One of the great incentives fuelling the proliferation of cybercash is precisely the prospect of being able to gain a lot from its issue.

Digital seigniorage may take the form of tangible income, whether through transaction fees, processing charges, membership subscriptions, interest, licensing fees, or royalty payments. Or it may come more indirectly, as in the case of enhanced brand recognition. The combined seigniorage gains will already be quite significant for those cybercash variants which serve as online extensions of existing money forms, such as e-checks or smart cards. But they may be even larger for new forms of cybercash operating autonomously as self-contained monetary spheres beyond the confines of traditional bank money, as in the case of beenz or Amadigi's digital tokens.

One major benefit accruing to any issuer of cybercash is the use of money creation as an effective mechanism with which to deepen its commercial relationships with network members using this monetary unit. Its supply of money breeds loyalty among merchants. As the cyber-cash issuer offers competitive user fees ('discounts') and royalty schemes to merchants willing to accept its money form, it will be able to boost demand for its other products at merchant locations. American Express, for example, would find much greater acceptance for its other card products among merchants who have signed up for its online-payment service. In a similar vein, any successful cybercash issuer will gain significant clout among consumers as a result of the enhanced name association and brand identification that come with using its money unit. This marketing benefit promises to be especially dramatic when consumers start pricing goods and services increasingly in its monetary unit. The company issuing this unit becomes a daily point of reference for millions of inter-acting agents.

Other advantages arising from the issue of online money derive from the inherently self-feeding nature of this activity which promises to boost volume. Provided the monetary unit in question maintains stable value and strong merchant acceptance, there will be an incentive to avoid conversion costs and continue transacting in that unit. To the extent that cybercash recipients keep spending their online money in that unit, each transaction duplicates itself when the payee becomes payor – a multiplier which greatly enhances transaction volumes denominated in that unit.

With rising transaction volumes the users of a particular online money unit (such as PayPal) are bound to discover its function as a store of value and build up savings in that unit for later spending. The accumulation of unused balances in client accounts allows the money issuer to invest these excess funds in income-yielding assets (securities) and so turn the act of money creation into an income-generating activity. The most important source of income associated with money creation comes from loaning out excess balances and so creating new money. Like the banks before them, cybercash issuers will inevitably engage in that highly profitable activity whereby they turn reserves into higher yield loan assets. What is especially attractive here is that any issuer of an autonomous form of cybercash (such as beenz) can determine its own monetary unit's short-term interest rate, and thus also lending revenue, by manipulating the supply of that money.

The manipulation of the money supply and short-term lending rates will inevitably involve cybercash issuers in open-market operations of the kind currently conducted by central banks. They will inject more of their money into circulation when buying securities (and paying in new units) and shrink the money supply by selling securities. To the extent that their money supply grows, cybercash issuers will accumulate a growing portfolio of income-earning securities (bonds) which back their zero-interest liabilities representing the money they have issued. This interest differential between their assets and liabilities is a source of profit for issuers of cybercash.

The capital for such open-market operations derives from the difference between the face value of the digital cash issued and the costs of creating and backing that electronic money. Such capital can be either spent or loaned out, thus giving the issuers of cybercash an easy way to expand the scale of their operations. These companies will find that money issue allows them to build up their capital base which in turn enhances their borrowing capacity with which to leverage their operations. Over time we can expect the balance sheets of any cybercash issuer to become increasingly a function of its monetary units in circulation, since this activity of money creation represents a direct means for that firm to generate more revenues and/or boost its capitalization. The temptation of cybercash issuers to enlarge their capital base and revenue stream by simply creating additional supplies of their cybercash will be kept in check by the danger of eroding the public trust with too much money in circulation. This is a difficult balancing act to manage.

Private issuers of cybercash will have to walk the tightrope of self-regulation between the desire to create ever-growing amounts of money in their quest for profit maximization and the need to maintain the public trust in their unit as a stable, well-managed medium of online exchange. While always tempted to expand the volume of their units in circulation as a source of profit, suppliers of cybercash will learn that public trust is the most important factor for their long-term viability and that this trust rests to a considerable degree on the avoidance of excess. Much of that learning comes about when seeing overextended and/or mismanaged issuers face a sudden crisis of confidence which triggers a capital flight by the public to safer issuers.

That balancing act between moderation and excess is complicated by the fact that any digital seigniorage will have to be distributed among several players involved in the creation and circulation of such online money. Even though they may very well continue to play a dominant role in the issue of cybercash, banks are not going to monopolize this activity as they have done for centuries with regard to paper money. As discussed earlier (in section 4.4), banks will have to cooperate with other firms without which they cannot launch and operate their e-money platforms. Long-standing partnerships with internet service providers, software firms and merchants willing to accept payment in their e-money variant will need to be built. Such cooperation is a new challenge for bankers who are not used to working together with all those different kinds of enterprises and retailers. Now for the first time they will have to share income gains from money issue with nonbank institutions, and the success of their joint ventures with those partners depends not least on how fairly these gains are distributed.

The precise modalities of such multi-firm alliances are shaped by the kind of cybercash system which the alliance partners construct and operate together. If banks wish to be at the center of any such alliance, they will have to define generally accepted rules for the sharing of costs and gains with their nonbank partners. They may, for instance, pay licensing fees to software developers whose products they are using, share user fees with ISPs bringing them clients and provide incentives to merchants while imposing only modest processing and reconversion charges. Partners, whose expertise is indispensable to the successful functioning of a particular cybercash system, may use their market power to secure a relatively large portion of the total gains associated with the issue of cybercash. Such multi-firm alliances will have a much better chance to survive and provide each participant with a satisfactory share of total gains, if they can design a system which generates enough income for all. This necessitates effective cooperation within the alliance, motivated by the collective interest in maximizing gains together.

Multi-firm joint ventures of cybercash suppliers leave any partner responsible for one particular aspect of the overall system in exchange for an appropriate slice of the total seigniorage benefits. The intra-group relations between alliance members can be characterized as *coopetition*, a combination of cooperation and competition (see section 3.3). They cooperate with each other in the issue of their cybercash and share the gains from that activity. But these partners also compete with each other, not least over the distribution of seigniorage gains or allocation of tasks. For example, look at the battle between banks, utilities and ISPs over electronic-billing protocols. Coopetition will move to outright competition when nonbank partners use their expertise with online payments to launch their own cybercash systems bypassing banks.

If digital seigniorage turns out to be a rich source of benefits as can be expected, then we should also see persistent efforts by nonbanks to occupy a dominant role in the creation of cybercash and so grab the lion's share of those gains. The inability of banks to exercise physical control over cybercash, which exists only as software and electronic data flows, renders them vulnerable to intrusion in their money-creation activities by nonbank institutions in pursuit of digital seigniorage. We already see several trends unfold in this direction – companies setting up their own in-house banks to process bills and fund transfers; the circulation of e-mail money (PayPal) or coupon money (beenz) without reconversion into 'real' cash; Amadigi's digital tokens which can be issued and exchanged by any party. Nonbank issuers of electronic money are thus likely to emerge alongside banks, and some of these new players in the monetary process will try to push their cybercash variants as far away as possible from traditional bank money to gain a certain autonomy from the banking system. PayPal, Flooz, Beenz, Oakington and Mojo Nation are early manifestations of this trend, each one a unique attempt to move cybercash out of the hands of banks. The precise balance between bank-controlled cybercash (e-checks, smart cards, perhaps e-mail money) and ISP-controlled cybercash (digital coins, coupon money, B2B payment arrangements) depends on the relative growth rates of the different engines driving the diffusion of specific e-money variants.

6.3 Risk Management

Validating a cardinal rule in finance concerning risk-return trade-offs, high returns from digitial seigniorage arise not least because of considerable risks associated with the issue of cybercash. Some of these risks, such as liquidity risks, credit risks and interest-rate risks, are generic to banking, but may well be more intense in the case of electronic banking than they were when banks still dealt with paper deposits and checks. Other risks, however, may be unique to electronic banking and digital money. This seems especially true for operational risks, reputational risks and legal risks. Those kinds of risks are unfamiliar, lack precedent and therefore, in their newness, pose special challenges for effective risk management.[6]

Commercial banking activity, which combines the taking of deposits and making of loans, is an inherently risky business:

■ Because of fractional-reserve banking, the banks typically have a lot more deposit liabilities outstanding than covered by cash reserves. A sudden wave of cash withdrawals from these deposits may create liquidity problems and force banks to rely on costlier funds which eat into their profits. If the public perceives heightened liquidity risks with regard to a specific bank, deposit-holders there may panic and seek to take their money out of that institution even more than before. Such runs on banks have been part of our history for centuries now. The appropriate response is to be prepared for any sudden spike in redemption demand and remain heavily invested in liquid assets. For issuers of cybercash such *liquidity risks* may be especially intense because of the magnified speed of withdrawals and technologically easy disengagement by users. The key here is to make such disengagements more difficult for users by developing long-term client relations (through membership subscriptions, for example) coupled with an integrated array of high-value services which the customers come to depend on for their daily forays into cyberspace. Good systems to monitor usage and comprehensive audits to check readiness on a regular basis are essential.

■ Banks always face the possibility that some of their borrowers default on their debt and so cause losses which have to be written off out of the bank's capital. Since banks typically do not have a large capital base, they cannot take too many such hits before being pushed to the brink of insolvency.[7] This kind of *default risk* needs to be carefully managed. Banks, of course, do this by evaluating the creditworthiness of their prospective borrowers before approving a loan application. But they often become less cautious in their evaluations during boom periods when euphoric optimism distorts the assessment of the future and the desire to increase profits results in eager accommodation of strong loan demand. Such lack of care in the balancing of risks and returns sets the stage for overextension followed by crash. Lending decisions and procedures need to be audited on a regular basis while high standards should be maintained throughout the course of the business cycle. Cybercash issuers need to be extra careful in their management of default risk, since the provision of credit through remote banking might involve a disproportionately large number of nontraditional borrowers for whom reliable data are either not available or difficult to come by.

■ To the extent that banks invest their funds in securities rather than loans, they are exposed to losses from sudden, unfavorable interest movements. A precipitous decline in the market valuation of their securities (such as bonds) may reduce the value of their assets relative to their outstanding liabilities. Any bank thus affected may end up no longer complying with regulatory requirements in which case it will have to take corrective action. Such *market risk* can produce sufficiently large losses to trigger a panic run on the faltering bank and so expose it to more liquidity risk at a time of great vulnerability. Banks can hedge against market risk by instituting appropriate interest-rate risk-management strategies with the help of derivatives (such as bond futures). Similarly, they can protect themselves against undue market risk arising from their currency transactions through foreign-exchange risk-management and hedging programs. Issuers of cybercash are particularly exposed to market risk. They will in all likelihood link their money issue to open-market operations, much like a central bank, so that their liabilities arising from the issue of cybercash are backed by assets. They may also be more heavily involved than traditional banks in funding their operations through money-market instruments rather than deposits. Thus they will carry relatively large amounts of securities on both the asset and liability side of their balance sheets. Issuers of cybercash are also likely to operate globally and so conduct a lot of currency transactions in the foreign-exchange market.

■ The globalization of financial capital has transformed banks into transnational organizations which spread their assets across a variety of countries. While on the one hand reducing market risk by diversifying portfolios, at the same time this strategy generates a different kind of risk. Countries can be subject to economic, social or political turmoil which may affect a bank's asset values and operations there. Such *country risk* needs to be assessed on an ongoing basis. In the case of electronic money, country risk also includes the possibility that an overseas partner becomes unable to meet its obligations within the scheme. The lead bank in that scheme may then have to sort out problems with local customers in that country and find alternative service suppliers while facing the possibility of lawsuits.

Whereas all these traditional banking risks seem accentuated when money and banking turn electronic, such risk elevation pales in comparison to qualitatively new risks which may arise in the context of cybercash. For one, this type of money depends heavily on advanced technologies which carry a variety of unique *operational risks*. Perhaps the most acute among those is unauthorized system access by hackers for criminal purposes, such as attempts to steal money. This may involve the interception of confidential customer information, as often happens in instances of digital identity theft. Cyberterrorists may inject a virus into the bank's internal system, destroy or corrupt data and deliberately disable a large portion of the technological infrastructure used by the issuers of cybercash. The costs of repairing damaged systems and a tarnished reputation can be quite high. One answer to such threats is the deployment of communication security technology, such as firewalls, data encryption, virus checks, password management and proper authorization of end-users. Security measures need to be monitored closely and subjected to rigorous penetration testing for vulnerabilities. Issuers of cybercash will also have to commit themselves to close surveillance of usage patterns in order to detect anomalies.

Cybercash issuers will face fraud by some of their customers who complete a transaction, then deny that it ever took place and demand reimbursement of funds spent. Expenses incurred in proving authorization of the disputed transaction can be reduced through security measures which enhance customer authentication, such as the use of personal identification numbers. In the realm of authentication, cybercash issuers face the risk of having forged certificates issued in their name, thus defrauding customers, or having certificates issued to criminals posing as bank customers without adequate verification of identity. The cost of revoking and reissuing compromised certificates can be best avoided through appropriate security measures and controls in conjunction with the certification authorities.

Operational risks may extend to fraud by employees of cybercash issuers who may steal smart cards, obtain confidential information about customers and alter data in attempts to draw funds from client accounts. In those instances customer losses will have to be reimbursed and data reconstructed accurately. Cybercash issuers may also face losses when electronic money is redeemed for which no prepaid funds have been received. If customers perceive a money-creating institution suffering from employee fraud to be unsafe, additional costs may arise from negative publicity, lawsuits, or regulatory action. Employee fraud can be reduced by screening job candidates carefully, using external auditors to assess employee performance, instituting internal controls, segregating duties and ensuring the safe storage of smart cards.

A third operational risk associated with cybercash is the possibility of counterfeit, whereby criminals alter or duplicate electronic money units to obtain goods and services without proper payment. The issuer is liable for the amount of the falsified money and, in addition, will need to repair a compromised system. Some cybercash issuers, especially those specializing in micropayments, will be able to impose low load limits which may make counterfeiting less attractive. Smart cards and merchant hardware will have to be fitted with tamper-resistant devices. The counterfeit threat can also be reduced by tracing individual transactions and maintaining cumulative records in a central database.

Another complication, which may undermine the operation of cybercash systems, derives from their complex architecture in which the issuer of money typically outsources specific services to a variety of specialists.

In such multi-party alliances great care must be taken by the money issuer as to the reliability of partners, since it may be held liable for any non-deliverance of service on their part. Failure to deliver services as promised can ripple rapidly through the system and cause major disruptions to the entire electronic-money network. Apart from exercising due diligence when selecting partners, cybercash issuers need to structure service provider contracts around specifications of performance benchmarks, contingency planning and auditing provisions. They will also have to make back-up plans, including the possibility of switchching service providers at short notice.

Cybercash poses unique operational risks not least because of its heavy reliance on rapidly evolving computer and communication technologies. In a world of fast-paced change issuers of electronic money run the risk of betting on the wrong technology. Additional *technology risks* arise from the rapid obsolescence of existing systems in light of new advances, inadequate management and staff expertise in dealing with new technology, and the possibility of a malfunction or breakdown of system components disrupting service. Providers of cybercash and cyberbanking services will therefore have to make the management of technology a top priority to address these risks effectively. A team of specialists should be made responsible for the evaluation of technology choices, testing of systems, training programs for personnel and implementation of contingency planning. This team could also be held accountable for ensuring timely upgrades of both hardware and software to avoid obsolescence. Finally, cybercash issuers have to excel in guaranteeing a very high degree of consumer privacy and safety in their operations. All these issues need to be discussed, coordinated and planned jointly by the key partners of any multi-party alliance.

Since any of the risk categories discussed above can undermine the performance of a cybercash system, they all have the potential of hurting the reputation of the issuer. Such *reputational risks* can weaken the issuer badly. First the customers directly affected by any mishap may leave. Then, when the problem becomes public knowledge, other customers may follow suit. Public trust, so essential with regard to money, is hard to come by and easy to lose. The best way to guard against such losses is to prevent the mishaps in the first place. This requires continuous testing of system components. When problems do occur, it is crucial to minimize disruption through the execution of effective back-up plans and capable handling of customer complaints.

Just as various mishaps end up hurting the reputation of any cybercash issuer, they also bring about a variety of *legal risks*. These may take the form of exposure to lawsuits by customers seeking compensation for damage they allege to have suffered as a result of breakdowns in online money management. The question of law is, however, likely to intrude in a much broader fashion on the internet than just the traditional fear of litigation. Its virtual nature and global reach raise a number of complicated legal issues. This is still largely uncharted territory, and many of those issues have yet to be resolved. Online firms thus operate in a murky and rapidly evolving legal environment where they may inadvertently violate new internet laws and regulations. They will have to keep abreast of the latest developments in that area and comprehend the differences in law and convention between those countries within which they operate.

Cybercash issuers will face an especially intense challenge in the area of legal risks, since their operation touches on so many issues of judicial controversy – taxation of e-commerce, digital signatures, privacy protection, safety, money laundering, other types of electronic crime, financial transactions and money itself. They will also have to pay special attention to the protection of consumer privacy because of their fiduciary responsibility to the public. Global in reach, they must be well informed about country-to-country differences in laws and regulations and the jurisdictional responsibilities of different national authorities. If they rely on multi-party alliances, cybercash issuers must also be prepared for liability arising from the fraudulent actions of their partners.

Complex risk-management strategies will thus become the bread-and-butter activity of any entity empowered to create online money. The balancing act between high returns and significant risks is sanctioned, one way or another, by public trust in any particular variant of cybercash. When risk management fails, the public's confidence in the tarnished e-money unit will prove as ephemeral as that money is virtual. The consequences of such erosion can be devastating. Wounded cybercash issuers, which the public no longer trusts, may well face a sudden and massive flight by customers and investors alike. Given the highly automated infrastructure and massive amounts of fixed costs involved in the issue of cybercash, even relatively small reductions in transaction volume may trigger extensive operating losses. Yet online banks and other issuers of cybercash, motivated by profit, may not want to incur the costs associated with effective risk management as they chase the benefits of digital seigniorage. How do we make sure that the internal drive for high returns fraught with considerable risks does not get out of hand? Practical answers to this question will determine how effectively this innately privatized money form will safeguard its public-good character as something that its users can rely on at all times.

6.4 External Stabilizers

It is useful to keep in mind the contradictory dual nature of money when analyzing cybercash. As a public good, money dramatically facilitates economic activity and thus helps to generate productive (output and income) gains which in the end make everyone better off. As a private commodity, it puts its issuer(s) at the nerve center of society. If those issuers are motivated by profit, they are likely to use this strategic position to impose unequal access, pursue the benefits of seigniorage to the point of excess and implement innovations capable of transforming the monetary process (see section 1.5). The tension between these two souls of money yields a capitalist system which functions remarkably well in its ability to produce and enrich, but which is also subject to recurrent financial crises and bouts of monetary instability. How well that system operates within its inherently cyclical nature depends therefore not least on proper balancing of money's dual nature as a public good and private commodity. The contours of such a balancing act change with the form of money and corresponding monetary innovation, as conceptualized in the notion of monetary regimes discussed earlier (in Chapter 2). In that regard, cybercash promises to be a qualitatively new phenomenon, both because of its virtual nature and, more importantly, its potential ability to escape the reach of governments and so become dominated by profit-motivated commercial enterprises extending far beyond traditional banking. It is the kind of money which the conservative advocates of fully denationalized money love, subject only to minimal restraints by government and thus firmly anchored in market regulation.[8]

If truly privatized, however, cybercash may be less benevolent than depicted by the protagonists of market-regulated money. Its private-commodity dimensions, tied to the profit motive of its issuers, are likely to dominate and could undermine its ability to serve as a public good to the benefit of all. It would then probably be prone to inequality of access, excess supplies and fast-paced innovation. The degree to which those tendentially destabilizing manifestations of money's private-commodity nature matter depends a lot on the type of cybercash system under consideration:

■ In its simplest form, cybercash will be just the online extension of traditional payment mechanisms. We think here above all of e-checks, cyberbanking built around EBPP and fund-transfer technology, or low-order e-mail money which cannot circulate on its own and has to be reconverted into hard cash (such as Yahoo!'s PayDirect and Western

Union's Bidpay). These cybercash variants are all tightly linked to the cash flow of traditional brick-and-mortar banks and thus have only limited autonomy with which to wreak possible havoc. Their potential for disruption is therefore relatively low. One can conceive of these e-money applications as a high-volume, low-margin business with correspondingly smaller risk.

■ Smart cards are a bit more complicated, to the extent that such chip-embedded plastic may in the future have dramatically enhanced capabilities and thus offer card-holders a variety of financial services. As primary access tools to one-stop banking offered by financial supermarkets, such smart cards may be programmed to provide a variety of online-payment services, such as overdraft facilities or credit lines to be tapped or accumulation of gift coupons and other marketing incentives. Taken together, these card-based services may in effect amount to an integrated cybercash system within which funds are transferred from card to card without reconversion into off-line currency. Such a card-mediated system of e-money escapes the government's traditional control over paper-based bank money and so is more inclined to manifest its private-commodity characteristics of inequality, instability and innovation.

■ When cybercash is primarily based on software, it will have even greater potential to act as a private commodity in the hands of profit-seeking issuers. This is especially true for coupon money in B2C commerce or online-payment platforms in B2B commerce, both of which consist of digital tokens created by computers for computers. In either software-based cybercash category, issuers may use that power of money creation to propel themselves to the center of large electronic markets which they organize and control as market-making intermediaries. We have seen this happen with Beenz which acted as the central bank of the beenz-denominated segment of e-commerce. And we can also imagine the same thing happening with issuers of trading currencies, such as Mojo Nation. Starting with Oakington's Amadigi, we can go one step further and imagine e-money software which allows interacting parties to design their own digital tokens and back those with any kind of mutually agreed assets whose property rights can be easily transferred from buyer to seller. Here we can see the evolvement of a highly customized form of e-money between two interacting parties based on a transfer of mutually acceptable liquid assets, not unlike derivative contracts tailored to specific individual portfolios which are traded over the counter (like swaps and collars). If and when digital-token designs *à la* Amadigi ever take off, they will comprise a large variety of liquid assets as payment choices. Some of these may allow us to turn contingent claims into spendable and tradeable assets (for instance frequent-flier miles), while others might involve claims to future income (such as expected royalty payments).

The stability of such privatized e-money will depend in large measure on the issuers' capacity for self-regulation. Much of the latter centers on managing the risk-return trade-off described above in the previous two sections – securing a number of reliable income streams associated with money issue, distributing those gains fairly among the partners participating in any given cybercash scheme and addressing the various risk sources effectively. It is quite conceivable that new types of insurance schemes and derivatives will be developed which enable the creators of e-money to protect themselves and their clients from the vicissitudes of that activity. Cybercash issuers must pay special attention to back their e-money liabilities with an equivalent amount of well-performing assets, whether loans or securities. Effective self-regulation also requires issuers to implement good accounting and book-keeping systems to keep track of their cybercash in circulation.

Cybercash issuers must constantly check their willingness to take risks and execute appropriate strategies to keep their money-creation activity below that threshold of risk exposure. As long as the online money under their control simply involves a transfer of funds from off-line accounts onto the internet, as would be the case with stored-value cards, the degree of riskiness is quite limited. In such a situation any online money is fully backed by off-line funds that had been created earlier. However, cybercash issuers face considerably greater risk exposure the moment they create new online money beyond existing funds. To the extent that such money creation yields more income, the issuer will be tempted to encourage users to demand more new cybercash and then meet this demand eagerly with new supplies. If the issue of cybercash involves lending (as in the case of a smart card with overdraft facilities or when loaning out excess reserves online in the form of e-checks), then the issuer incurs credit risks. These credit risks may well be more pronounced than in the case of traditional private bank money in paper form, since cybercash issuers will have access to a much larger and more diverse group of borrowers than commercial banks have typically had in their brick-and-mortar branches. Moreover, the act of credit extension may be much more spontaneous in cyberspace, where it is possible to lend potential shoppers new funds for their online purchases at short notice without lengthy loan application procedures.[9] Cybercash may also be issued as a reward. This could take the form of gift certificates or as e-pay for consumption-related e-work (see Chapter 7). In these instances the new money will have to be backed by additional securities, thus exposing the issuer to the market risk of adverse asset-price movements.

Given the endogenous nature of cybercash (see section 4.4), its issue is likely to be dominated by a strong marketing dimension. The issuers of cybercash will try hard to encourage more demand for their funds by users and then meet that demand with new supplies, since this process boosts their income. Their propensity for excess supplies may be kept in check by the need to maintain public trust in the stability of their monetary unit as well as by competitive pressures from other, well-trusted cybercash alternatives. Some especially greedy or careless issuers will not be held back adequately by those constraints and fail, but others will learn from such failures to maintain sufficient discipline. More problematic, however, is the systemic risk of generalized market euphoria during boom periods which could prompt most cybercash issuers, even the usually more careful ones, to lose sight of risks and succumb to the lure of profit to the point of collective overextension. These regular bouts of generalized excess in the credit system, perhaps even more pronounced in the relatively limit-less world of cyberspace than they were when money was still paper based, expose capitalist economies to recurrent patterns of boom, overextension ('asset bubbles'), financial crisis and recession. It is precisely this market failure which has made money and banking subject to regulation by external stabilizers, traditionally taking the form of government regulation and supervision.

External stabilizers are necessary to keep the destabilizing private-commodity dimensions of money in the hands of profit-driven issuers from interfering excessively with its public-good role. Such stabilizers of the monetary process are typically situated in the payments system, the locus of money's creation and circulation. The payments system provides for clearing and settlement of fund transfers, convertibility between different money forms and additional liquidity injections. It is there, in this nerve center of our economy, that we can establish and impose collective norms as to what constitutes money, who should issue it and how it can be accessed. The payments system has traditionally been the domain of each nation's central bank overseeing its key players, the commercial banks. This role of the central bank is not yet settled with regard to cybercash circulating on the internet. Neither the precise boundaries between this open communication network and the payments system nor the interlocking mechanisms connecting those two are yet fully established.

Central banks, such as the Federal Reserve or the European Central Bank, are thus obliged to let innovation run its course before deciding on a regulatory framework for cybercash.

The Fed has taken great care to prepare itself for the advent of cybercash without hampering its evolution through premature regulation. This stance reflects not only the dominance of conservative laissez-faire thinking in contemporary American politics, shared in unanimity among the members of the Fed's policy-making Open Market Committee, but also the changing role of the US central bank in managing the nation's payments system. When the Fed set up a check-clearing process in 1918, it anchored a monopoly role in running the nation's payments system for which it was authorized by law (in the Federal Reserve Act of 1913). That role began to be undermined by advances in communication and computer technologies used by banks for regulation-evading innovation, as manifest in the 1960s when the world's leading banks set up a parallel unregulated payments system through the eurocurrency market. Private-sector providers of payments services were further boosted by the DIDMCA of 1980 which, among many other things, asked the central bank to price its payments services explicitly in accordance with the market laws of cost recovery.[10] True to the spirit of the law, the Fed began to face stiffer competition from private bank consortia. Thanks to its large size, the Fed has been able to exploit economies of scale and so maintain a competitive advantage over private, often smaller competitors. According to Rivlin (1997), the US central bank clears about one-third of the 64 billion checks written by Americans each year, with the rest of the checks being cleared by banks directly, through clearing-house arrangements, or through the correspondent network. Having to compete with these interbank alternatives, the Fed has played an active role in pushing the development of ECP technology, digital imaging and e-check standards to maintain market leadership in this type of payment service. Its Fedwire service has kept the Fed in a monopoly position with regard to large-volume wholesale transfers between businesses, government agencies and financial institutions, after three private alternatives failed in the 1980s. The only other wire-transfer service, the CHIPS network, specializes in cross-border transactions and thus complements Fedwire rather than directly competing with it. The Fed also dominates the payments service for smaller retail transactions involving ACH arrangements, controlling about 80 percent of that market segment while the remaining 20 percent are shared by three private competitors.

Since the Fed maintains ultimate responsibility for the proper functioning of the nation's payments system in its entirety, it is also authorized to issue regulations designed to improve the efficiency of that system. It thus serves as both competitor and regulator of the banks, a potential conflict-of-interest situation which the Fed has at times exploited to secure itself competitive advantages over private alternatives. This was certainly true in the case of wire transfers when the Fed imposed new regulations in 1986 for daylight overdrafts among banks which contributed directly to the collapse of three privately operated wire-transfer systems that same year. The Expedited Funds Availability Act of 1987 gave the Fed power for the first time to regulate the clearing and settlement of checks that were not processed by its system's regional Federal Reserve banks. In 1996 the Fed introduced a new ACH operating system which processes transactions on a flow basis in real time 24 hours a day. These attractive features, not shared by the three private-sector ACH providers, have secured the central bank's domination in that area of the payments system.

Conscious that the appearance of cybercash may yet present the most advanced technological and organizational challenge to its domain over the nation's payments system, the US central bank approaches cybercash from that same dual position as competitor and regulator of the private sector. Its officials welcome the emergence of different e-money systems as cost-efficient and quality-enhancing alternatives to traditional payments services. As indicated by Ferguson (1998), the governors of the Federal Reserve board do not view this new money form as seriously affecting the Fed's short-term ability to supervise financial institutions, clear and settle payments, or implement monetary policy. This assessment rests on the assumption that, for quite some time, cybercash will consist mainly of prepaid payment schemes, similar to money orders or traveler's checks, which do not create new money. Such a limited form of cybercash may reduce the government's seigniorage gains by replacing coins and currency notes, a fact widely recognized by all the major central banks, but should otherwise have only marginal effects on the modus operandi of these institutions.[11] All that the Fed is concerned about at this early stage in the evolution of cybercash is to monitor developments in the private sector and update its intervention apparatus where required. For example, it has begun to improve the efficiency and safety of interbank settlement services for a number of retail payments clearing-houses, including private check and ACH clearing-houses, as well as several bank card clearing arrangements so that they may be ready to handle future e-money payment schemes. The Fed has also adjusted Regulation E of the Electronic Funds Transfer Act to allow for the necessary interactions between banks and customers concerning electronic fund transfers (such as disclosure of information by banks, preauthorizations by payors) to be handled electronically rather than in paper form.

At the same time the Fed is aware that the longer term evolution of cybercash may have major repercussions for its operations, especially when the presence of cybercash will have extended to the creation of new money and nondepository institutions. Should these extensions take root, the Fed foresees issuers of electronic payment obligations, such as stored-value cards or digital cash, setting up specialized issuing corporations with strong balance sheets and public credit ratings, not unlike similar arrangements used already in the derivatives and commercial paper markets.[12] While maintaining a strong belief in the virtues of private market self-regulation by e-money issuers, the US central bank also wants to ensure its ability to cope with the future challenges posed by cybercash. Towards that objective Chairman Greenspan created the Committee on the Federal Reserve in the Payments Mechanism in 1996 to examine the future evolution of the US payments system and the Fed's role in that process. The committee, headed by Vice Chair Rivlin, focused initially on retail payments where the Fed's role has traditionally been more controversial than in the area of wholesale payments. Wanting to launch a national debate on these questions, the committee held a series of national and regional meetings in 1997 with representatives from banks and other depository institutions, third-party service providers, clearing-house associations, consumers, retailers, academics and consultants. These participants discussed five possible scenarios for the Fed to consider – total withdrawal from retail payments services, privatization of its services, passive continuity of access to its existing services, a more active role in assisting private-sector efforts with the development of new and more efficient payment mechanisms, and a leadership role where the Fed positions itself at the cutting edge of change.

The consensus emerging from these discussions was for the central bank to engage its resources forcefully in shaping the transition to electronic retail payment services even though there were differences among the forum participants in defining what such leadership by the Fed would imply. Based on the results of this debate, the Fed has decided to play an active role in the promotion of electronic retail payment services, cooperating closely with the private sector in developing standards for electronic payments concerning authentication of payment instructions, privacy and safety of payment information, as well as the risks and liabilities associated with emerging payment services. The Fed will also get more heavily involved in public education efforts which aim to encourage the use of new services. Its governors are considering investments in new types of retail payment services even though they rule out for the time being the idea of having the Fed issue its own e-money.[13] As it has already demonstrated with the promotion of an industry standard for e-checks, the Fed will not shy away from a leading role in the development of promising electronic payment services.

While closely monitoring what is happening in the area of electronic money, the Fed is obviously more reticent in using regulatory powers to shape such developments. It does not see the need for any new regulations unless market failures by private-sector suppliers render such initiatives absolutely necessary. The Fed's leaders want to give the marketplace, specifically competition between different issuers and their interactions with users, the greatest possible space to determine what works and what does not. In a similar vein, Federal Reserve officials are at this point not too worried about nonbank institutions issuing cybercash. The Fed would simply ask such nonbank issuers to provide regular information about their activity, in particular about their outstanding e-money liabilities. This attitude contrasts quite dramatically with that of the European Central Bank and the Bank of Japan, both of which have decreed that e-money issue should be confined to banks. The ECB, following its 1998 report on e-money, has proposed several regulations concerning the issue of e-money. Nonbank issuers would have to obtain a special 'e-money institution' charter, which would treat them like a bank by subjecting them to the same reserve requirements, standards for prudential supervision and information disclosure rules. Any type of e-money would have to be fully redeemable at par with government currency. In Japan the Ministry of Finance's Working Group on the Future Framework for Electronic Money and Electronic Payment Systems has begun to develop the guidelines for a similarly proactive approach to regulating the issue of e-money. While these differences among the world's leading central banks may be philosophical or ideological in nature, they also reflect divergent views as to the nature of e-money. The Fed is much more inclined to view e-money as akin to money orders or traveler's checks while the more activist central banks of Europe and Japan regard e-money as equivalent to a demand deposit, thus as full-bodied money subject to regulation and supervision.[14]

Eventually the central bankers will have to iron out their differences one way or another. Cybercash, the most advanced form of electronic money, circulates on a global network which transcends national boundaries. It thus flows effortlessly across borders and national jurisdictions, requiring an unprecedented degree of international cooperation among central banks and harmonization of their rules concerning online money management. Central bankers have recognized this challenge. Working together under the auspices of the BIS, especially in its Basel Committee on Banking Supervision and in the Group of Ten's Committee on Payment and Settlement Systems, they have begun to explore areas of regulatory concern with regard to the issue and circulation of e-money. Reports have been published to discuss the implications of e-money on the internet for consumer protection, prudential supervision, sharing of jurisdictional responsibilities among national regulators in light of cybercash's global circulation potential and other cross-border issues. Special attention has been paid by the BIS to the question of e-money's security to identify the risks associated with this money form and specify benchmark standards for risk management that can be enforced by regulators through regular on-site examinations. As the BIS has shown with the implementation of the Cooke ratio imposing uniform minimum capital standards for banks on a global scale, this umbrella organization for central banks is capable of setting worldwide regulatory standards for money and banking which one day will have to be developed for e-money and cyberbanking transcending national boundaries.

As cybercash matures and its use spreads, national bank regulators will have to come up with global standards which put the creation and circulation of such digital money on a sound legal and technological basis. Agreements will have to be forged among monetary authorities with very different political and cultural traditions as to whether privately issued electronic money constitutes legal tender on a par with government-issued currency, who should be allowed to issue this kind of money and what regulatory as well as supervisory procedures need to put into place to manage online-payment systems. The establishment of such internationally harmonized rules governing the issue and circulation of e-money depends on the evolution of cybercash in coming years. The more advanced this new form of money becomes, the more extensive will the coordination and cooperation efforts of national regulators grow.

At the moment, the central banks are still mostly concerned with the rather limited applications of cybercash which emerged in its birth phase. These use the internet as the next in a long line of communication media (for example telephones, ATMs, POS terminals) to convey payment information, but otherwise rely on traditional payment mechanisms such as credit cards or checks. The underlying payment follows the same principles as credit-card payments over the phone or checks deposited in ATMs, thus allowing existing regulations and payment services to be extended to electronic payments arranged over the internet. From the Fed's point of view such online arrangements do not constitute true money inasmuch as they remain tied to existing payments systems transferring balances among accounts at banks. This situation, however, is likely to change with the appearance of more far-reaching cybercash systems which will use the internet to transfer 'value' in the discharge of payment obligations rather than have it just serve as an access device to communicate payment information to merchants and banks. Beginning with stored-value smart cards or e-mail money, such online value-transfer mechanisms represent actual money and should be treated as such by the monetary authorities for the purposes of regulation and supervision. It is only a matter of time before such e-money systems, notably software-based digital coins, will be used by their respective operators to create new money online. At that point cybercash will begin to impact directly on monetary policy and thus represent a more profound challenge to central banks than has been the case so far (see Chapter 8).

The emergence of e-money variants capable of money creation on the internet will force bank regulators across the world to address the question of who in the private sector should be allowed to issue such money and how they should be regulated. There is a strong argument to be made in favor of treating all issuers, whether banks or nonbank institutions, equally and subjecting them to the same regulatory requirements. If banks continue to face special regulatory burdens (in the form of reserve requirements, deposit insurance premia and compliance with supervision and examination procedures) while nonbank issuers of e-money do not, the latter will operate with lower costs and expand market share at the expense of the former. Moreover, the effectiveness of monetary policy would be undermined if a significant chunk of the money-creation process were to move outside the banking system and so beyond the reach of the state's monetary authorities. Central banks should be able to direct their monetary-policy tools at nonbank issuers of e-money as well as at the banks. Finally, no central bank can afford to be detached from nonbank issuers of e-money if these are capable of triggering gridlock in the nation's payments system when facing a liquidity crisis. Responsible for the smooth operation of the payments system under their jurisdiction, central banks have lender-of-last-resort mechanisms available, such as discount loans or open-market operations, to overpower any disruption in the flow of payments with a flood of emergency funds as the Fed, the ECB and other central banks did in coordinated fashion on 11 September 2001 when the physical destruction of the Bank of New York's settlement network in the wake of the terrorist attack on the World Trade Center threatened to paralyze the global payments system. All issuers of cyber-cash capable of disrupting the payments system will need to have access to such assistance.

Central bank responsibility for the safety and efficiency of the payments system will involve these institutions even more in the management of online money when cybercash variants are created and circulated within their own distinct monetary spheres. It is surely not too far-fetched to imagine that a leading internet service provider, such as AOL or Microsoft, may one day offer its subscribers access to a site-specific cybercash for all transactions on its platform or that a firm organizing an electronic shopping mall with many online merchants introduces its own cybercash variant for exclusive use within that network. The value of such autonomous cybercash units depends on the operational and financial strength of their respective issuers, which brings us back to Greenspan's idea of having the issue of cybercash vested in specially chartered corporations with strong balance sheets and public credit ratings (see note 12).

That idea makes a good deal of sense. The issue of cybercash needs to be kept institutionally separate from other activities in the economy. You do not want multi-product conglomerates, such as AOL Time Warner and Microsoft, or for that matter any issuer of cybercash, to be in a position of using the ability of money creation to finance their own expenditures directly with new money they create specifically for that purpose. Such mingling of funding and spending under one roof violates the equal-access requirements of money as a public good (see section 1.5). Microsoft, for instance, would have to issue its MSN dollars through a separately capitalized affiliate which could provide its other subsidiaries with funds in the form of loans, much like it lends to any third party. Keeping money creation vested in a distinct unit, which does nothing else, has the additional advantage of transparency. Not only can the public take a look at the financial statements of the issuer and judge the strength of its monetary unit without confusion about the possible impact of the issuer's other activities on the data, but regulators too will appreciate gaining accurate and undiluted information about money-creation activity. Just as they have done for decades with banks creating money in the form of checks, central banks will want to regulate those aspects of the issuers' money-creation process which need such constraints. We can imagine regulations pertaining to safety, privacy, technological standards, capitalization, risk management, dispute settlement and information disclosure. Minimum performance standards in these areas can be enforced and policed more effectively when they are applied to actors whose sole activity is the creation of electronic money.

It is quite possible that the issuing corporations will eventually evolve into full-blown monetary exchanges at the center of cybercash-based payments systems. While the value of any particular cybercash unit will be determined internally by its issuer's ability to match its supply and demand for settlement of payment obligations denominated in that unit, the attractiveness of any such unit will depend in addition on its liquidity in the broader sense of being automatically exchangeable with other money alternatives. The easier it is for any holder of a particular cybercash variant to swap his or her units for other types of money at acceptable rates of conversion, the greater its general acceptability and the more widespread its use – a classic example of network economies at work. Convertibility will thus always be a key criterion of popularity and competitiveness for issuers of cybercash. Most of them can be expected to seek opportunities of conversion for their cybercash units, provided they can collectively overcome the technological challenge of system incompatibility in their dealings with each other. With perhaps the exception of a few small-scale, self-enclosed cybercash systems providing barter-like online exchanges with a measure of value and medium of exchange (like the Ubarter units), cybercash issuers will all strive towards some degree of convertibility for their unit. At a minimum this means having one's unit automatically exchangeable with private bank checks or currency issued by the government to make that private e-money 'as good as' the country's official (paper) money standard. Central banks, in charge of maintaining the safety and efficiency of the payments system under their jurisdiction, will have an active interest in establishing convertibility agreements with private issuers of cybercash so as to ensure stability within an ever-growing pyramid of money alternatives. Such heterogeneity of private e-money variants must be given a modicum of homogenization through their respective links to the official payments system managed by the central bank, in accommodation of the public's desire to remain basically indifferent between private and public monies.

One can, however, foresee much wider monetary exchange activity on the internet. It is likely, as we have already seen in the case of Mojo Nation and the agreement between Beenz.com and Flooz.com, that private issuers of cybercash will want to make their units exchangeable with each other to gain more users and boost volume. Some of the larger issuers could well end up getting together to construct and operate full-blown online exchanges managing the convertibility of different cybercash units. We may get a sort of money market for cybercash where issuers may even start using each other's units as reserves with which to back their own unit. The exchange rates between the different cybercash units might be flexible, determined by the market forces of demand and supply. Such market regulation has the advantage of imposing a large dose of discipline on cybercash issuers having to face a devaluation of their particular cybercash unit relative to other alternatives in the wake of excess supplies or shrinking demand. Flexible-exchange rates for cybercash carry an announcement effect by informing the public what the market thinks of any given convertible unit, much like in the early 19th century when state bank notes of less-than-stellar banks in the United States were routinely discounted upon conversion. Cybercash issuers may have a collective interest in escaping such continuous market judgment. Nor may it be practical to tolerate different price systems in the various e-money segments of the online economy and have the relative-price differentials between those systems shift whenever exchange rates of their respective e-money units move strongly in one direction or the other. A better solution for cybercash issuers may therefore be to keep their exchange rates with each other fixed instead. Such a regime of fixed-exchange rates could be anchored by at-par conversion rules governing the exchange between any cybercash unit and government-issued currency.

It is precisely here where central banks have an entry point for effective intervention vis-à-vis cybercash. Any such institution will have to extend the nation's payments system so that it includes the whole gamut of domestically convertible cybercash variants, in effect adding a third layer to the pyramid of government-issued currency and private bank money in paper form. In the execution of such an extension, central banks will have the opportunity to bind cybercash issuers and their online exchanges to certain performance standards which will help to ensure continued at-par convertibility. In return for accepting such regulatory constraints on their operations, the cybercash issuers and exchanges are given the full backing of the state in terms of access to the central bank's payment services, settlement facilities and lender-of-last resort assistance. Of course, the central banks could consider running those online money exchanges themselves, just as they may wish one day to issue their own e-money as a liquidity and convertibility anchor for privately operated cybercash systems.[15]

Central banks will also have to take into account the supranational nature of cybercash flowing as mere signals through a borderless communication network. For law enforcement, tax collection and monetary policy reasons, governments will want to know about the domestic segment of the different cybercash systems under central bank supervision. This means that the authorities need to identify who is issuing and/or using cybercash units where. Such location capability will become possible soon with rapidly advancing geo-location software technology. The thorny issue of jurisdictional boundaries and cooperation between different national monetary authorities also renders such technology most useful. As long as we have not realized the utopian vision of one globally integrated and uniform payment system with a single supranational e-currency at its center, we will have national or regional payments systems for which equally national or regional central banks are responsible. Cooperation among central banks is essential as cybercash flows effortlessly across national boundaries, and such cooperation is likely to become even more of a reality when more and more of the currency trading in the foreign-exchange market moves online. But such cooperation is for the foreseeable future still going to be essentially bilateral in nature, following the principles of shared home-country and host-country responsibilities first laid down by the BIS in its Basel Concordat of 1975.[16]

Central banks will soon realize that in the era of electronic money they will have to cooperate a lot more extensively and regularly with each other than had been hitherto the case. They will strive for harmonization of their regulatory and supervisory practices concerning cybercash, since large differences on that score will surely shift the business of cybercash from more-regulated to less-regulated areas. Therefore we will see a sort of regulatory arbitrage until the nations involved all use much the same standards for this type of government intervention. Central bankers will also want to watch together on their radar screens certain private cybercash systems which function with their own distinct currency and thus reorganize monetary spaces across national boundaries. This, for instance, was the case with Beenz.com and its beenz-dominated slice of the internet spanning the globe. Such alternative private-currency systems can have powerful effects on the domestic monetary policy of nation-states, especially when their reputation for sound money management induces massive capital flight out of discredited currencies in high-inflation countries. The immediate availability of a better money alternative on one's computer might push such flight-to-quality reactions to a whole new level of mass behavior, compared to today when you still have to move your funds into another national currency. When such manifestations of monetary instability occur on an open communication network which knows no physical boundaries, central banks can no longer manage financial crises on their own. They need to work together when online incidences of financial turmoil spread across borders and threaten to disrupt the flow of payments in several countries at once. Finally, as has already been clearly illustrated in recent years by young hackers from Russia, China, Israel and the Philippines launching spectacular attacks on American web sites, cyberterrorism is a global phenomenon as are the criminal organizations specializing in computer crime. Both will target cybercash for their efforts at disruption and deception, a challenge which national governments will have to face together if they want to ensure continued public trust in this elusive money form.

Just as e-money platforms will technologically be part of online shopping protocols, so will any evolving regulatory framework for electronic payments have to be embedded in a broader architecture of rules and conventions guiding electronic commerce. Towards that objective there will have to be international agreements on customs and taxation practices, protection of intellectual property rights, privacy of information, online security, telecommunications infrastructure and IT standards, online content and technical standards. In addition, the spatially transcendental, virtual and real-time nature of online transactions requires a global framework for contractual engagements on the internet, a 'uniform commercial code for electronic commerce'. International fora exist to negotiate such agreements, be these the World Trade Organization (WTO), the Organization for Economic Co-operation and Development (OECD) or the United Nations Commission on International Trade Law. Whether these multilateral organizations will have the ability to balance the divergent interests of multinational corporations and developing countries and carry sufficient enforcement powers remains to be seen. What is likely to occur over the next couple of decades is the emergence of new global bodies using innovative regulatory approaches to meet the unprecedented challenges posed by e-commerce in general and electronic payments in particular.

PART III

The Internet-based Economy

CHAPTER 7

Virtual Capitalism

Even though it is difficult to project forward the course of major innovations, we can make several reasonably safe bets about the evolution of the internet as a locus of economic activity.[1] New communication technologies (such as broadband) will eventually give the internet dramatically enhanced performance capabilities in terms of safety and convenience of access, speed of operations, information-processing capacity and multimedia applications. Furthermore, infrastructure enhancements will allow the net to spread in all kinds of directions, rendering the currently dominant and centralized World Wide Web layer of the internet less important as other net layers emerge. I can think here of intra- and extranets, instant messaging, the wireless 'mobile web', decentralized P2P networks with interactive file-sharing and downloading capabilities and communication networks allowing smart machines to talk to each other. Also quite predictable is that paper will be crowded out by electronic data signals which save money and time. The vulnerability of mail delivery in the wake of the anthrax scare in the USA in late 2001 has already prompted accelerated efforts to move from paper to digitalized information. This transformation will affect the way we receive and pay bills, read books or newspapers and enter into contracts.

The most important switch from paper to electronic data concerns money, with paper notes or checks increasingly giving way to cybercash. This change in money form will have a major impact on all the activities relying on it. We have already discussed (in Chapter 2) how the transition from a monetary regime rooted in the gold standard to the more flexible postwar regime of state-administered credit-money laid the foundations for a more dynamic and stable capitalism driven forward by a 'debt economy' as its growth engine. We can expect similarly dramatic changes to unfold during the next couple of decades as cybercash grows into the dominant payment mechanism. That new money form will help to create a new type of capitalism, just as its predecessor – elastic bank money in paper form – did in the aftermath of World War II. Cybercash will turn the internet into a vector of structural change which will transform all economic activities organized as monetary circuits – exchange (section 7.1), production (section 7.2) and credit (section 7.3). The cybercash-powered online economy will fuel the growth of two qualitatively new types of capital, intangible (productive) capital and fictitious (financial) capital, which together with electronic money form the foundations for the development of 'virtual' capitalism (section 7.4).

7.1 The Online Marketplace

The act of exchange, involving a swap of goods, services or assets for money, will be profoundly impacted by cybercash. Such an impact will extend to the markets organizing exchange, not least by moving them online and structuring them there around a high-tech form of money which carries a lot more information content than any other money form preceding it. The repercussions of cybercash for the modalities of exchange will have many channels and will be felt across a large variety of markets.

7.1.1 Micropayments

Since cybercash, once installed as a payment system, will have marginal costs approaching zero, its processing costs will be so low that even very small transactions become feasible. It can thus penetrate a number of routine consumer transactions in ways that credit cards, with their much higher processing charges, never could. People will buy their movie tickets, newspapers, parking spaces and so on online. Vending machines, activated by smart cards, will spread to provide us with stamps, food, liquids, money, parking permits and other products of daily need. In general, we can expect such smart cards, equipped with sophisticated microprocessors for multi-functionality and biometric technology for safety, to become our principal means of personal identification and primary access tool to the online economy. Smart cards will be combined with many access devices for log-on capacity anytime, anywhere – at home, at work, in the car, from the street. The omnipresence of access will allow us to transact constantly on the internet, and we will get used to doing so extensively on a daily basis. Micropayments in cybercash, providing the online economy with the mass volume it needs, will also nourish many new services which can be directly produced on the internet. In particular this concerns information which we might buy regularly – news, weather forecasts, traffic conditions, location services, prices and inventories in targeted shops, medical assistance and so forth.

7.1.2 E-tailing (B2C)

Many products, once bought exclusively in brick-and-mortar outlets, will be traded actively on the internet once we have reduced the act of buying to a simple click of the mouse or push of a button on the cell phone. Such simplification will happen thanks to centralized online exchanges or other steps towards system compatibility which allow interaction and settlement between different cybercash systems whose units are convertible with each other. E-wallets exchanging personal information relevant to the transaction will help to automate the purchase steps online.

Once households across the globe have internalized online shopping and payment in cybercash to the point of automaticity, many consumer goods and services will shift their markets increasingly online. The best candidates for such a shift are products which carry high information content, do not require to be touched or tried by shoppers before buying and are distributed on a large scale. Considering these features, we can foresee e-commerce expand especially rapidly with regard to consumer electronics, software, books, subscription-based access to music, pay-per-view video for movies, so-called content (for entertainment, information and news) and travel services.[2] Other routine purchases, such as standard apparel and non-perishable groceries, may also thrive online. As B2C sites become better, they may provide an alternative virtual shopping experience that is more entertaining and informative than the one we are used to from our visits to traditional retail outlets. In that case even fashion and cars may be bought online, as will other products which up to now most consumers had always wanted to feel and/or try out before buying. Financial services, entertainment, health care and education are all services which by their very nature can be easily digitized and so should end up being transacted massively on the internet.

This shift to online selling in many key consumer-product categories will have tremendous repercussions for e-tailers. One key concern for any B2C firm will be its ability to handle the storage, distribution and delivery aspects of the sale. These aspects will be a major constraint to the scale capacity of any online seller and thus a key determinant of its competitiveness. The importance of logistics will give an advantage to the big multiproduct retail outlets, such as Wal-Mart or Sears Roebuck, because they will have the scale to offer relatively lower delivery charges through more efficient handling of online purchases. They may cement that advantage over smaller, single-product retailers by offering site visits which allow consumers to navigate in a nonlinear fashion around the virtual store. Such online roaming can do wonders for impulse buying, and much technology will be invested in encouraging such behavior. Consumers may be taken to places on their visits which they did not expect, but which are conducive to spontaneous purchase decisions. For instance, when looking for a CD from a favorite artist, the shopper may be informed to check out another artist making similar music. When seeing the earrings of one's favorite actress on television, the person watching the show may use interactive TV right then and there to buy the same piece of jewelry. Such impulse buying, often far more profitable than routine purchases, will be further encouraged by overdraft and consumer-loan facilities incorporated in cybercash systems designed for B2C commerce.

E-tailers will also want to hook consumers by giving them price discounts, often made possible by the lower costs of operating online compared to off-line, or by offering them coupons right then and there as an incentive to buy. They will have lots of information available about their regular customers to create an instant customer profile of habits and tastes with which to design effective incentive packages. They may also use that information to select potential members of fee-based clubs for upscale, trend-conscious customers whose membership entitles them to discounts on their favorite products or brands. But the information advantage of the internet works both ways. Consumers too will have much more information available about the product and will have done extensive comparison-shopping online to check price differences between competitors. Retailers will have to learn how to deal with much better educated consumers, relying for instance on instant matching of lower prices elsewhere, buy-now coupons which expire with the end of the visit, personal assistance on demand (for instance call-in centers) and attractive after-sales services.

Because online shoppers will be well informed and have easy access to alternative sites of competitors, e-tailers will try hard to boost the loyalty of otherwise fickle consumers and encourage repeat customers. That is why ideas such as instant coupons or fee-based clubs offering discounts are surely going to play an important role in B2C commerce. Very attractive in this regard is the concept of coupon money first introduced by

Beenz.com (see section 5.3) where firms participating in its network could offer consumers a fixed amount of free beenz for certain actions. While Beenz.com is now defunct, its idea of a limited-circulation cybercash transferred to users as coupons is not. People like to be rewarded, especially for things they enjoy doing. If this idea of coupon money ever catches on, it might become a way for millions of online shoppers to earn some additional income in exchange for doing things that enhance the revenue potential of the site issuing the coupons. People could be getting paid for site visits, application for membership, participation in surveys, supply of personal information, actual purchases and a host of other consumption-related activities. Such coupon rewards turn the leisure activities of net surfing and online shopping into income-generating 'work' which many consumers will be happy to carry out on a regular basis, thereby allowing merchants to deepen customer loyalty and encourage repeat visits. If frequent-flier miles are already popular today, imagine how irresistible such consumer rewards for e-work may be one day.

7.1.3 P2P Networks

Napster's music-sharing service, much discussed in the press because of the copyright suit against it by the music industry, shows what an online network of interacting peers is capable of. Peer-to-peer technology, such as Napster's MP3 software, lets PCs communicate directly with one another and exchange data via the internet without going through central computers such as web servers. This advance facilitates the spontaneous sprouting of decentralized peer-to-peer networks beyond the web's central reach, an innovation with many useful applications. Businesses can link their offices to those of their clients and access each other's computer systems for the swapping of data. Or they can link PCs anywhere within the company and so boost collaboration among employees. Stringing PCs together into a 'distributed computing' network creates virtual machines through aggregation of computing power which can be used to tackle big problems. Consumers may use P2P technology and networks to trade with each other. To begin with, they may trade content stored in their PCs such as music, software or movies – an ultimately unstoppable practice which will require some rethinking of copyright protection and an adequate fee structure for services rendered. But as P2P networks become better established, their use for market transactions may expand in all kinds of unanticipated directions, such as hobby clubs (to trade stamps or baseball cards, for instance) or online tutorials as a highly customized form of 'distance learning'.

Perhaps the most convincing illustration of P2P trading's potential so far is eBay, one of the largest and most profitable online companies ever. This company is in many ways a model of the future, the harbinger of the virtual capitalism to come. Its business model is proof that, when it comes to the internet, sometimes the craziest ideas are the ones that have the greatest success. Who would have thought four years ago that the idea of having people buy used cribs, Beenie Babies, or diet pills from someone they have never met hundreds or thousands of miles away would turn into one of the most successful dot-com start-ups to date? What the skeptics at the time underestimated was the ability of the internet to let individuals form uniquely self-sustaining global marketplaces. To realize that potential eBay introduced several crucial innovations tailor-made for the internet. One was the model of *online auctions* bringing together buyers and sellers to establish prices for goods and services which had never been marketed before. The value added by eBay, as the basis for its profits, lies in the organization of such auctions. As such, the company established itself as an indispensable online intermediary controlling an entire segment of e-commerce, a promising e-business model. Moreover, the company has played an important role in the diffusion of cybercash by establishing the popularity of e-mail money. Its proxy-bidding feature, which allows bidders to punch in their maximum offer and then have the auction site automatically bid on their behalf in preset increments up to the limit, is an early application of machine-to-machine (M2M) e-commerce. Perhaps most important is eBay's ability to harness the communications power of the internet. The company solicits input from its clients and also watches their movements carefully on its site to identify new products and services tailored to their observed needs.[3]

The online auction model developed by eBay marks an important extension of e-commerce, offering millions of individuals a low-cost opportunity to engage in a new type of economic activity which until now they had no chance of realizing. Gripped by the chase for capital gains from buying low and selling high, they can let loose their entrepreneurial spirits. Participants in eBay auctions learn the art of bargain hunting, value determination, marketing and price negotiation from the ground up in repeated encounters with the pure market logic of a nearly perfectly competitive market. If they are successful, many may become more ambitious and hone their entrepreneurial talents in a more organized fashion by starting a business. The availability of auctions frees them from the heavy overhead costs of running a store. Wishing to foster entrepreneurship, eBay has made special efforts to accommodate those who want to turn themselves into an auction-supply business. On its site people rate each other on every transaction, encouraging sellers with good ratings to stay on eBay. Its Safe Harbor program offers fraud reimbursement, identity verification and other safety features which have kept fraudulent activity on the site very low and thus created a great deal of public trust in the auction process on eBay. This makes it easier for anyone to set up shop on the site. Would-be entrepreneurs can also get help by attending eBay University for auction training. A monthly 'rent' of $9.95 allows sellers to open store-fronts on the eBay site, and the dominant payment systems used in eBay auctions (PayPal, eBay's Billpoint) have already adjusted their product offerings by introducing special fee-based packages for small businesses (see section 5.2). We can imagine these payments systems or even the auction sites themselves one day offering would-be entrepreneurs micro-credits to launch their businesses with a stock of supplies, a sort of venture capital for the masses.

Apart from encouraging entrepreneurship among a large number of individuals, the online auction model pioneered by eBay also turns into marketable assets a large variety of products which up to now had lacked such liquidity. Used goods, which otherwise would have been thrown away, are now given a chance of revival in the hands of someone else. The transfer of property rights turns a mere possession into an asset which yields its original owner income. From the point of view of income creation, what we have here represents a productive activity which may even be counted as a net addition to the nation's wealth in terms of expanding its total asset base. In a similar vein, online auctions are also handy devices to sell excess supplies at discounted prices which is better than not selling them at all. Apart from boosting growth through the orderly liquidation of excess supplies which otherwise might have remained frozen out of circulation, this process has the added advantage of improving the economy's allocative efficiency by better matching surpluses and shortages.

While we have had auctions in various off-line contexts (art, government licenses), this kind of market has found much room for expansion online because of the internet's ability to connect a large number of buyers and sellers with speed, efficiency and fairness.[4] Apart from the ascending-price auctions practiced by eBay and most other online auction sites, there are alternative auction models which may in the end prove more effective in the virtual marketplace. The market model pioneered by Priceline.com, where potential buyers can name their own price for the item and have the seller agree or not agree to the deal offered, has proved quite popular. Some sites, such as Basement.com, have begun to use descending-price auctions. In July 2000 eBay diversified into fixed-price sales by acquiring

Half.com where books and CDs are sold for half their list price or even less. Such experimentation in dynamic pricing is especially important for the business-to-business online auctions which will play a huge role in how large corporations will automate their purchases of supplies and thus transform their relations with suppliers. The B2B segment of e-commerce may, for instance, see the proliferation of group buying sites, like the one pioneered by Mercata.com.[5] More generally, B2B auctions may very well form the entry point for larger scale corporate reorganization seeking to exploit the opportunities of internet-based automation in all aspects of the production circuit – from buying the inputs to selling the output.

7.2 Automation of the Production Circuit

7.2.1 E-marketplaces

Early on in the dot-com boom, in 1998, the financial community became enamored with the idea of forming e-marketplaces which would bring businesses together in specific industries to trade supplies needed in that sector. Lots of capital poured into that segment of e-commerce, and B2B exchanges took off. In less than two years most industrial sectors had several B2B exchanges setting up operations at the same time, with an additional layer of general online exchanges trading across sectors. The impetus for this explosion was the irresistible prospect of transforming rigid supply chains, which tied manufacturers, wholesalers and retailers together on the basis of long-term supply contracts, into much more flexible *business webs* (b-webs).[6] Those e-marketplaces allow large corporations to cut costs, lower inventory levels, shorten time to market, facilitate entry into new markets and deepen their interactions with suppliers towards greater cooperation and coordination. All this boosts operating efficiency and helps the bottom line.

Since the heyday of B2B euphoria in 1999–2000, this sector of e-commerce has been hit hard by the e-crash on Wall Street. A massive shake-out is under way, a combination of outright failures and takeovers of weaker sites by stronger rivals. There were an estimated 1200 such e-marketplaces set up in early 2000; not more than 300 will survive. The shake-out, brutal as it may be, will strengthen the survivors by forcing them to move beyond the low-margin intermediation business of bringing buyers and sellers together on the net and expand their range of services. For example, they can help buyers to streamline the entire ordering process by securing financing from a third party, tracking down sellers of highly specialized products, assisting buyers when filling out bids and posting them on the site and arranging delivery. Diversifying revenue streams beyond transaction fees, online exchanges could sell information such as data comparing suppliers' delivery times and product quality. They may sell warranties and insurance. And they might want to offer consultancy services for a fee. In the process of reorganization, we will see e-marketplaces experiment with a variety of business models which may coexist within and across specific industrial sectors or product categories.[7] The insertion of cybercash into the e-marketplaces of tomorrow may add several attractive revenue streams, especially when those e-money systems contain features tailored to the B2B marketplace, such as credit lines, netting facilities, automatic tax collection, escrow accounts for post-delivery payments, and electronic billing.

7.2.2 Online Labor Exchanges

Businesses will use the internet beyond procurement of supplies to hire labor services. This trend is beginning to be visible today. Online exchanges set up as collaboration hubs, such as Bid.com, already allow firms to hire independent contractors for specific projects. The start-up eLance offers freelance workers the opportunity to market their skills online while trying to match these with corporate projects posted on its site. The tremendous success of monster.com, a job exchange, shows the potential for greatly improving labor market efficiency by harnessing the internet's information capacity. We can foresee online labor exchanges that specialize in pools of part-time workers, high-skilled workers in great demand, or temporary hiring of workers who normally work for other firms. The nature of the labor market will change, giving it an added degree of flexibility which will benefit especially those workers wishing to work part time or do freelance work for specific projects. Online exchanges will excel in identifying and overcoming labor shortages. Cybercash will help to cement the interactions between firms and workers they hire by settling their contractual obligations online.[8] I can even imagine future cybercash systems specifically designed to allow the servicing of debts through labor services in lieu of cash payments, translate their value equivalent in money and keep track of the flows – a 21st-century version of feudal peonage.

7.2.3 B-webs

Online exchanges will revolutionize the resource markets where businesses buy their inputs, prompting large corporations to reorganize their
hitherto rigidly vertical supply chains into horizontally flexible b-webs. In
the process these producers will end up revamping every aspect of their
production circuit from input purchases through the actual production
process to distribution and sales of output. Crucial will be the use of the
internet for linking the databases of cooperating firms in a b-web to keep
track of inventory levels, replenish supplies automatically and plan
production schedules together. Firms will use the same technology for
their inventory management to stay in touch with their wholesale or retail
distributors in charge of selling their output. Interactive communication
with customers will allow producers to take orders online which has the
advantage of building to demand rather than on the basis of imprecise
sales forecasts (see our discussion of Dell below).

The penetration of e-marketplaces on both ends of the production
circuit will spur a variety of e-business strategies to reorganize all aspects
of the company so that it can move at net speed. Such reengineering
imposes wrenching changes in corporate culture and management. Many
jobs will be eliminated through automation while remaining employees
face the task of acquiring new skills in a hurry. Key to successful e-
business strategies will be the ability to cooperate with suppliers,
customers and even former competitors. This requires not only changing
traditionally adversarial relationships into collaborative ones, but also a
willingness to share what used to be proprietary information with others
inside or outside the company. The vertical chain of command from the
top down will give way to much less hierarchical decision-making procedures tailored to in-house teams of employees working with each other on
specific projects and collaborating with teams from other firms. Whatever
set of tasks each team is responsible for and however these are distributed
among cooperating teams, what holds them together and coordinates them
will be a constant flow of data and interactive communication. This is one
reason why we can expect the internet to penetrate and transform every
organizational aspect of businesses, whether small or large, producing
goods or services. Cybercash will help to organize the interactions
between the members of such b-webs. Thanks to the tremendous information-processing capacity of money as software, we may soon have cybercash systems designed for b-webs which help to keep track of money
flows, net out mutual debts and regulate intra-web credit. Revenue- and
cost-sharing among b-web members, which is at the heart of their cooper-

ation, will be more easily handled by B2B cybercash systems which have the ability to release funds automatically upon receiving a signal of contract fulfillment or at a preset date.

7.2.4 The Dell Model

While still at the very beginning of the digital revolution, we can already see the internet make a difference in all aspects of business organization. Besides automating procurement and flexibilizing supply-chain management through extranets or online exchanges, e-business strategies focus today on creation of company intranets for in-house communication, expansion of online selling, engagement of suppliers and customers in product design, improvements in customer service and installation of knowledge-management systems to capture the know-how of employees for innovation.[9] These initiatives may be boosted by real-time reward systems, providing instant bonuses or coupons, which can be much more easily set up with cybercash than was the case with paper money.

A good glimpse of what a company may typically look like in a decade's time can be had by studying Dell Computers, currently the world's leading producer of PCs. The company obtained this position by implementing early on a complete e-business model that enabled it to outcompete larger, much less automated rivals. Founder Michael Dell's revolutionary idea of selling PCs over the phone or the net allowed the company to avoid the costs of building a sales force or paying retailers a distribution fee. By getting in touch with its customers directly, Dell takes customized orders and then builds the PCs to specification in three days with all the custom software installed. Corporate customers too can order their Dell computers online. Its built-to-order system works because of Dell's super-tight integration with its suppliers who are in constant touch with the company to regulate order flows and adjust inventory levels. Thus because it is capable of operating with much lower stocks, Dell can take advantage of the latest prices of components which are constantly declining. In cooperation with its suppliers, the PC maker has even pioneered an innovative product-design strategy known as modularity, the art of designing components that can be easily plugged together ('snap-in assembly'). This strategy has put Dell in a position where its b-web can assemble 25,000 different computer configurations within days to meet any combination of specifications ordered by customers.

With lower unit costs Dell can aggressively underprice its competitors, steal away their market share and thereby gain additional economies of scale for even lower unit costs. Forcing its rivals to slash R&D spending to its own comparatively low levels, Dell has let efficiency crowd out innovation and so turned PCs into commodities. Now the company is trying the same strategy in low-end servers and networking gear by driving down margins with cheaper products. The fate of its recent forays into high-end servers, data storage and software-based web site management services will depend on how easily these more R&D-intense products can be commodified.[10]

Dell's ability to underprice its competitors with better products delivered in record-short time is rooted not least in its highly advanced automation of production, with meticulous detail given to every aspect of the process from product design to inventory flows and capacity utilization of machinery all the way to delivery at the end. It relies on multi-layered communication between suppliers, in-house teams and customers which enables the firm to react rapidly to changing circumstances.[11] Advances in factory automation, driven by economies of scope from combining computers, software and robotics, will allow firms to collect performance data on their machines, send it to central headquarters with the help of remote monitoring (RM) technology, and plug it into their enterprise resource planning (ERP) system. Today we have ERP software which keeps track of everything – supply-chain management, customer service, accounting – and thus allows full integration of all aspects of the production circuit. Based on data analysis, central headquarters can make rapid adjustments in the production flow by reprogramming the performance parameters of the machines involved. Producers can give customers access to the data and so get help in catching defective products early on.

Such RM technology links factory equipment together into long-distance systems which can be managed from a central location. Its use of the internet for M2M communication will accelerate a trend already well under way, the transformation of multinational corporations with separate regional production and distribution systems into *global production networks* (GPNs) which locate different phases in the production of their globally standardized products wherever they find the best resource mix for that particular step (for instance design in Italy, engineering in Germany, labor-intensive assembly in Mexico). Those GPNs of tomorrow will do much outsourcing to smaller operators within their global b-web, reserving for themselves only those activities in which they excel or over which they prefer to maintain direct control.[12] Cybercash plays a supportive role in this trend towards global production networks and virtual companies by facilitating the centralization of cash management, specifically the netting and settlement of intra-network payments between b-web partners, as a means of improved control which goes hand in hand with the decentralization of production.

7.2.5 The Online Firm

The developments described here raise the question of what the purpose of a firm will be in the net-based future. Two generations ago Nobel Prize winner Ronald Coase (1937) asked why corporations existed in the first place. If markets were truly the best mechanism for equalizing demand and supply, determining equilibrium prices and getting maximum utility out of finite resources, then why not have individual buyers and sellers acting out the 'invisible hand' in the marketplace rather than have them grouped together in large corporate organizations which stifle competition? Coase's answer pointed to a variety of transaction costs – search costs caused by the need to find appropriate suppliers, contract costs arising from negotiation of prices and other contract details, and coordination costs of meshing different products and processes. Corporations can conduct these steps in-house and so save themselves the transaction costs which producers would incur if each step of the production circuit had to be negotiated as a separate transaction. The Coasian justification of the firm came to be embodied after World War II by such corporate leaders as Ford which tried to bring the entire chain of production under its control – from ownership of steel mills supplying its car factories to acquiring a thrift for its consumer-finance operations. Today, however, this notion of the vertically integrated firm is stood on its head by the internet's ability to reduce radically all three transaction costs. This information network promotes cost reductions, service enhancements, innovation and customization throughout the entire process of production. It thus adds knowledge value to goods or services at each stage of their production cycle which should be captured by the unit(s) best able to turn these improvements into a source of wealth at that stage of the cycle. Thanks to the internet, large companies are thus free to focus on what they do best and leave all the other steps to the most qualified partners in their b-web. Many of them may very well end up as virtual companies living off their ideas and otherwise engaging in contract management, running a network of partners to whom they outsource most production-related activities.

This radically different model of business organization is inevitable, since the old model of vertical integration and supply-chain management will see most of its primary sources of profit extraction sharply eroded, if not altogether destroyed, by the internet. As Hamel (2000) noted, the 'frictionless' capitalism heralded by the arrival of the internet tends to reduce all kinds of friction which once boosted corporate profits: customer ignorance (the so-called asymmetric information problem); local monopolies or oligopolies controlling a neighborhood whose residents are hostages for lack of alternatives; margin-boosting tie-ins which customers will now be able to escape thanks to the internet's facilitation of unbundling and recombining products; bargaining-power advantages vis-à-vis suppliers and distributors; and price discrimination between different local markets. All these barriers to perfectly competitive markets, which companies have traditionally used as sources of monopoly power to extract more profits, are tied to the physical world of the industrial economy and tend to disappear in the virtual world of the internet economy. Much of the dot-com crash of 2000–01 was about this realization, the failure of business models which tried to 'virtualize' existing businesses and applied the old rules of the industrial economy to the new game of virtual capitalism. Deprived of profit-boosting, margin-protecting and competition-reducing frictions, many dot-coms went bust. They simply could not boost enough revenues to match their large start-up costs, either because of lacking volume or an inability to charge sufficiently high prices online.

The lesson from these failures is quite clear. The virtual capitalism unfolding in cyberspace necessitates entirely different business models from the old industrial ones in order to generate sustainable profits. Any online producer faces more or less the same set of operating problems. Start-up costs are high with heavy initial investments in data centers, web programming, promotional campaigns and a variety of other intangibles (such as intellectual property rights, skills, brand recognition). Most operating costs are fixed, a cost structure conducive to economies of scale from high volume. Marginal costs are negligible to zero, since it costs practically nothing to expand online distribution of products to additional customers once the site has been set up. The trouble with such a cost structure is that if we let nearly perfectly competitive online markets drive prices down to marginal costs in line with mainstream microeconomic thinking, then online firms will go bankrupt in droves. They need new sources of monopoly power, something which replaces the lost frictions of the industrial age. Understanding that any monopoly in virtual capitalism is only temporary until rendered obsolete by better technology, online firms will try business models that build volume for economies of scale, knowledge-based value added for economies of scope and a combination of both to exploit network economies.

The ability of online firms to build temporary monopolies on the internet must be rooted in the special nature of that medium. To begin with, it makes sense to offer products and services online which cannot be supplied off-line, as eBay has done. It also helps online producers to engage in genuine and ongoing innovation, since one powerful source of monopoly power arises from being the first with a new product that catches on. The internet is like a huge ideas factory, creating and distributing knowledge on a mass scale. Successful internet-based producers generate ideas and make them accessible to others who might want to use them for their own benefit.[13] This means turning information into a commodity which people are willing to pay for, whether in the form of licensing fees for the use of software, transaction fees in online exchanges, membership subscriptions for access to multi-product content packages as offered by AOL Time Warner, or whatever else innovative e-business strategies can turn into a steady revenue stream. In this context it is useful to remember that the internet is particularly well suited for the delivery of custom content. While this medium crowds out old line intermediaries, such as travel agents or brokers, who had built their power on the basis of asymmetric information advantages, it opens the way for a new kind of intermediary who collects, rebundles, personalizes and distributes information online to a large variety of users according to their specific needs. *Infomediaries,* such as eBay, AOL Time Warner, Microsoft, DoubleClick, or E*Trade, represent a new type of intermediary specifically designed for the knowledge-based internet and, unlike the hands-off public utilities of yesteryear (such as telephone companies), strongly engaged in content.[14] This e-business model seems to be at the cutting edge of the cyber-revolution, especially when it propels the infomediary to the center of large networks and marketplaces which it organizes. Any issuer of cyber-cash is itself a type of infomediary at the center of the monetary sphere that uses its unit for money.

7.2.6 Intangible (Productive) Capital

Irrespective of which e-business models will ultimately turn out to be the most profitable, internet-based producers will seek new forms of monopoly control by accumulating productive capital that is inherently intangible in nature. While the traditional industrial enterprises grew by expanding their stock of physical capital (plant and equipment), online producers grow by generating new ideas, transforming those rapidly into marketable services and distributing these knowledge products on a large scale. That kind of producer relies heavily on intellectual property rights, the 'human capital' (for instance skill levels) of its workforce mustering its collective knowledge pool for service-enhancing innovation, the ability to generate economies of scope in product development, a corporate culture conducive to teamwork as well as individual initiative among employees, the quality of its b-web coordination and brand recognition built on a reputation for quality which merits public trust. All these resources represent intangible forms of productive capital in the sense that, in contrast to a machine or a plant, they lack a physical presence which would make them easily measurable.[15]

The more firms operate online, the greater their reliance on intangible capital to boost income. But how do you value something that is inherently unmeasurable, like an idea, the use of information, the contribution of knowledge to value added? This is becoming an increasingly urgent question. Managers will need to develop a good sense of the loss-profit potential of investments in intangible capital without having hard cost or revenue numbers to work with when evaluating their projects. Investors will have to assess fairly accurately what the intangible capital of a firm is worth when trying to work out the fair-market valuation of that company, and they will need new accounting standards for assets that cannot be given a precise dollar value. The same holds true for creditors examining the creditworthiness of corporate borrowers. The prevalence of intangible capital is also a challenge for government officials, to the extent that it wreaks havoc with public policies designed for an industrial age. The internet economy renders obsolete existing accounting principles, antitrust practices, patent and copyright laws, trade rules and even monetary policy (see Chapter 8).[16]

Apart from presenting measurement problems and challenges to prevailing public policy, intangible capital also imposes its own unique accumulation dynamic on those firms seeking to use it. Take, for instance, products whose primary value lies in intellectual property, such as software, movies, records, pharmaceutical drugs or e-business models. Such knowledge-based products carry large development costs up front, but then have zero marginal costs especially when they are distributed electronically. After their initial development costs have been recouped, every additional user basically represents pure profit. In addition, knowledge-based products are subject to positive network externalities, where the growth in the number of users renders those products exponentially more valuable for each individual user. If, for instance, large amounts of people and businesses use the same cybercash system that I have access to, I will be able to carry out that many more transactions. This combination of zero marginal costs and network economies makes it possible for producers of knowledge-based products to win big. At the same time, they are at great risk whenever a better idea emerges which prompts users to switch massively to the improved product version. In such instances of technological obsolescence, the supplier of the older, now obsolete product may face large losses quite suddenly. Internet-based producers may contain this risk through continuous innovation, which keeps them technologically ahead of competitors, and by devising strategies which make it more difficult for their customers to switch to alternative suppliers (such as subscription-based membership or multi-product packages). In the absence of such counter-strategies, producers may find the internet a much more discriminatory and unstable environment for business than they are used to. In the industrial era, with its supply constraints and inert structures, there was always place for smaller, less competitive suppliers coexisting in fairly stable fashion with the leader (as in the car rental industry with Avis and Budget versus Hertz). In the virtual world of the internet, on the other hand, producers face more of an all-or-nothing situation in which they either win big or lose a lot.

The diffusion of cybercash will greatly facilitate the accumulation of intangible capital in internet-based production activities. For one, it will anchor the principle of paying for services rendered and products used, thus making it much easier for suppliers of knowledge-based products to charge adequate prices and generate revenue streams. Moreover, the design flexibility of cybercash systems, each tailored to the needs of the e-commerce segment it serves (B2C, P2P, B2B and M2M), will itself enhance the quality of intangible capital. For instance, the aggregate operational efficiency of b-webs will greatly improve with an effective cybercash system keeping track and settling the transactions between partners on an ongoing basis. Cybercash can be used for automatic performance bonuses encouraging collaborative teamwork, rewards for innovative ideas, revenue-sharing arrangements between partners, tuition payments for 'distance learning' programs used by workers, funding of employee assistance services and a host of other automated processes used by the global production networks of tomorrow. Finally, habituation with online payments should make it easier to evaluate the performance of intangible assets. Given its information-rich nature, cybercash will offer much enhanced record-keeping and tracking capabilities with which to identify the cost and revenue flows specifically associated with an investment in intangible capital. With improved measurement facilities, such investments will be implemented more easily and in less risky fashion.

7.3 Cyberfinance

Finance, the vehicle for credit, is particularly susceptible to automation-enhancing innovation, since it involves contractual arrangements rather than physical products. This activity has until now involved swapping one set of paper (money) with another set of paper (IOUs or securities). The internet replaces these swaps of paper with flows of electronic data, and that change will reorganize financial transactions quite radically. The computerization of finance, a process already well under way (see section 2.4), will be given added impetus by combining fund transfers in cyber-cash with financial claims in digital format. This combination will move the entire credit system onto the internet and in the process transform the role of finance in our economy. The financial revolution discussed earlier in the book, a process driven by the simultaneous deregulation of money, securitization of credit and computerization of finance (see Chapter 2), will gain a whole new dimension once it sweeps online.

7.3.1 Cyberbanking

Overcoming its difficult birth (see section 2.5), online banking is bound to take off with electronic billing and cybercash. Both mass applications will enable banks to use the internet as a principal vector for their aggressive push into universal banking made possible by recent deregulation. Besides offering considerable scale economies typifying the mass distribution of electronic services, online banking distinguishes itself above all as a source of network economies where a growing client base satisfies individual customer preferences for liquidity, safety and convenience. It also helps that cyberspace transcends geographic boundaries and so gives financial institutions access to customers across the globe. With universal banking putting a premium on product development, cyberbanks will find the internet a powerful vector for innovation and source of scope economies yielding synergies when different financial services are combined. Leading banks will design multi-product packages which allow their online customers to take care of all their financial-services needs on one site – checking and savings accounts, loans and other credit facilities (credit cards), mutual funds or alternative vehicles for portfolio investments, brokerage services, investment advice, bill payments, insurance coverage and cash management (including conversion facilities for different cybercash variants). To what extent these package deals will be exclusively targeted at wealthy clients, a major risk when money becomes a private commodity as it will with cybercash, depends on the desire of financial-services providers to maximize their client base and on government efforts to ensure equal access.[17]

Ten years from now the structure of the financial-services industry will be quite different from the one we have been used to for over half a century. Gone will be a whole layer of small and medium-sized banks which used to serve their communities as local monopolies or oligopolies. These institutions will be victimized by the transformation of traditional banking services into low-margin commodities and their failure to respond to this challenge with higher value online services earning them membership subscriptions or transaction fees. They will be squeezed from above by the giant banks which enjoy reputational, capitalization and network-access advantages, while also feeling the pressure from below by specialists carving out a market niche within which they excel. In addition, banks in general will face an onslaught on their traditional service base from investment banks, brokerage houses, mutual funds and insurance companies which they will try to counter by expanding into the turf of these nonbank institutions. The greatest threat, however, will come from ISPs using their strategic position as entry ramps to the information super-highway for a launch into financial services. Microsoft's MoneyCentral, Yahoo! Finance, and AOL's link to Citibank's c2it are the first efforts in this direction, each providing a financial portal which offers online payments by e-mail and personalized financial planning.[18] It is quite possible that these financial portals offered by ISPs, using the absence of supervision and regulation by bank regulators as a comparative advantage, will try to expand into commercial banking activities and issue their own cybercash variants. Such a push goes to the heart of a crucial question, namely how to ensure a level-playing field between bank and nonbank issuers of cybercash. The ECB approach, insisting on a uniform set of regulations for all e-money issuers under its jurisdiction, might ultimately be adopted globally once cybercash gains widespread use (see Chapter 8).

7.3.2 Online Financial Markets

Apart from its impact on banking, the internet may have an even more important role to play in the transformation of financial markets. We have seen (in section 2.4) that most of these markets – for stocks, bonds, currencies, futures and so forth – are already in the grip of online trading. They are now being rebuilt on the internet, with online exchanges trading digitalized financial claims and setting up central clearing and settlement facilities for such trades. Cybercash will integrate every facet of these online exchanges into a seamless flow of funds and information. The use of cybercash for liquidity injections, trade credit and netting of mutually off-setting positions will make online exchanges highly attractive and efficient marketplaces.

Internet-based financial markets generate high-quality, real-time information about market conditions which improves hedging strategies and attracts lots of risk-taking investors hoping to make a profit. Countless institutional as well as individual investors will jump at the opportunity of electronic trading. Today investors can easily acquire a sufficiently diversified basket of, say, 20 stocks for a small fee based on sound advice. In doing so, they may well beat the (frequently below par) returns of professional fund managers while at the same time avoiding costly brokerage or management fees. Widespread online trading will present a major challenge to brokerage houses and mutual funds unless those institutions transform themselves into facilitators of this activity. Much of their focus in the future will be on educating their clients about the ins and outs of finance, filling a considerable knowledge gap among the vast majority of households concerning securities and personal financial planning. They will also focus on giving their clients highly customized advice about investment opportunities and risk profiles.[19] In the end bankers, fund managers and brokers will all compete intensely for the lucrative business of centralized cash and asset management for wealthy clients through multi-product packages earning user fees or membership subscriptions. Both individual and institutional investors will run internationally diversified portfolios, helped by advisors whose forte is global portfolio management.

Once the trading of securities and currencies has moved online, barriers to the global integration of financial markets will come down. Online markets transcend physical boundaries, allowing them to become increasingly interconnected across regions and also across product categories (for instance bonds, stocks and derivatives). Financial product connections, manifest today in such crossover instruments as stock-index futures or bond-stock convertibles, will multiply as innovation in that direction intensifies. Pressure for market integration comes not least from the liquidity preference of traders converging to the site where sellers can find the most buyers and vice versa. New technology, in particular 'intelligent order routing' software which lets investors interested in a particular stock or bond scan all relevant exchanges, ECNs and brokers for the best combination of price, order size and speed, will do its share to link markets more closely. The precise configuration of such market integration depends on the kind of harmonized accounting, surveillance, oversight and listing rules that online financial markets will eventually be subjected to on a global scale. Just as traditional financial markets depend on an elaborate infrastructure of credit facilities (including broker loans, credit lines, overdraft facilities), so will future online exchanges be supported by cyber-cash-based supplies of funds in support of trading activity.

7.3.3 Fictitious (Financial) Capital

While the internet will spur cyberbanking and online financial markets, its impact on finance will be even deeper. Specifically, it will accelerate the trend away from loans to securities. These two credit channels represent fundamentally different types of financial capital. Bank loans, until now the primary locus of money creation, may be characterized as *interest-bearing loan capital* which ties the lender's funds to the borrower's income-creating activity. This linkage expresses itself through various aspects of the contractual engagement between the two sides of the credit relation: the borrower promising the lender a predetermined sum of the income gain in interest; the sharing of losses in case of investment failure; and assets acquired by the loan serving as collateral.

Unlike loans, securities are contracts which can be traded in organized financial markets. Their value derives principally from the capitalization of future income streams which their holders expect to earn.[20] Yielding capital gains as a primary source of income, this type of financial capital depends on the evolution of market expectations rather than on the actual workings of productive capital as in the case of loans. Such disassociation from the underlying 'real' economy of production leads us to characterize securities as *fictitious capital*, a more dynamic mechanism of finance which enables borrowers to tap a much larger supply of funds at lower costs and helps investors to manage risk more effectively.[21] The principal attractiveness of fictitious capital for investors lies in its ability to generate returns which may – at least temporarily – grow much faster than other types of income.

Fictitious capital is certainly not a new phenomenon. It began in earnest with the appearance of stock markets and government bonds during the late 19th century. This type of financial capital had a major boost during the interwar period when we moved from the gold standard to elastic credit-money. Several economists (see note 21 above) have actually characterized credit-money itself to be a sort of fictitious capital, based on its creation 'ex nihilo' by banks investing their excess reserves of which additional supplies can be generated at will. While such money typically gives rise to interest-bearing loan capital due to its creation in acts of bank lending, it also anchors its fictitious-capital nature through its ties to government bonds which the central banks buy to increase bank reserves available for money creation. This link will intensify dramatically in the era of cybercash. Once this new type of credit-money will have moved beyond being just an online extension of traditional payment mechanisms to become an autonomous money form capable of self-expansion, issuers of cybercash will be able to expand their money-creation capacity by acquiring all kinds of securities with which to back the new money. We can therefore expect new supplies of cybercash to be directed to a much larger degree toward securities markets than was the case in the era of paper money. As credit-money, newly issued cybercash tokens will be transferred from issuers to users not only via e-loans, in the form of gift certificates or as reward coupons, but also through security purchases by the money issuer who thereby injects liquidity into financial markets.[22]

The emerging fusion of electronic credit-money and securities can already be discerned in the fact that stocks, a quintessential form of fictitious capital giving corporations a 'market value' quite apart from the 'book value' of their productive assets, now serve increasingly as money. Companies pay their managers and salaried employees with stock options. They also issue stock for employer contributions to their employees' private pension plans, such as the popular 401(k) accounts. And stock swaps are the preferred payment method for mergers and acquisitions, especially during a bull market. Once money and securities are both just digitalized bits of information, they can be connected so that they become interchangeable.

The ability to connect different financial instruments in digitalized format will spur increasingly complex, multi-layered financing arrangements. We have already witnessed the propensity of fictitious capital to organize its own self-expansion by tying different credit channels and securities together, as in the case of rebundling loans into asset-backed securities or when linking stocks, bonds and currencies to financial futures and other types of derivatives. Such linkages serve the dual purpose of generating more funds while at the same time spreading risks over a greater number of investors. For every dollar mobilized to fund production and exchange activities in the 'real' economy, the market-makers of fictitious capital organize several dollars worth of interdependent financial transactions – a trend greatly intensified when playing itself out on the internet where such information-based innovation has a chance to thrive like never before. In the absence of regulatory constraints on its issue and circulation, cybercash may very well nourish the spread of fictitious capital online by providing liquidity support for its various components in any given set of contractual commitments and tradeable claims. Cybercash issuers, whether banks, ISPs or any other type of online infomediary, will thus in all likelihood come to play a crucial role in the financial markets which comprise the infrastructure of fictitious capital.

7.3.4 Derivative Trading and Credit Securitization

Once operating online, fictitious capital will fuel the proliferation of derivatives (futures, options, swaps) whose value is linked to some underlying financial instrument such as currencies, bonds or stocks. Financial derivatives have already become the principal tool of risk management, because they enable investors to hedge against adverse future price movements. They are also attractive to speculators seeking to earn capital gains from correctly anticipated price movements. Speculators' returns on capital are larger for any given price change, the more debt they use to finance their positions – the so-called *leverage effect*. This incentive to indebtedness by speculators provides an opening for banks to profit from the derivative business, as lenders as well as counterparties in trades. According to data supplied by the US Comptroller of the Currency, the nominal value of derivatives on the books of US banks, not counting off-balance-sheet transactions, grew from $6.8 trillion in 1990 to $51.3 trillion in 2001. Derivative trading may grow even more spectacularly on the internet where cyberbanks can accommodate the speculators' search for leverage by tying their electronic credit-money to overdraft facilities, margin credit and contractual commitments concerning collateral or revenue sharing.

What drives both hedgers and speculators to derivatives is price volatility in the commodity and financial markets. But these kinds of contract, which can be traded either on open exchanges or less publicly over the counter, will move beyond price risk to apply to all kinds of other situations carrying risk.[23] Companies, investors and lenders will design new derivatives designed to reduce their exposure to a variety of financial risks. Take, for instance, credit derivatives which insure against corporate bankruptcy by promising to pay back the lender's money in exchange for a premium. This instrument, only introduced in 1995, is today a $360 billion market. Other insurance products, such as performance bonds which protect people doing business on the web, could conceivably be reconfigured into tradeable derivatives to spread the risk associated with such guarantees. Enron, before its fall from grace, pioneered a number of innovative derivatives for traders to bet on electricity prices, telecommunications bandwidth and even the influence of the weather. The likely proliferation of new types of derivatives traded online is part of the internet's proclivity to develop secondary markets for various products not currently listed on futures exchanges (such as VerticalNet's market for dynamic random access memory). Apart from being ideally suited for the task of bringing together a large number of buyers and sellers, the internet also lends itself to innovation with regard to information-rich products, such as derivatives.

The internet will provide financial engineers, who view every investment as a bundle of separable risks and rewards to be parceled out to the highest bidder, with plenty of opportunity to come up with new products. Not only will their innovative design work lead to a greater variety of derivative contracts, such as strips or swaps, but it will also push us much farther along the securitization of credit which repackages loans into securities.[24] Today real estate finance in the United States is entirely dominated by the market for mortgage-backed securities. Efforts are under way to do the same for home equity loans, car loans, student loans and credit-card debt, all of which will be increasingly repackaged into securities whose value is backed by the payment streams from the underlying loans. Credit securitization may very well extend to short-term inventory loans, commercial leases, and perhaps even small-business loans. Very useful for banks and other lenders will be the possibility of liquidating nonperforming loans by repackaging them into attractively priced securities, an innovation which has already taken a first step with the spreading practice of selling bad debts online for pennies on the dollar (for example DebtAuction.com and Debtforsale.com).

Asset-backed securities will continue to thrive, because they benefit lenders as a source of fee income and convenient method to unload their loans while offering investors attractive risk-return profiles. As they become a mainstay of our online credit system, these instruments will go beyond securitizing existing pools of loans and actively open up new avenues of credit financing. I am thinking here in particular of microcredits to individuals setting up their own businesses which may be pooled and repackaged into securities to provide venture capital for the masses. Such a financing mechanism would help to unleash a wave of entrepreneurial initiative which up to now has been blocked by lack of affordable access to external funds. More generally, asset-backed securities may open the way for a whole new system of retail credit aimed at helping individuals to invest in their human capital. In the not-so-distant future we can expect qualifying households to have access to a variety of funding options for self-improvement efforts, such as education credit, training bonuses, launch funds for new business projects, installment credit for purchases of knowledge-based capital goods and services and so forth. In return, individual borrowers will provide their backers in the asset-backed securities markets with lots of details about their financial condition, akin to the balance sheet and income statements supplied by corporations today. It is even quite conceivable that individual households will be subject to market evaluation on the basis of publicly accessible *wealth accounts* comprising all their assets and liabilities as well as current and future income-earning potential. Depending on their wealth-account position, individuals will have more or less access to funds and pay lower or higher returns, similar to the rating of corporate creditworthiness by Moody's or Standard & Poor. We may one day see hundreds of online rating agencies evaluating and grading the wealth accounts of millions of households.[25]

The widespread presence of wealth accounts presumes, of course, that individuals will be willing to furnish voluntarily lots of details about themselves in return for capital backing. Such commodification of information, surely one way to get around privacy-protection issues, is greatly facilitated by the internet's data-collection capacity and cybercash's recording of such information flows. But if and when personal wealth accounts become standard practice, it will be only a small step for individual agents to use their assets as collateral for additional funding from others. Rather than providing these funds through illiquid loans, investors may prefer to offer their funds in exchange for liquid securities that can be resold. Who knows what prospective borrowers will be able to securitize in the future? Any source of future income creation could be used to issue securities against, provided that investors can be found who are willing to bet on that asset's future.

Cybercash is ideally suited for the accelerating trend of credit securitization. While there will always be space for loans, the primary form of credit will be securities traded in organized financial markets. The greater the proportion of money created in acts of securities purchases rather than loan extension, the larger the volume of transactions in financial markets and the broader the variety of securities issued by borrowers. When banks began a couple of decades ago to beef up their stock of securities in lieu of lending, all kinds of new securities came to the fore – brokered deposits, negotiable certificates of deposit, euromarket notes, commercial paper, junk bonds and a large variety of derivatives contracts (such as bond futures, interest swaps). Projecting this trend forward, we can foresee an explosion of innovation concerning tradeable financial claims made possible by the liquidity support of cybercash. We will see many new types of securities arise in coming years.

7.4 Intangible Capital and Fictitious Capital

The exercise of projecting possible scenarios about the internet's impact
on the modus operandi of our economy drives us to the prediction that this
new medium, once reinforced by its own unique type of electronic money,
will give rise to two new forms of capital – intangible (productive) capital
in knowledge-based production and fictitious (financial) capital mobilized
through online securities markets. Cybercash feeds the growth of both
intangible capital and fictitious capital by codifying the information underlying both and facilitating their valuation. An immaterial money form, it
corresponds to the virtual nature of these new forms of capital and is
particularly well equipped to intensify linkages between them. The integration of cybercash, intangible capital produced by b-webs and fictitious
capital mobilizing online credit will give our economic system an additional dimension, a sort of *virtual capitalism* in cyberspace, thriving on
global competition and fast-paced innovation. This triangular force will
eventually reshape existing norms of socioeconomic behavior as well as
traditional organizational models wherever it is allowed to sink in.

7.4.1 The Fusion of Intangible and Fictitious Capital

The advantages of virtual capitalism are manifold. Perhaps its most important benefit is much faster productivity growth which will raise the speed
limit of the economy. Such improvement will come about with a combination of more efficient corporate organization and customization of
product offerings. The extension of markets on the internet creates broader
categories of tradeable assets and a wider variety of income-generating
opportunities for many actors. These benefits will be pursued most aggressively by a new brand of entrepreneurs who master the fusion of intangible
and fictitious capital for online products that yield significant scope
economies and/or network economies. In the process these innovators will
create all kinds of new infomediaries which end up dominating their niche
of e-commerce.

Attempts to integrate its two pillars, intangible (productive) capital and
fictitious (financial) capital, will be the hallmark of virtual capitalism.
After all, did not the internet itself emerge in such a fusion? The proliferation of e-commerce models by dot-com start-ups was funded by a combination of venture capital, stock options, IPOs and booming share prices for
high-tech stocks (see Chapter 3). Once established, e-commerce provided
a fabulous outlet for online infomediaries creating new markets that they

managed to control, as demonstrated by eBay, E*Trade and a host of other dot-com pioneers. Today we are pushing the fusion further. Take, for instance, the partnership between insurance company Swiss Re and M-Cam to appraise and insure a firm's intellectual property so that it might be used as collateral for loans. This is a first step towards using intangible capital for the issue of derivatives or asset-backed securities funding its accumulation.

7.4.2 The Enron Scandal

While the profit opportunities opened up by such an integration of intangible and fictitious capitals are bountiful, the process is also fraught with new dangers. A perfect case study of the latter is Enron. In the 1990s, this regional natural-gas and electricity utility used deregulation of the energy industry and the emergence of the internet to transform itself into an info-mediary which in a matter of a just a few years managed to become the seventh-largest US company. At least initially the phenomenal growth of Enron was a well-deserved reward for path-breaking innovation. First it used the internet to add or draw power from a grid of wired power plants in response to sudden demand or price changes. This technology enabled Enron to parlay itself into the nation's leading wholesale trader of electricity just when this activity exploded in volume following deregulation. Enron then set up an online marketplace where companies all over the world could buy or sell electricity, oil, natural gas, coal, metals, plastics, pulp, paper and broadband. As its trading capacity and expertise expanded, the company engaged more and more in trading new types of derivatives which ultimately made it resemble more a hedge fund than an energy company.

Its innovation-driven growth ambitions required Enron to raise a lot of capital which in turn depended on an investment-grade credit rating and rising share prices. In order to maintain both, the company moved many assets off its balance sheet into complex partnerships, creating in the process 4000-plus special-purpose entities, many of which were controlled by its own financial managers. Once it began to use these partnerships to hide debt, cover up losses, boost reported earnings and pay off insiders, the company turned into a criminal enterprise for whom discovery of its illegal manipulations would ultimately spell instant death. Amidst all the public outcry over the misdeeds of Enron's top managers responsible for the largest bankruptcy in US history, we forget that those very same people were once heralded as pioneers building the model company of the New

Economy. Nor is it easy in the wake of the scandal to focus on some deeper lessons from that fiasco.

For one, Enron's tragedy proves the danger of success. Having achieved market domination on the basis of brilliant and well-executed ideas, the firm's top managers became greedy, arrogant and megalomaniac to the point where they were willing to break the law in order to ensure continued success. This self-destructive human trait was also evident with Drexel's Michael Milken cornering the junk-bond market he had set up in the late 1980s. And that same mixture of overconfidence and greed drove John Merriwether's hedge fund Long-Term Capital Management in 1998 to bet the house on price adjustments in derivative trades modeled by three Nobel Prize winners which, in the context of a global financial crisis, could not possibly come true. If success catapults ambitious business leaders over the edge of lawful behavior, we need a strong system of checks and balances to contain this dangerous propensity. One truly remarkable thing about Enron was how effectively this company used a pro-business climate and political muscle to demobilize every single institutional check on its actions – auditors, government regulators, creditors, rating agencies, stock analysts, institutional investors and even its own board of directors.[26]

Another important lesson from the Enron scandal concerns the proliferation of creative accounting practices designed to present corporate performance in a more favorable light than is actually the case. Such misrepresentation of balance sheets and income statements is very much a byproduct of fictitious capital whose very nature allows separation of actual cash flows and valuations from what companies report, a striking feature of contemporary capitalism which began to make its presence felt in the 1970s when historic cost accounting allowed companies to declare massive inflation-induced paper profits from underreporting their costs. Since then companies have perfected the art of paper profits by manipulating the amounts, timing and classification of items in their financial statements to their advantage. They can stretch out payments by classifying them as capital expenditures to be amortized over years rather than expensed all at once, treat debt as capital, book income before they have received it and set up partnerships for transactions designed to hide liabilities or boost income artificially. The possibilities of self-serving manipulation through creative accounting are endless, as Enron and many others have demonstrated.

The desire to embellish actual performance thrives in a climate where managers' foremost objective is to boost their firm's stock price. Their pay, much of it composed of bonuses and stock options, depends largely on how much earnings they report and stock-market reactions to those

numbers. Unlike bank loan officers who prefer conservative earnings esti-
mates and realistic capital valuations, shareholders demand better
numbers, no matter how, for their capital gains. Thus there exists enormous pressure to maximize stock-market valuations and for that purpose
use accounting practices which hide bad news or generate more paper
profit. When the techniques to do so have become so complex that the
chief executive officers and board directors no longer understand them, it
is easier for the firm's financial specialists to manipulate operating results.
They are supported in this exercise by compromised accounting firms for
whom audits have become loss-leaders to generate more lucrative
consulting business. How can a firm be properly audited by outside
accountants who in their other role as consultants may have helped to
design that firm's architecture of deceit? Collusion extends to stock
analysts inclined to make favorable announcements regarding a firm's
stock so that their employers can get more investment-banking businesses
and so pay them higher bonuses.[27] Nor does it help to have the Financial
Accounting Standards Board (FASB), the private-sector agency defining
generally accepted accounting practices in the United States, dominated by
the big five accounting firms and intense corporate lobbying efforts. At the
same time the government regulator, the SEC, lacks the resources for
effective enforcement of financial-reporting rules.

A third lesson from the Enron scandal concerns the dangers of fusing
intangible and fictitious capital into a *Ponzi scheme*, where the firm guarantees investors high returns which are paid out from funds supplied by an
ever-greater numbers of investors.[28] In the new world of virtual capitalism, Ponzi schemes are often fuelled by the schemer's reliance on ever-
rising stock prices which attract new rounds of funds to pay off earlier
investors. Such a scheme can enrich many people while it works, but will
implode when it fails to achieve the exponential increase in fund suppliers
necessary for its sustenance. Enron's spectacular rise and fall is an important case study of such a Ponzi scheme gone wrong.

During the 1990s Enron amassed a considerable amount of intangible
capital – a combination of highly skilled human capital, well-connected
management, a gung-ho corporate culture and path-breaking product
development – to transform itself from a regional energy supplier into a
global commodities trader and hedge fund. Riding a wave of successful
innovations and filling the spaces opened by deregulation, Enron projected
very rapid revenue growth to boost its stock price and then used its
increased market capitalization to borrow billions in the world's capital
markets. From the very beginning of its ambitious transformation, the
company relied on creative accounting techniques to artificially boost

reported revenues. Using its exemption from brokerage regulations and oversight by the Commodities Futures Trading Commission (CFTC), Enron recorded as revenue the total amount of its energy trades rather than just the profits made on each trade as is typical at brokerage firms.[29] An accounting technique known as 'mark to market' allowed the company to book immediately future earnings it forecast on energy deals. Enron's financial engineers also structured several of its now-infamous partnerships so as to make the parent company appear to generate cash from operations rather than from its financing activities.[30]

Matching its rising capitalization on Wall Street with similarly spectacular increases in debt to finance its highly leveraged trading operations and ambitious product-development plans, Enron soon began to face what Minsky (1982) has described as Ponzi finance: the need to borrow more just to service the old debt. Such a situation, compounded in Enron's case by notoriously inadequate cash flow due to a series of underperforming assets and low-margin trading, threatened its investment-grade credit rating and stock price – the two pillars of its breathtaking expansion. Trying to make its debt-heavy balance sheets look less vulnerable, the company's financial engineers set up an intricate web of thousands of partnerships to take billions in underperforming assets and liabilities off its books.[31] Many of these partnerships were backed by Enron stock to lure outside investors and had 'trigger point' provisions (expressed in terms of stock-price floors and credit-rating downgrades) which required the parent company to pump more stock into the vehicle or declare partnership losses as its own.

These timebombs began to go off when Wall Street's euphoria with Enron turned sour in the wake of the dot-com crash and questions began to arise about the wisdom of its aggressive expansion into broadband and fiber optics. A sustained decline in Enron's stock price and mounting losses accumulating in several key partnerships began to put relentless pressure on the company's Byzantine and fragile financing structure. In March 2001 Enron secretly bailed out a quartet of partnerships known as Raptors which had originally been set up as risk insurance for its now sharply devalued portfolio of volatile technology stocks. More trouble soon brewed with other key partnerships, notably Chewco and Jedi. After announcing large losses from contingent liabilities tied to its Raptor and LJM partnerships in October 2001, the entire house of cards that was Enron vaporized in a matter of weeks.[32]

7.4.3 New Systemic Risks

The story of Enron's rise and fall provides us with a window into the future of virtual capitalism. The picture which emerges is contradictory. On the one hand, the internet will render our system more stable by making it more flexible. Highly automated and horizontally organized b-webs operating online will respond much more rapidly to shifts in demand than the vertically integrated manufacturing giants of yesteryear were able to. Intangible capital embodied in humans is much more easily redeployed than the physical capital of plant and equipment. Shortened life cycles of online products put a premium on fast-paced innovation which aggressively managed firms with a promising e-business model, especially infomediaries at the center of newly emerging markets, can finance through mass mobilization of funds from eager investors. But herein lies a huge danger. Enron has demonstrated in stunning fashion how rapidly fictitious capital can disappear when euphoric sentiments in financial markets are proved wrong. While bankers usually stick with troubled borrowers to avoid having to write off a loan as a loss, investors in securities have an exit option which they tend to use en masse once bad news has created enough fear. Their flights to safety will often have avalanche-like quality, because market expectations tend to homogenize towards the extremes and highly leveraged investors are often forced to sell into a declining market. Such an avalanche can make a $70 billion company like Enron disappear in a couple of months.

Enron-like incidences of financial instability have to be put into the broader context of the credit cycle which plays an important role in the cyclical fluctuations of our economy by supplying too much credit during booms and not enough during downturns. Credit overextension through the bank-lending channel is usually tempered by the more cautious credit-risk evaluations of relatively conservative bank loan officers and the finite limitations placed on interest by the borrower's income-creation capacity. No such restraints operate in securities markets where asset-price bubbles can build to generate capital gains which no other form of capital income can match in growth potential. Asset-price bubbles, like the one NASDAQ's high-tech stocks experienced in the late 1990s, may very well become more potent in the future when fed by additional supplies of cybercash which its issuers create through purchases of securities and also in the wake of their securities portfolios gaining in value. Bigger and longer-lived bubbles tend to burst more violently than small and short-lived ones.[33] The highly pro-cyclical pattern of fictitious capital generates considerable *systemic risk* that a financial crisis may spread out of control to the point of paralyzing economic activity. This is especially likely if and when the bursting of a bubble forces cybercash issuers to cut back their supplies or triggers flights out of private e-money.

With fictitious capital, the systemic risk of a financial crisis spinning out of control does not just concern avalanche-like collapses of securities prices, but also the potential for contagion through increasingly inter-twined financial markets. Derivatives, for instance, are by their very design connected to other securities markets and will affect those immedi-ately in moments of crisis. As was made clear during the last decade by several instances of huge losses suffered in derivatives trading (as in the case of Orange County, Metallgesellschaft, Barings, Daiwa Bank, Sumitomo, Long-Term Capital Management and Allied Irish Banks), these instruments are dangerous in their complexity, have markets that dry up easily during episodes of instability and often affect underlying stock, bond and currency markets to which they are tied. Asset-backed securities also carry considerable systemic risk as untested financing instruments with unpredictable behavioral patterns (for instance prepayment risk) and in their linkage to bank lending. As the locus of instability has increasingly shifted from bank-based credit crunches to turbulence in financial markets, the Fed has been able to adjust its crisis-management operations quite effectively – from its audacious intervention in the stock-market crash of October 1987 to engineering the bail-out of Long-Term Capital Manage-ment in August 1998. Let us see whether the central banks will be able to cope equally well with future financial crises, especially those that involve a considerable degree of monetary turmoil in the wake of massive e-money destruction and panic flights out of private cybercash.

The Enron story points here to an entirely new systemic risk, namely that the revelation of a seemingly successful company having been nothing but a high-risk Ponzi scheme masked by accounting trickery destroys investor confidence in the transparency, fairness and self-regulation capacity of financial markets. The media are inclined to present Enron as the imperfect child of an otherwise healthy system. More appro-priate perhaps would be to look at Enron instead as the perfect child of an unhealthy system. In the aftermath of its spectacular collapse, we have seen how inaccurate financial statements can be when there is widespread use of creative accounting, how compromised auditors and stock analysts have become in the face of acute conflicts of interest and how ineffective government regulators are when they are subject to intense lobbying pres-sure and ideological animosity towards their job. Unless addressed, these problems will only deepen in the world of virtual capitalism. How do you value a firm using mostly intangible capital as production input? Which accounting standards are appropriate for tomorrow's online b-webs engaged in a myriad of intra-network transactions? How do investors maintain reasoned judgment during the euphoria of asset-price bubbles and protect themselves when those bubbles burst? What can be done when the sudden collapse of confidence turns market liquidity into an illusion and destroys the capital base of firms? These and other questions force us to contemplate new public policy responses to the challenges arising from the integration of intangible capital, fictitious capital and electronic money in cyberspace.

CHAPTER 8

Cyberspace and Public Policy

As the internet assumes a central role in our lives and remakes our economy, it posits major challenges for policy-makers. Its growing presence has already raised serious concerns about privacy protection and safety, complicated the collection of indirect taxes (value-added taxes, sales taxes), enhanced the possibilities for tax evasion or money laundering and undermined the ability of governments to control the territorial space under their jurisdiction. With the internet anchoring itself ever more as a vector of change, it will impact on many public policies. These will have to be adjusted to a new reality, the omnipresence of cyberspace as a medium of interaction and the implications of its virtual nature for the organization of society.

The internet's power as a global information network operating with lightning speed is also what makes it so dangerous to public policy-makers. By allowing instant interaction between any number of actors anywhere and anytime, the internet eviscerates traditional constraints anchored in physical space, tangible (thus relatively inert) resources and slower moving time. Long-established mechanisms of control and modes of operation are rendered obsolete, needing to be replaced by new ones better fit for the virtual world of cyberspace. E-businesses and e-marketplaces require effective e-government, anchored within a very different kind of governance through which we give society its normative context. What used to be a world of direct interaction based on physical contact between actors now becomes a world of computer-mediated communication where the actors relate to each other only indirectly, by means of networked machines, without being in touch with each other. In such a computerized world, where the meaning of the social in us no longer rests on commonly shared experiences, the government's source of legitimation, modes of intervention and policy objectives will all change fundamentally. If we let the internet develop its own money, traditionally the apex of state authority, then governments all over the world will soon have no choice but to adapt to the new realities of virtual capitalism.

Policy-makers all over the world have already begun to get a sense of the internet's wide-ranging effects on their domain. Challenges abound across the entire spectrum of government intervention. It is quite evident that the facility of cross-border money flows online seriously threatens government control over its territory and subjects. If e-money can flow from one corner of the world to another as if national boundaries no longer existed, then it becomes considerably more difficult to track funds. Money laundering, already a serious concern in light of globally organized criminal organizations (such as the Mafia, drug cartels and al-Qaida), will find many new routes with cybercash. The same holds true for tax evasion. Indirect business taxes charged on goods and services, an important source of government revenue (sales taxes in the United States, value-added taxes elsewhere), will be difficult to collect online. The Microsoft case has made clear that existing antitrust policies, designed for an industrial economy dominated by manufacturing of goods, do not apply very effectively when technology is the issue of contention or when companies extend their reach across a variety of industries. Fast-paced innovation concerning online products also puts into question the efficacy of intellectual property rights, as the internet vastly accelerates both the diffusion of ideas and the pace of competition-driven product development. And what will happen to prevailing trade rules when a growing number of products are directly produced and distributed through a global communication network that ignores national borders? Over the last five years policy-makers across the globe have started to debate how best to respond to these questions raised by the arrival of e-commerce (section 8.1).

Rather than responding to the policy challenges of cyberspace on an ad hoc basis, politicians will realize that the internet requires a more coherent approach. Such coherence will inevitably seek to establish itself around the question of *information management*. This question has already sneaked up on policy-makers as a problem of privacy protection, with the uncontrolled gathering of data by businesses posing a barrier to the public trust necessary for the sustenance of e-commerce. It becomes an even more urgent question when applied to safety, with new types of electronic crime – from digital identity theft to cyberterrorism – raising the specter of massive disruption. Soon regulators will have to decide how to revamp accounting and financial-disclosure rules for tomorrow's e-businesses. It is at that point, when deciding how to value intangible capital and record the intricate arrangements of fictitious capital, that policy-makers will come to appreciate the public policy challenge of the internet as one of information management (section 8.2).

As the internet pervades our economy, it will surely affect the conduct of macroeconomic policy by which governments seek to stabilize an economy prone to cyclical fluctuations and inequalities. Typically governments use both fiscal and monetary policies for the purpose of macroeconomic stabilization, and both will be significantly impacted by structural changes due to the internet. Apart from having to work out how to tax online activity, governments will also be pressured to reorient their spending priorities. With capital more mobile than ever, countries will compete intensely with each other for their fair share of global investment flows. This means creating promising resource pools capable of attracting foreign investors, a task that will require more government spending on the infrastructure (energy, transportation, communications) as well as on the human capital embodied in the nation's labor force (health care, education). Monetary policy too will undergo many changes once central banks have to deal with cybercash fuelling online activity. As central bankers struggle with the management of online money supplies and the dynamic of interest rates in a world of computerized finance, they will inevitably have to rethink their regulation of online finance and their crisis-management interventions (section 8.3).

Since cybercash is a supranational money form, the monetary regime emerging in its wake is equally global in nature. International monetary arrangements will thus be at the center of this regime. Central banks will have to cooperate intensely, if they want to ensure a properly balanced distribution of money flows and the good behavior of globally interconnected financial markets. Such cooperation centers in all likelihood on co-management of the payments system within which e-money circulates and is kept convertible. Over the long run we may see those efforts move us closer to the utopia of a single international currency. This idea, which dates back to the end of World War II when Keynes proposed his Bancor Plan, becomes more realistic once the monetary authorities have to deal with a truly stateless money form and globally integrated financial markets (section 8.4).[1]

8.1 The Internet as Public Policy Challenge

When the internet emerged in the mid-1990s as the engine of an unprecedented boom fuelled by massive business spending on information technologies, it soon gave rise to the optimistic notion of a New Economy in which rapid productivity gains would ensure faster economic growth at low inflation rates. That vision had global reach, prompting many traditional societies to question how to adapt their risk-averse and stability-bound cultures to the turbulent New Economy thriving on change and risk. As less dynamic societies in Europe and Asia looked with envy at the American model of entrepreneurship, innovation, mobility and flexibility, many governments there began a painful process of structural reforms.

Now that the e-crash of 2000–01 has cooled off the once-relentless hype about the New Economy, governments all over the world have a chance to consider the long-term impact of the internet on their economy. Some will surely use the breathing space to delay painful choices that must be made for the sake of necessary reform. But any responsible government will have to realize that the internet is here to stay, that its power to transform economic activity is truly profound and that this transformation will have major repercussions for economic policy. In the United States these realizations seem to have spurred some serious thinking in both political parties about appropriate high-tech policy agendas. During the 2000 elections the Democrats' E-Agenda competed with the Republicans' E-Contract 2000 for support of the crucial information-technology community, with both platforms pledging increased cybersecurity, investment-enhancing tax breaks, a tax moratorium for e-commerce, benefits for telecommuters, more work permits for high-skilled foreigners, promotion of high-speed internet access and better digital opportunities for the disadvantaged.[2] As these policy debates are taking root, certain already-manifest issues associated with the internet weigh in as priorities in search of a pragmatic solution.

8.1.1 Money Laundering

The internet enables economic actors to regroup and transact in a virtual world which compresses time and transcends space. Governments worry with good reason about the ability of subjects under their jurisdiction to operate online beyond their reach. That concern has crystallized not least around the question of money laundering. Criminals need to 'wash' their 'dirty' (meaning illicitly earned) money by moving it from their illegal sources to legitimate businesses used as cover. Willy-nilly the banks and other financial institutions help them to accomplish this task, thus making it possible for criminal organizations to organize on a large scale much like multinational corporations. Whether they trade in drugs, arms, people, confidential information or smuggled goods, modern crime cartels have become a major threat to the law-and-order capacity of governments. All across the world we see corrupt government officials using their power for the benefit of criminal organizations or countries plunged into civil wars fuelled by the vested interests of the global 'underground' economy (for instance the role of diamonds in wars devastating a large swath of Africa from Sierra Leone to Congo). One can fight these organizations effectively only by choking off their money-laundering and transfer networks. Unfortunately, the internet provides new outlets for illicit movements of funds which are even harder to control than traditional routes.

Since a large portion of laundered money flows across borders, the problem requires cooperation among national authorities under the auspices of international organizations. The OECD has for this purpose launched the Financial Action Task Force on Money Laundering where the leading industrial nations have a chance to develop a coordinated approach to the problem. The United Nations, the BIS and regional groupings such as the EU and the Organization of American States have all issued reports and policy recommendations with regard to money laundering. The key issue addressed by these organizations concerns reporting requirements imposed on financial institutions, especially in off-shore banking areas providing clients a great deal of secrecy. Those efforts have intensified dramatically in the aftermath of the 11 September attacks on New York and Washington which have prompted an intense effort by the US government to rein in terrorist financing. Hitherto reluctant banks are now being pushed much harder to adopt tougher regulations and cooperate with the authorities. Policy-makers will soon have to start thinking about money laundering via cybercash, an issue not yet apparent on their radar screen.

8.1.2 Tax Collection

One of the more hotly contested policy challenges concerning the internet has been the question of taxing e-commerce. How do you collect sales taxes or value-added taxes in cyberspace where buyers and sellers can be easily located in different states or nations? The US Congress has pre-empted this issue with the Internet Tax Freedom Act of 1998, a three-year tax moratorium on e-commerce transactions which has been extended by another two years. While this moratorium only applies to new levies, local and state governments have not been able to collect their existing sales taxes from merchants outside their borders. Such power requires Congressional authorization. Even with such authority, e-commerce taxation will be difficult due to the incredibly varied nature of sales taxes. The United States has over 7500 state, county, city and special tax districts, each with its own system of sales-tax rates, qualifying items, exemptions and collection procedures.

With sales taxes in the United States averaging 6.3 percent, e-commerce has enjoyed a significant subsidy in excess of $2 billion (in 2001) from uncollected taxes. Brick-and-mortar retailers are complaining loudly about this unfair advantage given to their competitors online. And both state and local governments look with dread at the growing erosion of their revenue base which depends so heavily on sales taxes. There is no reason why online merchants should be getting such a free ride on taxes. While any sudden imposition of indirect taxes on e-commerce will considerably cramp online spending by typically price-sensitive e-shoppers in the short run, such price elasticity of online demand is sure to be less pronounced in the long run.

The ability of states and municipalities to collect sales taxes depends, however, on radical simplification of the tax code, a prerequisite for congressional tax-collection authority and cooperation of the business community. For that purpose thirty-two states have launched the Streamlined Sales Tax Project which would establish a single rate in each state, harmonize rules across state lines and create a more centralized tax-collection system. This project has had a difficult time producing results due to opposition from local governments seeing their taxing power undermined and from four states strongly dependent on high-tech industries (California, Massachusetts, Virginia and Colorado). The same type of problem exists elsewhere with regard to value-added taxes in cross-border transactions. The European Union has pointed the way to a solution here. After harmonizing the VAT systems of member nations as part of its single-market project a decade ago, the EU has had little trouble imposing such taxes on e-commerce and since December 2001 has even required non-European companies to collect value-added taxes on sales of digital products to EU customers. In the meantime, the OECD continues its work of building a consensus among industrial nations on new rules for taxation of e-commerce.[3]

8.1.3 The Digital Divide

Capitalism puts a premium on efficiency over equality. Its operation, under the impersonal laws of market regulation, gives rise to significant inequalities in the distribution of income, wealth and opportunities. If allowed to grow too far, these inequalities can undermine the workings of the system by limiting markets, creating social tensions and inviting political turmoil.

Even though their own games of political favoritism often make the inequality problem worse, governments have the ability to counteract distributional gaps thanks to their tax, spending and regulatory powers. Ever since the end of World War II the governments of rich industrial nations have been committed to use these powers for redistribution purposes, through a combination of progressive taxes and income-maintenance programs. Now they face a new source of inequality caused by class differences in access to the internet which may leave a significant portion of the population deprived of this medium's benefits. Part of the problem is transitional, with the internet first being used by those best able to afford the investment in machinery and literacy. As spreading usage lowers access and set-up costs, more people from less privileged strata will try the leap online. This uneven diffusion pattern has been empirically confirmed by much faster user growth rates among lower income groups in the United States during recent years. Such a catching-up pattern can also be witnessed in other parts of the world, above all Europe and East Asia, where the internet is gradually becoming a mass product as well. Still, the 'digital divide' between rich and poor persists, raising worries about the long-term implications of systemically unequal access to the internet for society.[4]

We ought to consider internet access a public good whose enormous social benefits should not be kept from anyone. Those unable to access the net will find themselves condemned to a poverty that comes with a lack of information. Universal access to the internet should thus be a major public policy goal in the information age. Governments have indeed undertaken major initiatives in this direction. The Clinton/Gore administration in particular made the digital divide a high policy priority. Its e-rate program, run by the Federal Communications Commission (FCC), reimbursed thousands of inner-city schools and public libraries for as much as 90 percent of the cost of wiring those buildings for internet access. Its Technology Opportunities Program provided matching grants to state and local-government agencies as well as community organizations for technology projects at schools, libraries, health agencies, police departments and nonprofits. Oddly, Bush has cut these popular programs, relying instead on block grants to states for education-technology programs. He also opposes the Democrats' push for tax breaks to companies bringing broadband internet access to poor and rural areas.[5] These political squabbles will only go so far, considering that today half of the new jobs for US workers without college degrees require daily use of computers, often including the internet. Behind the so-called digital divide lies a skills gap which harms the employability of low-income groups most vulnerable to unemployment, a loss from which the entire society suffers.

The question of unequal internet access will eventually move from the stark all-or-nothing dichotomy to a more nuanced problem. While the internet will be universally accessible in industrial nations, the degree of access will still vary greatly – from limited one-time access in schools, libraries and internet cafes all the way to superfast broadband service with multiple access tools. Even more pernicious than this hardware problem is the software problem of cyber-discrimination. As more and more online information becomes commodified and only available for a charge, e-businesses are likely to discriminate in their product development efforts in favor of carefully selected upscale customers being offered attractive packages for membership fees. Dot-com firms will be quite eager to lock in such high-margin customers willing to spend a lot and repeatedly. They will use the information they collect about site traffic to weed out high-risk and low-return consumers. When cybercash becomes a pillar of e-commerce, its presence will only reinforce digital inequality both in terms of its enhanced information-processing capabilities and its ties to credit allocation.

The internet's impact on inequality will extend beyond national boundaries to the world economy where the question of access to the latest technologies will shape globalization's greatest challenge, the growing gaps in income and living standards between rich and poor nations. Just as access to global capital markets makes all the difference to the industrialization potential of developing economies, so will access to the internet have a huge impact on a poor country's capabilities of insertion into the world economy. The rich countries too have a vested interest in extending easy internet access across the globe, not least because of network externalities from increased use and benefits accruing from a freer flow of information in the tackling of global problems, such as environmental protection or epidemics. Their e-businesses will surely want to have the option of reaching millions of newly middle-class consumers in the emerging-market economies of Latin America, Africa and Asia. The internet can also serve as useful communication and organization tool for democratic movements intent on improving the governance of their societies, just as it will surely boost grass-roots initiatives for political reform and corporate accountability in advanced capitalist societies. Most promising is the prospect of new telecommunication technologies, based on satellites, fiber optics and cable, giving poor countries instant internet-delivery capacity for a reasonable price and so offering them the chance to skip or shorten several stages in their industrialization process. The question, yet to be addressed, remains whether the rich countries will have the collective will to supply such reasonably priced internet-hardware access to the poorer countries. This objective should guide development aid and assistance programs aimed at poverty reduction.

8.1.4 Antitrust Policies and Intellectual Property Rights

The internet is bound to wreak havoc with established antitrust policy which was designed a century ago (for example America's 1890 Sherman Act and 1914 Clayton Act) to deal with the manufacturing giants of the industrial era. As already discussed in Chapter 7, corporations will organize entirely differently and the concept of monopoly power will gain new meaning in the internet era. The very notion of markets will become a lot more fluid when e-commerce firms bundle different kinds of products that stretch across several, hitherto separate sectors. Take, for instance, the multi-sector e-business model of AOL Time Warner or universal cyberbanks combining commercial banking, investment banking and insurance. For the same reason there will be a lot more technological tie-ins of the kind practiced by Microsoft when it bundled its web server and operating system. Indeed, the antitrust case brought against the software giant is a classic case study of the challenges imposed by New Economy firms in high-tech sectors on competition policy. Traditional responses, such as a break-up, might have deprived the company of significant scale and scope economies. Instead America's trust busters preferred an approach that gave Microsoft customers more choice of product alternatives and its competitors better terms for the sharing of technology.

When confronted with the accumulation dynamic of internet-based production, antitrust enforcers from the US Justice Department or the European Commission will continue their recently more relaxed attitude towards mergers and acquisitions. If anything, the minimum scale efficiency required for online producers is significantly larger than traditional manufacturers, in light of the internet's combination of scale, scope and network economies and the high costs of achieving brand loyalty among mobile, well-informed online shoppers. Instead, those regulators will shift their attention to new practices thriving on the internet, in particular the prevalence of joint ventures in research and development, possible collusion among large corporate buyers in B2B exchanges, the multivariate interactions between partners cooperating with each other in global b-webs and the (ab)use of asymmetric information advantages by online infomediaries. All this will require globally harmonized antitrust practices in the face of corporations without borders. The WTO may be an appropriate forum to that effect. Such harmonization has already made it onto the to-do list of policy-makers after the EU rejected the General Electric–Honeywell merger which the Americans had approved. The two sides will have to bridge fundamental differences in policy approach, with the Europeans stressing competition while the Americans emphasize consumer benefits and thus efficiency considerations. I suspect the latter point of view will gradually win out.

Going back to the precedent-setting Microsoft case, it is not surprising that its resolution relied heavily on technology transfer and information-sharing. These issues are normally assigned to the domain of intellectual property rights, an area of regulatory policy even more deeply affected by the internet than antitrust. On the one hand, such protection will become even more important for innovation-driven online firms whose ability to be first with a new product gives them the kind of temporary edge needed online for monopoly rents. On the other hand, what good does such a property right do when the protected innovation can be easily copied and ever so slightly altered by imitating competitors? The internet does not allow innovators to turn intellectual property rights into a claim to monopoly. Instead those rights are more like options with which to manage the revenue potential of their technological know-how. I expect intellectual property rights to expand their repertoire beyond individual patents, copyrights and trademarks by designing new collaborative property contracts which facilitate the sharing of know-how and accommodate the speedy diffusion of innovations.

8.1.5 Trade Rules

E-commerce depends on open global markets. National markets may simply be too small to justify high-risk investments in innovation. And the network economies prevailing on the internet encourage massive scale. While it costs very little to add new customers to a network, the benefits accruing to customers from expanding the network are quite large. This makes it irresistible for online firms to increase market size, especially for innovators seeking to exploit the advantages of being first. Free trade is also needed on the internet because of the innovation factor. For the first time in history we have a technology which makes data available world-wide. Engineers in developing countries, for instance, now have instant access to vast amounts of data and can communicate easily with their colleagues in other countries to learn what works and what does not. The unimpeded circulation of information will accelerate the global transmission of innovation which in turn will boost growth rates worldwide.

Yet free trade for the online economy is by no means assured. While we tend to conceive of e-commerce as inherently borderless, the reality is quite different. Online activity can be, and indeed often is, subjected to a myriad of barriers imposed by national governments for the purposes of protection. The country-specific address system for the internet, from which only American sites are exempted, gives repressive governments in China, Iran and elsewhere 'watchdog' control over domestic online traffic. Similar impediments arise from telecom monopolies and regulations in many countries, while excessively strict privacy rules may well end up hampering the flow of information across borders. Even more worrisome is the tendency of many governments in rich countries, such as France, Germany and Japan, to extend century-old protections of domestic producers or retailers to the internet.[6] Those barriers to e-trade hamper the flow of commerce even though many of them can be circumvented by ingenious e-shoppers conducting business on sites in other countries or downloading internet-based products which do not rely on physical delivery. Circumvention is only a second-best solution in light of additional search and transaction costs. Better would be removal of such barriers, supported by a uniform set of free-trade rules for borderless e-commerce.

Despite the good intentions of policy-makers there is no guarantee that we will ever see such free trade over the internet. Growing income inequalities and structural unemployment have created a worldwide backlash against the further liberalization of trade. Protectionist pressures from worried workers will only intensify in response to the heightened threat of job losses posed by the internet's revolutionary potential for automation of services. Services, the mainstay of the internet-based economy, have only recently become subject to international trade rules under the auspices of the WTO, notably with the General Agreement on Trade in Services (GATS) in 1994 which was followed by sectoral WTO agreements in 1998/99 for financial and telecommunication services. Many administrative and regulatory barriers to e-trade persist and have yet to be addressed by the WTO. They will only be tackled if and when WTO members move towards more uniform rules for competition policy and intellectual property rights.

As the WTO prepares for the next round of global trade negotiations, its agenda should include defining best-practice principles for e-commerce. Foreign online firms should not be discriminated against, governments should refrain from unnecessary measures restraining e-commerce and technological neutrality in regulatory treatment of online products versus real-world products should prevail wherever possible. Also needed are guidelines for the harmonization of indirect taxes collected from online sales which should include a prohibition against internet tariffs. The WTO will in all likelihood have a leadership role to play in this as well in the formulation of global privacy-protection rules, lest it allows regulatory differences between its members hamper the cross-border flow of information.

8.2 Information Management

So far governments have addressed the public policy challenges of the internet in piecemeal fashion, responding to isolated instances of regulatory obsolescence with limited and narrowly designed reforms. There is understandable hesitation among policy-makers to impose regulatory restraints prematurely, preferring instead to let the fast-moving medium evolve as much as possible on its own. At some point, however, the internet's growth may give rise to qualitative changes in the modus operandi of our economic system (see Chapter 7) which require a more comprehensive and proactive regulatory approach. Such a strategic change in policy-making is probably going to focus on the defining feature of the internet, its unequalled ability to create, circulate, process and commodify information. On the internet, information becomes both a resource to buy and a commodity to sell. Government officials will discover that the different facets of their internet policy all center around information management, and it is there that they will have a chance to develop a coherent regulatory approach for virtual capitalism.

8.2.1 Online Safety

The internet, a global network of computer-mediated communication and interaction, poses a severe safety challenge. Given relatively unprotected computers, software design flaws and still-breakable encryption codes, this network generates much criminal activity by highly skilled operators. Electronic misdeeds, such as digital identity theft, unauthorized entry into sites, hijacking of computers and tampering of data, will be committed with the intent to steal or destroy. The prevalence of such e-crimes is likely to rise proportionately with the diffusion of cybercash use online.[7] If people do not feel secure to operate on the internet, they will deprive themselves of its use and so let the social benefits from this innovation go to waste.

As already indicated (in section 4.3), much of the solution to the problem of safety lies in better technology applied to both hardware (firewalls) and software (encryption). Significant learning curves exist in both areas from the ongoing battle between online security specialists and equally skilled cyber-criminals testing each other's wits and driving each other to continuous improvements. The challenge here is to provide maximum security at a reasonably low cost and without undue disruption of internet traffic. This objective can be helped along by appropriate government assistance. For instance, governments need to launch educational campaigns which raise the awareness of internet users about what they can do to improve safety. Governments should actively promote the development of encryption technology and safety standards. A legal code defining electronic crimes and specifying sanctions will have to be introduced and then enforced. Such enforcement will require much-enhanced crime-fighting capabilities within the national security apparatus of the state. These will have to be well grounded in procedural law so that private citizens do not have to fear the state acting as Big Brother.

Internet safety has been given a big boost as a policy issue by the terrorist attacks of 11 September. American security officials have been impressed by al-Qaida's extensive use of the internet for information and communication, prompting major efforts to protect the infrastructure of the internet from cyberterrorism.[8] These attacks have produced a major shift in the thinking of both national-security specialists and corporate managers. Whereas until then the occasional denial-of-service attack or computer virus were deemed a nuisance too small to warrant massive investments in IT security, they now foresee possible scenarios for much more devastating attacks on the IT infrastructure and are much more willing to pay for improved protection. Both the Office of Homeland Security and the Pentagon's ARPA have made cyberterrorism a top priority to defend against.

8.2.2 Privacy Protection

Related to the question of safety is the issue of protecting the privacy of internet users from unauthorized use of personal information collected about them. Self-policing by e-commerce firms has worked rather poorly so far. Privacy policies have been promised but not delivered, or they have been delivered but not administered effectively (see section 4.2). Temptations for abuse are simply too great, since the collection of personal information can be turned into revenues when sold to third parties or used for better targeted sales pitches. Thus governments have inevitably become involved in seeking solutions to this problem. But their regulatory initiatives in this area face a difficult trade-off between lax rules that can be easily circumvented and tough rules which impede the flow of information. Nor does it help that the United States and the European Union have adopted different responses to this trade-off, since regional differences in privacy-protection rules constitute themselves a barrier to trade. A much-needed compromise for uniform standards of behavior should empower customers to determine the level of privacy protection they want adhered to.

The appearance of cybercash, a money form with potentially unprecedented information-collection and -processing capabilities, will intensify the privacy-protection problem and at the same time push us more strongly toward globally coordinated policy solutions. At one point, however, policy-makers may very well realize that a cybercash-powered online economy creates a radically different privacy problem than the one encountered in the birth phase of the internet, namely a desire by customers to give away too much information about themselves. Coupon money, payment schemes for consumption-related e-work and individual wealth accounts tied to credit securitization may combine with other online incentives to prompt individuals to divulge a lot of information about themselves in exchange for rewards. Given the impersonal nature of online relations and some people's desperate need for money, there is a lot of potential for abuse here. We have to guard against turning the data of our personal lives into a publicly accessible commodity that all those willing to pay can access for their own commercial benefit. How will those knowing about us make use of that information to control us?[9] If the Faustian dilemma of selling one's soul to the devil for material benefits ever were to have a revival on the internet, the government may have to step in and regulate the conditions and procedures under which such transfer of information may take place in a fair manner.

8.2.3 Accounting and Disclosure Issues

Government officials have already begun to zero in on the privacy-protection and safety issues as their first encounters with the information-management challenges posed by the internet. But soon they will come to realize that these issues, relatively static in their embodiment within computer-mediated exchange between transacting parties, are quite simple compared to the dynamic nature of information in online production or finance. What makes management of information so central to the internet is its flow quality as resource input and marketable output, subject to transformation in the production process whereby it engenders intangible and fictitious capital as income sources.

What, for instance, should we do when infomediaries control inside information and use such asymmetric information advantages for excessive or illegal gain? Market manipulation, discrimination, pressure tactics and collusion all thrive in an environment of unequally distributed information. One can argue that the market will take care of abusive infomediaries by robbing them of public trust and thus their clientele. This presumes that we will have a chance to find out about such abuses. Unfortunately, web sites are often paid in ways that create inevitable conflicts of interest, as happens when a seemingly objective product review suddenly leads you to the site selling that very product or when customers are steered to the sites of business partners. E-commerce firms have a vested interest in hiding these ethical conflicts and may be able to do so quite effectively in the virtual, immaterial world of the internet. Yet consumers should know all about these practices and relationships so that they can make good decisions on the basis of objective, balanced, accurate and transparent information. Otherwise they will not be comfortable or confident enough to engage in much e-commerce. While competition for brand loyalty and reputation will force the majority of e-commerce firms to earn the public's trust, there is always the temptation to gain a competitive advantage by violating the rules of good behavior. Governments must therefore enforce standards of full disclosure and transparency of business ties with the power to sanction violators. They may even have to ask strategic infomediaries for details pertaining to their use of information, be authorized to approve e-business models presented to them before implementation, and supervise those practices. These tasks may be carried out by self-regulatory boards made up of representatives from industry, consumers and government agencies, provided they are subject to official oversight and follow rules set in the public interest.

When governments get ready for the task of regulating the handling and disclosure of information online, they will have to make sure that internet-based firms provide the outside world with an accurate picture of their performance. This involves a fundamental reform of accounting and financial-disclosure rules. The Enron scandal has revealed the inadequacy of prevailing practices which in turn has spooked global capital markets by making investors question the trustworthiness of reported data. When investors do not have accurate information with which to judge the performance of those seeking their capital, how can they make good decisions?

This post-Enron crisis of confidence is serious enough to push government regulators into reform. US officials from the FASB, CFTC and SEC are examining how to tighten accounting rules and raise accuracy standards for financial statements while Congress is working out ways to strengthen institutional checks on corporate managers and sanction their illegal behavior. The Americans, who used to hold up their own higher accounting and financial-disclosure standards as the key reason for the vibrancy of US financial markets, have now seen their laxity in rule-setting and supervision erode this comparative advantage. The initiative has shifted to the London-based International Accounting Standards Board (IASB) which plans to formulate global accounting and disclosure rules tougher than those currently prevailing in the United States.[10] This is a good development, since such raising of standards is necessary and must be done globally in light of borderless online firms and interconnected financial markets.

As standard-stetting agencies redefine accounting and financial-disclosure rules, they will have to tackle a number of thorny issues. For one, they will have to compile a record of all questionable corporate practices of creative and pro-forma accounting, analyze these practices for their distortion potential and come up with new rules that ensure greater accuracy. Moreover, rule-setters will have to decide how to deal with the intra-network transactions of b-webs, from transfer pricing designed to reshuffle reported earnings between subsidiaries and affiliates all the way to the consolidated statements of virtual companies operating in cyberspace at the head of complex multi-firm alliances in which much activity is outsourced. A third problem, already mentioned earlier (in section 7.2), arises with the growing prevalence of intangible capital as productive assets to which traditional accounting principles do not apply.[11] Finally, regulators will have to face the fact that the dominance of fictitious capital requires greater transparency of performance indicators from borrowers seeking funds and sufficient amounts of data about their intricate financing arrangements.

8.3 Macroeconomic Policy Implications

Assuming that electronic money will eventually develop beyond being just an extension of traditional fund-transfer mechanisms and grow into an autonomous money form, the cybercash-powered internet will alter the modus operandi of our economic system. Then governments all over the world will have to examine the implications of cybercash for macroeconomic policy which they use to stabilize their domestic economies. Both pillars of macroeconomic stabilization – fiscal policy and monetary policy – will be profoundly impacted by the widespread use of such digital money.

8.3.1 Fiscal Policy Challenges

The tax-evasion potential of cybercash is such that it will play havoc with existing tax systems. We have already discussed (in section 8.1) the challenge of collecting sales and value-added taxes in e-commerce transactions. But the problem goes deeper than that. While it may still be possible to collect payroll taxes, employment-related personal income taxes and even some property taxes through withholding arrangements, corporate income and personal incomes other than wages and salaries could become increasingly difficult to tax. They may be sheltered, moved abroad and hidden in the undetectable crevices of cyberspace. Obviously good information management includes making income flows transparent for the purposes of taxation. But how can we rely on voluntary compliance when corporations and wealthy households have so many opportunities to shield their incomes? This will become a crucial question, not least because tax evasion may well provide the motivational impetus for the world's most productive citizens to withdraw from their respective societies and form supranational economic communities in cyberspace where they create wealth and conduct transactions with each other, immune from the sovereignty of their governments.

Non-wage income must be subject to effective taxation if corporations and the wealthy elites are to pay their fair share in taxes. If, however, these two pillars of society transact predominantly over the internet, then governments will have to work out how to tax them there. One solution is tax reform aimed at radically simplifying the income tax code, perhaps even a flat-rate tax on all incomes which could be automatically deducted and routed to the tax authorities at the point of income generation. Cybercash may have the technological capability of being programmed in such a fashion. The government could refund tax exemptions, deductions and credits, but should keep these at a minimum for the sake of simplicity and neutrality. The centralized collection process implied by such an automatic-deduction system requires agreements between federal, state and local governments as to the distribution of tax revenues among them. Global tax harmonization, already a necessity with regard to indirect taxes charged on goods and services sold online across borders, may eventually extend to income taxes so that cross-border movements of funds are subject to the same degree of taxation as purely domestic flows.

Government spending priorities will also undergo considerable adjustment under pressure from the online economy. Increasingly dependent on the allocation of capital by global production networks and transnational financial markets, governments all over the world will be forced to consider the competitiveness of their national economy as the highest priority. Countries will only attract capital if they can offer investors high-performance resource pools capable of generating sufficient income. We can therefore expect governments to spend a lot more on the physical infrastructure of their domestic economies. Transportation, energy and communication systems will all be stressed by the internet economy, and so will need modernization and expansion. Developing countries will also require better storage and delivery systems if they want to participate in e-commerce. Given the importance of worker skills in the internet economy, governments will put greater emphasis on improving their education systems.[12] Such a push for enhanced human capital should include worker-retraining programs, widespread internet access in schools and other public institutions, labor-market reforms enhancing worker mobility, incentives for training in high-tech skills (for software designers and engineers) and the promotion of an entrepreneurial culture. Luckily, the internet will probably make that task easier as an outlet for distance learning, which saves countries significant investments, and by giving everyone online access to so much information.

Cybercash will alter the financing of budget deficits and so affect what may easily be the most important aspect of fiscal policy, namely the government's ability to stimulate the economy out of downturns through tax cuts and/or spending increases. Institutional arrangements pertaining to money play a crucial role in the financing of budget deficits. Governments have traditionally financed their deficits by exerting control over domestic banks for privileged access to bank loans. In an early manifestation of the credit securitization trend, bank lending has gradually been crowded out by the issue of government securities for deficit-financing. To the extent that a central bank buys new government securities and thereby increases the pool of bank reserves available for money creation, it helps the financing of budget deficits by matching public-debt increases with automatic increases in the money supply. Such *debt monetization* may very well continue in the coming era of electronic money, especially if a central bank issues its own e-money or private cybercash issuers buy government securities with which to back new cybercash supplies. At the same time, a cybercash-based system of online finance may reduce the privileged role of banks as well as government securities in the credit system which forces governments to rely more heavily on international capital markets.

We have already seen this happen with many emerging-market countries and even smaller industrial nations.[13] In that case governments will have to compete more intensely for global fund supplies. While such competition encourages greater fiscal responsibility, it becomes a problem when governments find it difficult to finance recession-related increases in budget deficits needed to reverse cyclical declines.

8.3.2 Monetary Policy Challenges

The modalities of deficit-financing inevitably tie fiscal policy to monetary policy, a link that has so far crystallized mostly around the central bank's trading of government securities (in open-market operations). As already mentioned in section 6.4, central banks are worried that cybercash will cause such trading activity to decline substantially. To the extent that digital money replaces the public's demand for traditional bank money, it will surely lower the volume of the central bank's open-market operations backing the latter. As evident from various reports published in the late 1990s, central bankers expect cybercash to reduce seigniorage, the income they earn from these open-market operations by acquiring interest-yielding assets (government securities) to back their zero-interest liabilities (currency and bank reserves).[14] These officials can even foresee the day when the proliferation of e-money beyond their direct control will rob them of the ability to set the required reserve ratio, the fraction of deposits which banks must keep on hand at all times. Historically this power has been the central banks' most powerful tool to alter the money supply. Central bankers, pointing to the experience of Canada, Britain, Australia and New Zealand after reserve requirements had been abolished there, do not believe that this erosion will weaken their monetary policy effectiveness. In the future such policy will no longer focus on altering the money supply, but on controlling interest rates as is already mostly the case today.[15]

Cybercash will conclude a gradual shift in monetary policy orientation from money supply to short-term interest rates which we have seen unfold over the last quarter of century with the progressive deregulation of money. A central bank, like the Fed, today typically targets the interest rate for overnight funds in the interbank market (bank reserves) and then conducts open-market operations to regulate the supply of bank reserves relative to demand so that its rate target is hit. Such market manipulation allows the central bank not only to control a key interest rate in the money market, but also to shape expectations about future rates. The central bank's influence over investor expectations affects financial market prices, in particular long-term interest rates, stock prices and exchange rates, which in turn impact on economic activity. Optimists, such as Woodford (2001), believe that the internet might actually improve the effectiveness of monetary policy to the extent that it enhances the processing of information and efficiency of financial markets.

Such optimism assumes, however, continued central bank control over the targeted interest rate. This presumption will surely be tested by the growing diffusion of cybercash. The key question is cybercash's long-term impact on the interbank market for reserves, especially once this money form evolves beyond being a prepaid storage device tied to existing cash balances in the banking system and becomes an autonomous money form capable of self-expansion. At that point cybercash will surely reduce the demand for bank reserves to meet reserve requirements. This does not greatly worry central bankers, as long as banks still need reserves for clearing purposes.[16] What the monetary authorities have not yet contemplated is the possibility of cybercash eventually breaking that link too. At the moment banks need reserves for clearing purposes, because they settle claims against each other (in the form of checks) by transferring reserves. In the future, however, banks may increasingly settle claims against each other differently – by transferring title to all kinds of assets which back their deposits. This alternative settlement mechanism will thrive with credit securitization making all kinds of bank assets more liquid, information technology improving our ability to price such assets in real time, and asset purchases becoming the preferred mechanism for the issue of new cybercash. Settlement by title transfer will open the way for nonbank agents to issue cybercash, ending the long-standing bank monopoly over money creation. Unfortunately, this alternative also replaces settlement demand for reserves, rendering the prevailing monetary policy procedures ineffective.

If this scenario bears out, the central banks will have their work cut out for themselves. They will have to come up with new ways to conduct monetary policy. It is quite possible that many smaller countries will simply adopt the currency of stronger powers, in particular the dollar or the euro. That trend, already evident (for example the recent dollarization of El Salvador and Ecuador or the coming enlargement of euroland), may well accelerate once national currencies have to compete against cybercash denominated in 'harder' units. The central banks of the leaders, notably the Fed and the ECB, will have to work out the right kind of e-monetary policy. Perhaps they will introduce new operating procedures with which to influence strategic short-term interest rates in the money markets. Or they can rethink their strategy and target another variable, such as credit volume and distribution. I find interesting the suggestion by

Palley (2002) to impose reserve requirements on assets across the entire financial system. Apart from using this weapon to cool off sectoral over-heating without having to hurt the rest of the economy with the blunt weapon of interest-rate hikes, asset-backed reserve requirements can provide the institutional foundation for effective counter-cyclical monetary policy in a world dominated by e-money.[17]

8.3.3 Financial-crisis Management

Ever since the traumatic collapse of the global banking system during the Great Depression, central banks have had the responsibility of preventing financial instability from turning into a crisis of systemic-risk proportions which paralyses the economy. Much-feared bank runs have been effectively contained by the simple device of bank-deposit insurance, which raises the question of whether and how such protection should be extended to cyber-cash balances. Perhaps the best approach would be to create an insurance mechanism for all e-money units whose issuers are classified as credit insti-tutions subject to banking regulations and supervision. A second dimension of crisis management involves the central bank as a *lender of last resort* pumping liquidity into a stressed banking system, either through short-term loans or open-market purchases of government securities. As credit supplies have shifted from bank lending to securities markets, the central banks have had to adjust their lender-of-last-resort interventions to deal with asset-price collapses in financial markets. The Fed can claim a pretty good record in that regard, as proved with its dramatic interventions during the stock-market crash of October 1987 and the rescue of Long-Term Capital Management in August 1998. The International Monetary Fund, acting as global crisis manager, has been less successful, especially when considering its controversial approach to the Asian crisis of 1997–98.

Cybercash promises to complicate considerably this aspect of central banking. Financial instability will come in greater variety, have more dramatic contagion potential and be harder to combat. We are not just talking here about the vagaries of new derivatives or asset-backed securi-ties and the yet-untested behavior of their markets. We must also consider what happens to the herd behavior of panic-stricken investors when they are all online, leveraged to the hilt and given access to superfast transac-tion and settlement systems. Nor can we afford to ignore the growing link-ages between different financial markets which may spread an initially local crisis in all kinds of directions. All of these forces carry systemic-risk potential to which central banks will have to respond.

One of the more troubling aspects of cybercash must surely be its highly pro-cyclical supply behavior. If the issuers of e-money create additional supplies by acquiring assets in financial markets, they may feed price increases in those markets by boosting demand there. To the extent that this further enhances their money-creation ability by increasing the value of the asset base backing their e-money units, issuers of cybercash may recurrently set off asset-price bubbles whose inevitable bursts can trigger dangerous bouts of financial instability. Price collapses in financial markets, feeding on highly leveraged investors forced to dump assets into declining markets, may cause much cybercash to be destroyed. Such sudden elimination of liquidity reinforces the financial crisis under way and may cause harm to the level of economic activity. Central banks will have to pump liquidity into financial markets threatened by paralysis. They may also wish to use selective credit controls, whether in the form of moral suasion, reserve requirements on assets, margin requirements limiting leverage, or other types of regulatory devices, to nip such bubbles in the bud.

Whatever crisis-management strategies central banks will develop in the wake of e-money, there is no question that they will have to face the uneasy coexistence of private cybercash and public money under their control. Monetary instability associated with cybercash may force central banks into difficult balancing acts. We may see spectacular instances of malfunction or overextension on the part of private e-money issuers whose collapse threatens the integrity of the payments system. Those kinds of events could also trigger flight into safer money forms and thus cause sudden spikes in the demand for bank reserves or currency which will have to be accommodated. Such switches in settlement preferences constitute a new type of bank run, this time targeting issuers of cybercash suffering an erosion of public trust in their capacity to settle claims properly. Cybercash issuers themselves may recurrently alternate their settling of claims with each other between asset transfers and reserve transfers, depending on price developments in financial asset markets which affect the value of their securities holdings. The ability of central banks to cope with such monetary instability depends on their handling of the payments system, in particular their interaction with the central clearing facilities settling different cybercash claims. No matter how the architecture of the payments system is transformed by cybercash, the monetary authorities will have to maintain guaranteed convertibility between the different money forms, specifically between central bank money (that is, currency, bank reserves) and private e-money variants.[18] Otherwise local problems with failing cybercash systems may grow into system-wide liquidity squeezes which could really hurt economic activity.

8.3.4 The Regulation of Online Finance

The monetary-policy and crisis-management responsibilities of the central bank, so crucial to the public-good nature of money, depend ultimately on its ability to influence the modus operandi of private money issuers through appropriate regulatory constraints. As cybercash matures, it will force corresponding adjustments in financial regulations. Soon the Fed will probably recognize the validity of the EU's approach to subject all issuers of cybercash, whether banks or nonbanks, to the same kind of rules and regulations.[19] Generally speaking, any agent empowered to issue money will have a special fiduciary responsibility which justifies meeting stringent chartering standards, capitalization levels, rules of behavior (such as fair access or loss protections for customers) and reporting requirements. Given the transnational nature of cyberspace, such rules should be applied across the globe, thus eliminating off-shore banking centers.

The great potential of globally harmonized banking regulation has already been proved by the imposition of the *Cooke ratio*, the risk-weighted minimum capital-asset ratio uniformly imposed on banks across the globe, in 1988. This BIS rule, which together with provisions for *universal banking* defines the new regulatory framework for banking, has recently been reformed to improve the banks' risk management as those institutions greatly expand the range of their liabilities and assets. With cybercash, risk management gains an additional, technology-determined dimension (see section 6.3), something that the leading US banks are already trying to come to grips with.[20] Even though self-interest will drive banks to face these technological challenges, regulators should be able to conduct on-site examinations of the banks' information systems and review their internet plans and activities – in addition to the commercial, trust, trading and compliance examinations already in place. Ultimately all issuers of cybercash should be checked on a regular basis. The more money is deregulated, the more its issuers will have to be supervised effectively.

Unlike traditional money forms, cybercash will not be confined to banking. Its reach will extend to financial markets. Electronic trading will be made easier when conducted with cybercash. In turn securities will play a crucial role in both the creation and circulation of cybercash, as its issuers buy liquid assets to back new e-money supplies and swap titles to these assets when settling e-money claims with each other. The strategic linkage between securities and e-money will amplify the advantages of electronic trading – lower transaction costs, more liquidity and greater transparency. But at the same time the use of cybercash in financial market transactions will also exacerbate the disadvantages of online finance, in particular the propensity for asset-price bubbles and greater market volatility.

Regulators have begun to worry about the implications of electronic trading.[21] But they have yet to contemplate the long-term impact of cyber-cash on financial markets. While specialized financial-market regulators (the SEC and CFTC in the United States) may in the future still make the rules pertaining to information disclosure, market-making intermediaries and trading, the dynamic interaction between cybercash and securities will prompt central banks to become more engaged in the workings of financial markets. They will want to focus in particular on how the markets' online trading protocols use cybercash for their payment and settlement aspects. It might be prudent to impose special safety standards on those issuers of cybercash who are directly engaged in the operation of financial markets. Such standards may relate to reporting requirements, permissible asset cate-gories, minimum capital base, credit extension limits and in-house controls. Since cybercash may turn into a potent propellant of asset-price bubbles once securities come to play a crucial role in its (asset-backed) creation and settlement (via title transfer), central banks may want powers to stop such overheating before it explodes. The Fed's power to limit the degree of debt used in stock-market purchases with margin requirements or the idea of asset-based reserve requirements could serve as a good starting point here. When asset prices collapse, central banks must be ready to pump liquidity into the markets thus affected. In such moments of stress, the central banks will also want to counteract the contagion potential of market crashes. They will be able to do so much more effectively if they cooperate well and have a bird's-eye view of the growing linkages between different markets.

8.4 Cybercash as Transnational Money

To the extent that cybercash represents a radically different money form, it will give rise to a new monetary regime. The reforms discussed in the previous section with regard to monetary policy, lender-of-last-resort inter-vention and financial regulation are designed to make that new regime a coherent one, capable of appropriate credit allocation and containment of intrinsic instability. The most important monetary-regime dimension with regard to cybercash is, however, the international monetary system it engenders. Cybercash is ultimately transnational in nature, and this unique feature makes the question of international monetary arrangements for this new money form a crucial one. No other monetary regime in history, not even the 19th-century gold standard with its specie-flow adjustment mechanism between countries, has depended so fundamentally on a global institutional framework regulating cross-border flows of money.

8.4.1 Digital Globalization

Over the last quarter of a century the world economy has become steadily more integrated. Major advances in transportation and communication technologies have combined with market deregulation to boost trade as well as investment flows across borders. In industry after industry producers have pushed beyond national boundaries into foreign markets. Such globalization of our economic system, which creates an intensely competitive environment with many winners and losers, will take a quantum leap forward with the emergence of the internet as an engine of growth. This truly borderless network will one day carry huge volumes of electronically distributed services which can be accessed in real time from any corner of the planet. It will help multinational corporations to reorganize into global production networks. Even small businesses will find it easy to trade with customers or form partnerships all over the world. Online trading of securities will induce investors to diversify their investment portfolios globally, while at the same time accelerating the worldwide integration of hitherto national stock, bond and money markets.

As a truly transnational money form circulating on the internet, cybercash should greatly facilitate the production of online services, formation of global b-webs and management of global investment portfolios – the three pillars of digital globalization. We have already seen what happened to the intensification of globalization when the emergence of the euromarket in the 1960s removed effective national controls over the cross-border flows of capital (see section 2.2). At least eurocurrencies, which are time deposits whose circulation involves a transfer of ownership title to equivalent demand deposits in the country of original issue, are still connected to domestic banking systems and national money supplies. Imagine what happens to globalization when you introduce a money form whose creation and circulation transcends nation-states even more. Much of what cybercash can and will do to the world economy remains to be determined, since its impact on digital globalization depends very much on the precise modalities of its issue and circulation. A cybercash backed on a one-to-one basis by real cash balances (made up of government-issued currency or bank reserves), with which it is automatically convertible, will be a much more limited globalizer than a less conservative version of cybercash of which additional supplies can be created without full real cash coverage. The latter, which we assume to be a realistic possibility in a few years hence, represents truly supranational money and is a much more potent propellant of internet-based economic activity.

8.4.2 Cross-border Interdependencies and Spillovers

Even in its less ambitious variants cybercash promises to intensify both the positives and negatives of globalization. By reducing the transaction costs of cross-border flows to practically zero, it will help to open the space for transactions to such an extent that economic opportunities for income and wealth creation explode. In transnational cyberspace such opportunities have a chance to be distributed widely among many countries. Yet at the same time cybercash may accentuate international inequalities and economic instability, two sources of friction which have already given rise to a vocal anti-globalization movement.[22]

One of the more problematic consequences of globalization, sure to get worse in coming years, is the synchronization of business cycles. We have seen this development already take root in the global downturn of 2001–02, which demonstrated quite dramatically the interdependence of national economies in the face of simultaneous declines of stock markets, cutbacks by multinational corporations and reversals of cross-border flows of capital. These forces of synchronization will only get stronger when routed through a transnational medium such as the internet, making international coordination of macroeconomic policy more imperative than ever. Such coordination must be based on an ongoing consultation process among policy-makers in the United States, Europe, Japan, emerging-market economies and developing countries which evaluates an agreed-upon roster of performance parameters for different countries to determine trigger points for specific policy changes. While the convergence criteria in the context of the EU's economic and monetary union show that such policy coordination is possible, the exercise I have in mind in response to business-cycle synchronization should be anchored less rigidly in fixed policy rules and allow for greater discretion. Policy rules, such as the ECB's exclusive focus on a 2 percent inflation target or the 3 percent limit on domestic budget deficits across the EU, make policy-makers more accountable and credible. But such fixed rules also weaken the ability of governments to counteract business-cycle fluctuations effectively.[23] And this they can ill afford. Globally synchronized business cycles produce potentially self-reinforcing fluctuations which demand a good deal of discretion on the part of policy-makers for effective counter-cyclical stabilization.

Unfortunately, the task of jointly coordinated policy responses will be greatly complicated by the potentially unstable coexistence of real and virtual economies. Exceptionally rapid expansion of online economic activities may divert resources which used to be available to traditional brick-and-mortar sectors. Even more problematic spillover effects may arise if cyberspace is hit with a serious crisis which hurts the rest of the economy, a phenomenon we have witnessed for the first time in the aftermath of the e-crash of 2000–01. Such disproportionalities in the growth pattern will pose a major challenge to policy-makers who at this point do not even know how to measure the virtual economy accurately. This challenge will be felt most acutely by central bankers, since inter-sectoral tensions between virtual and real economies will manifest themselves first and foremost in shifting money demand patterns. Cybercash may be in very strong demand during e-booms and then suddenly be subject to massive flight when an issuer of digital money goes bankrupt or in the aftermath of other types of online financial crises. Sharp flow reversals into or out of cybercash will impact on interest rates and exchange rates.[24] Central banks will have to learn how to live with a highly unstable component of the money supply over which they have very little, if any, control. They cannot afford to let cybercash disrupt the payments system or trigger recurrent credit crunches.

8.4.3 International Monetary Reform

How well policy-makers deal with synchronized business cycles, inter-sectoral disproportionalities and shifting public preferences for private cybercash versus state-managed 'real' money depends on how well they adjust their international monetary arrangements to the realities of cybercash. Take, for instance, exchange rates. Even if digital-money units continue to be denominated in national currencies (e-dollars, e-euros), their relative prices may deviate somewhat from those of their real cash equivalents because of much lower transaction costs. Independently denominated e-money units, such as future successors of flooz or beenz, will have their own exchange rates among themselves and with regard to national currencies. If one of those cybercash variants depreciates, it could trigger a mass exodus which might bankrupt its issuer and spread to other private e-money units. On the internet such panic runs can unfold very swiftly indeed. Conversely, we may also see massive movements of funds out of beleaguered national currencies into 'harder' cybercash units, a digital version of capital flight out of high-inflation and/or politically unstable countries. These potential sources of currency-price instability will require some counteracting institutions capable of maintaining orderly market conditions, probably centered around online exchanges set up to clear and settle transfers between different money units.

However, such exchange-rate stabilization will become more difficult to the extent that cybercash encourages more speculation. Much lower transaction costs and vastly increased cross-border trade in cyberspace will dramatically expand the number of participants in the foreign-exchange market. Take, for instance, consumers who until now have shopped mostly locally and kept most of their money in the domestic currency of their nation of residence. In the virtual world e-shoppers will buy globally and for that purpose store digital currencies of several states on their hard disk. Over time they will surely come to regard their various e-money holdings as a diversified portfolio which needs to be actively managed for loss prevention and profit opportunities. Currency speculation will thus gain a mass base which it still lacks today. Given the swift homogenization of expectations on the internet where information travels quickly and the whole world is logged on continuously, one can imagine how much more turbulent the already-volatile swings in exchange rates may become when millions of consumers place their daily bets on currency prices. If such a scenario actually unfolds, it might be time to reconsider the interesting idea by Tobin (1978) of imposing a 0.05 percent tax on all currency exchanges. Such a small transaction tax, which discourages speculation while being barely felt in trade and longer term foreign investments, could be programmed into e-money units for automatic tax collection whenever their denomination is changed.[25] Of course, the hundreds of billions of dollars we stand to collect each year from such a tax could help to address global problems, such as environmental protection, AIDS, poverty reduction or the digital divide.

Digital money will also have a major impact on the choice of world money. In cyberspace, money creation moves beyond the domestic banking system. Issued as coupons or backed by a large variety of assets, e-currencies can be created anywhere in the world. Given that liquidity preference drives money users towards a single international medium of exchange, digital money may actually reinforce the privileged status of the leading currencies serving as world money, in particular the dollar and perhaps one day also the euro. This will be especially the case when the citizens of weak-currency countries prefer to hold their funds and conduct their activities in a stronger currency, prompting a growing number of countries to adopt the dollar or the euro as their official currency. The logical extension of any such monetary centralization trend is a single currency for all cross-border transactions.[26]

The process of monetary centralization, which seems to fly in the face of the presumed heterogeneity of cybercash as a private (deregulated and denationalized) money form, may gain additional impetus from a second direction. Prompted by the self-feeding nature of monetary instability and/or financial crises online, central bankers will seek intervention powers vis-à-vis digital money. While it may be technically feasible to renationalize cybercash and put all cybercash issuers under the jurisdiction of national regulators subject to strict controls, such territorial segmentation is difficult to maintain in practice and undermines the benefits of the internet. A better solution would be to establish a new monetary authority in cyberspace, akin to a central bank in the real world. Such an institution would regulate all issuers of cybercash, organize the payments system for e-money, maintain the convertibility between e-money units and real cash in cooperation with the national central banks and manage financial crises as the lender of last resort. In pursuit of those objectives, the cyber-authority would have to be able to issue its own e-money. Just as government-issued domestic currency does today with regard to private bank money, so could this official e-money serve as the monetary base for private cybercash issuers and in this way move us closer to an eventual single-currency system for international transactions.

The story of cybercash remains to be written. Still very much at the beginning of its life cycle, this innovation has yet to move beyond a subsidiary status. At this point it is impossible to tell how cybercash will evolve. There are, however, forces under way – in particular the computerization of finance and the internet as a locus of economic activity – which will push cybercash forward. Once it becomes a dominant money form, its powerful presence requires a whole new institutional regime in terms of monetary policy, financial regulations, crisis management and international monetary arrangements. Such a monetary regime, through which we manage the contradictory dual nature of money as a public good and private commodity, will in the case of cybercash be particularly difficult to construct. We have here not only a uniquely privatized money form, but also one whose transnational character threatens to move the management of money beyond the reach of nation-states. The coming era of electronic money may also by necessity be an era of global governance and international policy-making.

Notes

Chapter 1

1. The costliness of the Fed's traditional check-clearing system is highlighted in Bleakley (1994) and Wilke (1996).
2. Early on Visa joined forces with Microsoft to develop a secure electronic payment system for credit cards. MasterCard responded by concluding a cooperation agreement with IBM and Netscape. In February 1996 the two groups, realizing that they could both benefit from a uniform standard, announced a joint agreement for a single SET format which immediately became the industry standard for credit-card transactions on the internet.
3. Debit cards and ATM networks are also used by the US government to pay government benefits (for example welfare, food stamps) to people who do not have a bank account. Its electronic benefits transfer (EBT) program gives those recipients debit cards with which to withdraw cash at designated ATMs or pay for food at POS terminals in participating grocery and convenience stores.
4. Some of America's largest retailers, including Wal-Mart, Sears and Safeway, have recently brought a class-action suit against Visa and MasterCard, seeking billions of dollars in damages for having to pay excessive debit-card processing charges. See Beckett (2001) for more details.
5. For more detail on the spread of EBPP technology see Radecki and Wenninger (1999) as well as Foust (2000).
6. As noted by the Basel Commission on Banking Supervision (1998, p. 3, note 5), the term multi-functionality could also mean that smart cards combine a variety of payment mechanisms, as is the case when they function simultaneously as credit cards, debit cards, or stored-value cards.
7. See Bank for International Settlements (1996a, pp. 5–10) for a more detailed description of distinguishing criteria setting the various e-money systems apart from each other. Useful in this context is also the Committee on Payment and Settlement Systems (2000) which provides a detailed account of different e-money experiments in the member states of the BIS.
8. Liquidity of an asset depends on how rapidly you can turn it into cash without losing value. Stocks are more liquid than, say, real estate, since they can be resold much more easily than your home. Money is the most liquid asset, since it already represents cash. Liquidity is valued by investors, because it represents less risk of loss and more command in the marketplace.
9. The procedure described here recognizes the time value of money according to which future money units are worth less than the equivalent amount of units today and riskier funds are worth less than funds deemed not so risky. When discounted returns still exceed current cost outlays, we deem the investment project profitable. The fair-market

value of any investment is the sum of the present values of expected returns associated with that asset, net of costs.

10. Very interesting analyses of the origins of money being rooted in the social practices of prehistoric communities can be found in Festinger (1984), Goodhart (1998), as well as Heinsohn and Steiger (1983).

11. That promise was often given symbolic expression by the depiction of animals, slogans, rulers and other iconic representations of the empire on metal coins which in this way came to legitimate centralized state authority more effectively than other instruments of power.

12. The specie-flow adjustment mechanism led to an outflow of gold in the wake of balance-of-payments deficits which in turn reduced the money supply in countries suffering such deficits. The ensuing reduction in prices there would improve competitiveness and thus restore external balance. At the same time surplus countries underwent the opposite adjustment. Over time prices became more downwardly rigid and trade more interdependent, thus making such adjustments less effective.

13. See Guttmann (1994) for an extensive analysis of the fundamental differences between commodity-money and credit-money.

14. In this contex, De Brunhoff (1978) characterized the lending activities of banks as acts of 'private ex-ante validation' of the borrowers' income-creating activities, motivated by the anticipation of sharing in the latter's future income gains. The state's monetary authorities, backing these loans through their guarantee of private bank money, practice with this guarantee a sort of 'pseudo-social ex-post validation' of the banks' lending decisions.

15. Whereas electricity had taken root during the 1870s, it took quite a while for this innovation to transform the production process. Manufacturers were slow in replacing their obsolete plant and equipment with single-floor factories and electrical machinery. In 1911 the Ford Company introduced the first assembly-line plant (see Ford, 1911) which combined with Taylor's 'scientific management' techniques of work organization (see Taylor, 1911) to provide the basis for the new industry model of mass production.

16. The tokens issued by banks (that is, empty checks) only become money in the hands of others, their borrowing customers. The issuing banks cannot use these tokens for their own spending purposes. In other words, they cannot write checks drawn on themselves. Banks must pay for their purchases of goods and services out of their own revenue. Similarly, the government cannot create money directly to fund public expenditures. The central bank as the issuer of currency is for that reason institutionally separated from the rest of the government.

Chapter 2

1. A long boom, such as the one we experienced in the 1950s and 60s, will also tempt borrowers to take on more and more debt. See in this context the prescient warning by Minsky (1964) that increased reliance on debt over several business cycles would eventually cause borrowers to experience increased financial fragility. Minsky defined this state as one where debt-servicing costs absorb a rising share of corporate income, the maturity structure of debt becomes increasingly short term, and firms need to cover their debt-servicing charges by taking on new debt.

2. These so-called borrowed liabilities comprise in essence short-term money-market instruments for which there exist nowadays very large and liquid markets. Key among those are negotiable certificates of deposit (large-volume time deposits which can be

sold to someone else before maturity), federal funds (intra-bank loans), repurchasing agreements (short-term loans secured by government securities), commercial paper (equivalent of a short-term bond), and eurodollar deposits which are bank deposits denominated in US dollars offered outside the United States.

3. For an excellent empirical as well as theoretical account of these recurrent credit crunches between 1966 and 1982, see Wolfson (1986).

4. The convertibility of US dollars into gold, at the guaranteed rate of $35 per ounce of gold, had been the cornerstone of the Bretton Woods system. Despite its linkage to gold, the postwar international monetary system could not be qualified as a gold standard. From its very inception in 1945, the dollar had been consciously overvalued against gold to make it the principal form of world money. Gold was reduced to a reserve asset in the hands of central banks and served as a value anchor for the determination of fixed exchange rates on the basis of the currencies' respective gold weights.

5. The eurodollar market involves dollar-denominated deposits and loans in banks located outside the United States, and this market makes up about two-thirds of the overall eurocurrency market which totals about $5000 billion today. As Frydl (1982) notes, eurodollars are in effect time deposits and therefore not strictly speaking money in a narrow transactional sense. But since these time deposits overseas are backed by checking deposits located in the United States, they can be loaned out and are therefore private bank money in the broader sense of liquidity creation.

6. For instance, by offering corporate customers unregulated eurodollar deposits and then borrowing those funds from their euromarket subsidiaries abroad, America's leading money-center banks found a way to bypass the Fed's Regulation Q ceilings on domestic bank deposit rates.

7. The global market volume of currency trading has risen from about $10 billion a day in the late 1960s (just before the first wave of currency speculation brought down Bretton Woods) to $100 billion in 1973, when fixed exchange rates gave way to market-determined ('flexible') exchange rates, to the current daily average of $1500 billion. Only 15 percent of this astronomical figure represents traditional trade and (long-term) invest-ment activity, while 85 percent consist of short-term transactions for hedging or specula-tive purposes. See Wachtel (1997) for more on this.

8. Speculation has been analyzed by orthodox economists (see Friedman, 1953) from the point of view of the rational individual trader who, spotting a deviation of an existing exchange rate from its presumed equilibrium, will try to benefit from this deviation and so bring the two prices into line. Such a perspective lends itself to viewing speculation like individual arbitrage and thus a stabilizing force. In reality, however, not even well-informed currency traders have a precise idea of presumed equilibrium prices. Nor do they operate in isolation from each other, but instead affect each other's expectation forma-tion in potentially irrational ways – as in the case of a market panic when everyone is trying to sell into a declining market.

9. The J-curve, a concept first presented by Magee (1973), takes account of the fact that in the wake of a currency devaluation the prices of exports and imports will change much faster than their respective volumes. This leaves the country with larger import bills and lower export earnings in the immediate aftermath of a currency decline, prompting further pressure for the currency to devalue.

10. The banking crisis of 1990–91 was preceded by a costly taxpayer bailout of hundreds of insolvent thrifts (in the Financial Institutions Reform, Recovery, and Enforcement Act of 1989). The crisis itself necessitated the recapitalization (in the Federal Deposit Insurance Corporation Improvement Act of 1991) of the government-sponsored lender of last

resort for US banks, the Federal Deposit Insurance Corporation (FDIC), which had been pushed into de facto bankruptcy by a large number of expensive bank bailouts.

11. For an interesting account of this trend towards greater interest in online payment and billing systems by corporate America in response to 11 September and anthrax, see Boslet (2001).

12. The Federal Reserve (see Maki and Palumbo, 2001) has concluded, on the basis of empirical data, that the wealth effect has been significant among the richest 20 percent of Americans, precisely that segment of the population likely to own assets and earn capital gains. This group significantly reduced its savings during the bull market of the 1990s to the point of having a negative savings rate after 1998, while the saving and spending behavior of the remaining 80 percent of Americans changed very little during that period.

13. For more information on the ECNs and the threat they pose to the traditional exchanges, see Buckman and Lucchetti (1998), Henriques (1999) and Ip (1999). More details on the regulatory challenge posed by these developments can be found in McNamee (1999). Similar developments in Europe, including the emergence of online brokers and ECNs threatening established brokerage houses and traditional stock exchanges in London, Paris and Frankfurt, are discussed in Reed (1999).

14. For more on the electronic revolution in the bond markets, see Gutner (1999), Hershey (1999) and Ante (2001). The last reference concerned an article about Cantor Fitzgerald's eSpeed experiment, written a couple of weeks before that firm's physical destruction in the World Trade Center attack in September 2001. Since then Cantor Fitzgerald has had to rely a lot more on its electronic trading capacity to survive.

15. Interesting discussions of the pros and cons of open-outcry trading versus electronic trading in the world's futures exchanges can be found in McGee (1995), Ewing (1998), Hiday (1998), as well as Sarkar and Tozzi (1998).

16. The spectacular rise of E*Trade into a leading online financial-services company in less than four years is well discussed in Lee (2000).

17. Details on consumer complaints about internet banking can be found in Barker (1999). The issue of security in internet banking is discussed in Wildstrom (1999).

18. In 2000 alone Citibank upgraded its online banking service known as DirectAccess, introduced an online brokerage service called CitiTrade, consolidated all of a customer's financial accounts on one web site called MyCiti.com, and entered into a partnership with America Online. For more on these initiatives, see Beckett (2000).

19. Timmons (2000) provides more detail of Merrill Lynch's new Cash Manager program.

20. The internet-only banks tried to counter this comparative disadvantage by not charging their customers for withdrawals from ATMs of other banks and by refunding on a monthly basis a fixed number of surcharges imposed by those banks for use of their ATMs. But this response was little more than a Band-Aid to a much more fundamental problem.

Chapter 3

1. In retrospect, it is no exaggeration to argue that the bullish investment analysts, having become widely watched entertainers on television reaching a mass audience of new investors, acted out of self-interest. Talking up stocks translated into higher valuations which in turn facilitated the deals enriching the investment banks for whom these analysts worked, causing them in the end to earn higher bonuses.

2. For more on the spread of less-stringent valuation standards for internet stocks during the 1998–2000 bubble, see Morgenson (2001).

3. The use of such stock options as a form of employee compensation, once the exclusive domain of highly paid corporate executives, now includes, according to a recent study by the nonpartisan Employment Policy Foundation, quoted in Dreazen (2000), as many as 26 million hourly workers in the United States alone.

4. At almost the same moment Britain's Vodaphone launched a hostile $160 billion takeover bid for Germany's Mannesmann, further cementing the era of mega-mergers made possible by the amazing stock prices of high-tech firms. The merger of Europe's leading wireless networks formed in a single transaction the global leader of the 'mobile web' accessed by cell phones.

5. Sellers pay those exchanges 1 percent of any deal in commission for the privilege of being allowed to participate in such electronic auctions.

6. Forrester's forecast matched that of the US Commerce Department which predicted the volume of e-commerce, the buying of goods, services and assets on the internet, to rise from $48 billion in 1998 to $1.3 trillion in 2003.

7. Japan had its own speculative stock-market bubble in the late 1980s pierced by the Bank of Japan in 1990 with devastating consequences of spreading deflation for the entire economy, in particular huge losses for banks. Nervous Japanese households decided to put more money aside, once their capital gains had stopped making up for saving less during the boom. And this propensity towards more saving has greatly complicated government efforts to revive the economy through fiscal largesse and easy money.

8. Mandel and Hof (2001) present detailed survey results and case studies of corporate online expansion strategies.

9. See Weber (2001) for more on the problem of valuing intangible capital and the role of the internet in that challenge. See also our discussion of intangible capital in sections 7.2 and 7.4.

Chapter 4

1. Earlier polls about public fears concerning privacy protection on the internet, summarized in Green (1998), showed that this problem has persisted since the very beginning of e-commerce. Such fears seem particularly widespread with regard to potential abuse of personal financial information by online firms. In a January 2000 poll done for IBM, 61 percent of respondents said that they had decided against using a financial web site because they were unsure how personal information about them would be used, exceeding comparable figures for insurance sites (58 percent), retail sites (57 percent) and health-related sites (39 percent).

2. Because of their inaccessibility privacy policies are not widely read. The IBM poll mentioned in the previous note found that barely one in two business site visitors has ever seen a privacy policy. Only 38 percent of e-commerce consumers always read the privacy policy of the company from which they buy. Nor do most internet users know that they can turn off cookies or how to do that.

3. Two examples, widely reported in the media, suffice to illustrate this problem. In September 1999 E-Loan, an online lender known for its strong commitment to safe-guarding confidentiality, had to admit that certain firms it had acquired continued to use cookies and other secretive tracking technology in violation of its privacy policy (see Moss, 2000). In January 2000 DoubleClick, the top ad-server company on the net, was charged with having given its business partners detailed online profiles about consumers with their actual identity rather than providing only anonymous data about web surfers to marketers, as promised (see Green, 2000).

4. Several technological approaches to privacy protection are currently in the works. One centers on security programs which provide for cookie management, such as Norton Internet Security or Cookie Crusher. Another approach, developed by the standard-setting World Wide Web Consortium and now adopted by Microsoft for its next-generation Internet Explorer 6 browser, is the so-called 'platform for privacy preferences project' (P3P). This technology allows PC users to set their preferences for privacy protection (for example whether personal information can be shared with third parties), notifies users when the privacy practices of sites being visited are in conflict with what the users want and rejects cookies that violate the users' preferences.

5. In addition, as reported by Simpson (2000b) and Borrus (2000), the FTC decided in May 2000 to ask for legislative action in Congress that would give it new powers to oversee how companies comply with privacy-protection standards. Several bills to that effect have been introduced in both chambers of the US Congress, but action on those initiatives has been slowed by sharp ideological disagreements among policy-makers concerning the role of government in regulating the internet and the fall-out from the 11 September attacks in terms of shifting legislative priorities.

6. This 'safe-harbor' agreement offers US firms a few loopholes. Instead of subjecting them-selves to the oversight of EU regulators, they can also obtain safe-harbor protection from litigation or prosecution in Europe if they sign up with an accepted self-regulatory organ-ization subject to oversight by the FTC or can demonstrate that US laws are comparable to those of the EU in the area in which they operate.

7. In contrast to the opt-in approach of the EU, US legislation pertaining to financial infor-mation only gives consumers the right to opt out, which puts the burden of protection on the consumers themselves. The FSMA contains an opt-out clause only for information sharing with unaffiliated third parties, but not with affiliates. Under the Fair Credit Reporting Act Americans have the right to opt out of sharing of information among affil-iates, but can do so only with data about their creditworthiness.

8. The safety issue has bedeviled online payments from the very beginning. According to a 1999 study by the Boston Consulting Group, 44 percent of internet users said fear of revealing their credit-card number was the primary reason they refused to shop online. This fear is not without solid foundation, in light of the fact that, as reported by the National Consumer League in January 1999, one out of every five online buyers has been a victim of fraud.

9. In the 1970s IBM and the US government developed a cryptographic method, a so-called block cipher known as the 'data encryption standard' (DES), which the US National Bureau of Standards and the National Security Agency approved as the official standard for use in commercial data transmissions or financial transactions via computer. DES transforms any message, up to 56 bits long, into a code which permutates and substitutes the original message in sixteen consecutive steps. The 56-bit key fixes the precise sequence of permutations and substitutions involved in this scrambling of 0s and 1s making up any electronic data flows.

10. The standard SSL system used by most e-commerce sites for secure communication has other disadvantages as well. It only allows the buyer to identify the seller's digital identity, but not vice versa. This flaw forces web sites to rely on passwords or cookies to identify their online customers. Another obstacle is the lack of standard software which forces most companies to use add-on software for public-key encryption. Finally, it would be easier to have one central authority store all the public keys of users rather than have many 'certificate authorities' which are difficult to keep track of.

11. See Takahashi (1996) and Brown (2000) for more details on that battle over encryption-software export restrictions.

12. Cox (2001) provides a useful comparison of fraud-protection practices concerning credit cards and those applying to different cybercash systems.

13. For more information on the new AES standard, go to www.csrc.nist.gov/encryption/aes.

14. A good discussion of Windows XP and its implications can be found in Buckman (2001). Microsoft's .Net MyServices strategy is discussed extensively in Lemos and Ricciuti (2001).

15. Contrary to the standard notion of an exogenously fixed money supply under the direct control of the central bank (see Friedman, 1954), new money is in reality created endogenously by profit-seeking issuers in response to demand (Rousseas, 1986). Apart from transactions, cash can also be demanded for precautionary and speculative purposes (see Keynes, 1936) which can be modeled as an inverse function of interest-rate movements (see Tobin, 1958). Keynes (1937) stressed a fourth source of money demand, namely the boom-related finance motive which arises when businesses undergo massive investment spending at or near the cyclical peak (see also Davidson, 1978).

16. The European Central Bank (1998) provided guidelines for the issue and regulation of e-money as the basis for EU directives and legislation which are now being implemented by the European Commission. Among the report's recommendations is that the issue of e-money be confined to banks and bank-like depository institutions (such as savings banks), subject to exceptions authorized by special waiver. See also the Committee on Payment and Settlement Systems (2000, pp. 22–8) for details on the ECB's e-money policy guidelines.

17. Prior to conducting a transaction, both parties agree to register with the same online escrow service (for example i-Escrow, Escrow.com, Tradesafe.com). The buyer then sends funds to the service which verifies the payment. Upon verification, the seller sends the merchandise to the buyer for inspection. If the items sent are accepted, the service transmits payment to the seller.

Chapter 5

1. See O'Mahony et al. (1997) or Wayner (1997) for good summaries of different cybercash experiments at the very onset of e-commerce. For more recent digital-money developments, see the Committee on Payment and Settlement Systems (2000) or Kuttner and McAndrews (2001).

2. Smart cards are safer than traditional plastic money inasmuch as the chips they carry are harder to forge than the magnet stripes on standard credit and debit cards. Moreover, those smart cards are also cheaper in terms of telecommunication costs, because the smart-card readers to which they connect do not have to use a phone line to connect to a central computer for authorization, as is the case with standard credit or debit cards.

3. As a scientist Chaum had made important contributions concerning the software design of cybercash. See, for instance, Chaum (1983, 1985, 1994).

4. Some e-mail-based payment systems, such as C/Base's Ecount.com, gmoney.com, and PayMyBills.com's payme.com, use credit cards as a fund-transfer mechanism. PayPlace.com also allows the use of debit cards. Systems of e-mail money, which transfer funds between checking accounts, include Achex (www.achex.com), the eMoneyMail system of Bank One's internet-only WingspanBank subsidiary (www.emoneymail.com) and the PayDirect payments service offered by Yahoo!.

5. Much of the information presented here on PayPal comes from its web site as well as Arar (1999), Spangler (1999) and Sapsford (2000). These articles also detail PayPal's push

into the mobile web to enable fund transfers via cell phones and Palm devices. See Cringely (2000) for details on the launch of PayPal and its subsequent merger with X.com.

6. For more detail on PayPal's struggle for profitability, see Forster (2000), Clark (2001) and Kane (2001).

7. As reported in Cave (2001), many of PayPal's customers have also become frustrated with its aggressive anti-fraud tactics which have included freezing of accounts without prior notification. But PayPal has suffered considerable exposure to fraud-related losses, being penalized by credit-card companies for its comparatively high chargebacks from fraudulent or disputed transactions.

8. In February 2002 Louisiana declared its intent to have PayPal classified as a bank and be treated for its fund transfers within that state to the same kind of regulatory oversight and restrictions as its commercial bank rivals. This and a patent suit did not prevent PayPal from launching the first successful dot-com IPO after the e-crash of 2000–01 a week later. In July 2002 eBay bought PayPal for $1.5 billion.

9. Online-payments specialist CyberSource has a similar service where it issues gift certificates to recipients designated by its customers on behalf of participating merchants in its network and settles payments between purchaser and merchant.

10. For more information on the innovative gift-currency service offered by Flooz.com, see Gutzman (2000).

11. More information on the collapse of Flooz.com can be found in Joyce (2001), Miles (2001) and Wearden (2001).

12. For more examples of e-tailers using beenz as promotional incentives for e-work, see Weber (1999).

13. Much of the information discussed here about the collapse of Beenz.com was taken from online news reports, notably Enos (2000) and Junankar (2001).

14. For a summary of product-development efforts by credit-card companies in response to competition from rivals, see Junankar (2000).

15. As reported by Sapsford and Beckett (2001), the antitrust suit led to a ruling in October 2001 which forced Visa and MasterCard to stop barring member banks from issuing cards from rivals. For the first time American Express and Discover will now be able to pursue relationships with banks that issue cards by Visa or MasterCard. The enhanced competition should encourage greater product differentiation in the $1.3 trillion credit-card industry, thus providing a boost for the development of smart cards.

16. Excessive market fragmentation caused by a lack of standardization and compatibility between different wallets has prompted the development of electronic commerce modeling language (ECML), which provides merchants with a standard format for their payment pages so that shoppers can use any wallet to fill them out.

17. After the terrorist attacks on the World Trade Center and the Pentagon, the use of smart cards has been given added impetus by the need for greater security. Combined with biometric technology, smart cards promise to become a widely used tool for personal identification, as demonstrated by a recent pilot program at Amsterdam's Schipol airport.

18. Examples of e-check systems under development are the eCheck.Net of AuthorizeNet (www.authorizenet.com), the Electronic Check Service offered by E-Commerce Exchange (www.ecx.com), the Troy Group's eCheck Secure (www.echecksecure.com) and the Electronic Check Systems by CyberSource (www.cybersource.com).

19. For more on Citi's c2it service, see Beckett and Buckman (2001).

20. In the face of inadequate demand, Mojo Nation was forced in February 2002 to abandon its ambitious plans. A simpler version of its data-transmission software, known as Mnet, has since been launched.

Chapter 6

1. See, for instance, Vernon (1966, 1971).
2. Electronic Funds Clearinghouse uses software to put into place an EFT system specifically designed for internet payments. This software completes the transaction according to the fastest and least expensive ACH conduits (for example the Fed, New York Clearing House, Arizona Clearing House, VisaNet) to debit the payor's bank account and credit the payee's bank account automatically.
3. An informative consumer report comparing the major e-mail money systems, in particular PayPal, eBay's Billpoint, Yahoo's PayDirect, Western Union's Bidpay and Citibank's c2it, can be found in Morton (2001).
4. Let us assume that Firm A owes Firm B $100,000 while being owed $80,000 by Firm C which in turn holds a claim against Firm B for, say, $60,000. That triangular relation of $240,000 in gross payments can be 'netted out' to $60,000 in actual payments (that is, $40,000 from A to B and $20,000 from C to A).
5. The true meaning of global seigniorage can perhaps be grasped better when considering that the country issuing the key currency serving as world money is able to buy foreign goods, services or assets with its own money, with pieces of paper that it does not have to earn but can simply print. Similarly, the country issuing the world money can accumulate and service foreign debts in its own currency.
6. An excellent summary of the different risk categories and scenarios pertaining to electronic money and banking can be found in the Annex of the BIS report by the Basel Committee on Banking Supervision (1998, pp. 17–21).
7. While industrial enterprises in the US manufacturing sector average about 50 percent in the capital-asset ratio, banks typically have an 8 percent ratio as required by international banking regulations (the so-called 'Cooke ratio') agreed to in the Basel Accord of 1988 by the members of the BIS.
8. The case in favor of fully denationalized money, freed from government control and thus subjected to market regulation, has been made quite convincingly by Hayek (1978) and Friedman (1989).
9. US banks have recently introduced so-called 'automated loan machines' (ALMs) which process and accept loan applications electronically, allowing applicants to walk away with a check at the end of the session. Such ALMs will in the future be turned into a software product so that they can also be accessed online for e-loans by qualifying borrowers.
10. DIDMCA 1980 asked the Fed to price its payments services so that, in the long run, all direct and indirect costs would be recovered. At the same time Congress widened the Fed's reach by subjecting all depository institutions, and not just member banks, to reserve requirements and granting them equal access to the Fed's payment services.
11. The Fed gains seigniorage from the issue of its currency notes as zero-interest liabilites which are backed by interest-yielding government securities. To the extent that e money replaces such notes (or coins), it will correspondingly reduce the amount of government securities held to back that currency and thus lower the Fed's interest income.
12. This idea of issuing corporations regulating the issue of cybercash as an effective method of self-policing by the e-money industry was first voiced by Greenspan (1996).
13. Fed governor McDonough (1996) specified the conditions under which the Fed would consider issuing its own e-money. Pointing in the direction of money as a public good, McDonough thought such a step justifiable only if private-sector suppliers fail to provide such a service with the same 'effectiveness, scope and equity' as the Fed could.
14. The FDIC decided in 1996 that most stored-valued cards do not meet the legal definition of a deposit and therefore do not qualify for protection through federal deposit insurance.

Patrikis (1998), then Vice President of the Federal Reserve Bank of New York, also made it quite clear that the Fed does not regard privately issued electronic money as legal tender, the official definition of fully fledged money issued and/or backed by the state.

15. Such central bank issue of e-money need not replace paper money or private cybercash variants and so operate in their place, as has been suggested by Warwick (1999) in his case for federally issued electronic currency. Rather it may coexist with private competitors, much like the Fed is facing today with its check-clearing and ACH services. Such coexistence may reassure the public that the Fed backs qualifying private cybercash units with its own e-currency.

16. That 1975 agreement under the auspices of the BIS defined the sharing of intervention responsibilities by central banks of home and host countries when euromarket subsidiaries of transnational banks fail. This agreement for bilateral cooperation concerning shared lender-of-last-resort assistance was later extended to the question of how central banks should share their supervision responsibilities when dealing with banks in the euromarket.

Chapter 7

1. Economists focusing on technological change, such as Mowery and Rosenberg (1998), have argued that even relatively mature technologies, seeking to extend their life cycle through innovation, can often develop in entirely unpredictable ways.

2. Market-research firm Jupiter Research estimated in late 2000 that nearly half of all PC hardware and software would be bought online by 2003, as well as between 10 and 15 percent of all hotel reservations, air travel tickets, books, music and event tickets. A broader discussion of B2C commerce's transformation of consumer goods and services can be found in Bakos (2001).

3. For a good description of how eBay uses customer input and observed behavioral patterns of the 38 million buyers and sellers trading on its site to develop new products in response to perceived client needs, see Hof (2001).

4. Auctions are the mainstream economist's ideal model of self-regulating markets tending towards equilibrium. Yet they also raise some issues, such as winner's curse or collusion (see Klemperer, 2000), which may actually be accentuated by the virtual nature of the internet and which the intermediaries organizing online auctions need to address if they want to remain popular.

5. Mercata.com is an online bazaar specifically designed to encourage 'buyer's cartels' by grouping individual buyers together so that they can leverage their combined purchasing power into bulk buying at discounted prices.

6. B-webs, which involve groups of suppliers, distributors, commerce service providers, infrastructure providers and customers using the internet for communication and transactions, are discussed at length as the corporate organization model of the future in Tapscott et al. (2000).

7. Based on current trends, Hof (2000) distinguishes several distinct business models for e-marketplaces, such as neutral exchanges backed by major industry players (for instance Covisint for the auto industry) or run by independent dot-coms (e-steel for example), auctions for unique items, collaboration hubs which help companies to carry out projects, buyer-driven procurement hubs for specific industries (notably MetalSite.com for steel, Chemdex.com for chemicals) or product categories (such as VerticalNet or FreeMarkets.com), seller-driven online catalogs, and virtual communities offering firms in

a specific industry information and communication facilities. See also the discussion of e-marketplaces in Lucking-Reiley and Spulber (2001).

8. As noted by Autor (2001), improvements in communications between employers and employees made possible online extends to more of the actual work being done on the net rather than on-site. Online labor markets also make job seekers less dependent on local market conditions.

9. For more details on the amazing width and depth of internet-based innovation across the entire flow sequence of the production circuit, reshaping companies in practically every sector of our economy, see Reingold and Stepanek (2000), Brynjolfsson and Urban (2001), or Rocks (2001).

10. The recent diversification initiatives of Dell Computers are discussed in Park and Burrows (2001).

11. When US borders were closed and air travel shut down following the terrorist attacks of 11 September 2001, Dell survived that disaster much better than any of its competitors thanks to its more advanced use of the net. It worked out rapidly where supplies would be disrupted and switched production as well as order-taking elsewhere (Europe, Asia). Its real-time tracking of the order flow allowed it to prioritize orders and take care of the most important ones first. And its online sales staff were given models to push which the company's supply network was better able to assemble during the post-attack turmoil.

12. The recent reorganization of the French telecom company Alcatel gives us an idea of how far firms may go in outsourcing almost all of their operations and retaining just a few high-value activities such as product design or b-web coordination.

13. Borenstein and Saloner (2001) present an interesting discussion on value creation and reallocation of monopoly rents on the internet.

14. Even though most infomediaries provide custom content, they have convinced the public and government regulators to consider them passive middlemen, like the phone company, who should not be held accountable for the digital bits moving over their networks. This hands-off attitude, enshrined in legislation (Communications Decency Act) and defended strongly by eBay, Napster, and Yahoo! in precedent-setting lawsuits, runs directly counter to the public interest in such hot-button issues as safety, protection of personal privacy, and intellectual property rights. For more on this contradiction, see Weber (2001). In this context, see also the discussion of online intermediaries in Lucking-Reiley and Spulber (2001).

15. The challenges posed by intangibles and their many profound implications are discussed meaningfully, among others, in Shapiro and Varian (1998) and Lev (2001). See also the annual conferences on intangibles organized by New York University's Stern School of Business.

16. Policy implications of the emerging information economy, in particular as regards its heavy reliance on intangible capital, were discussed at length at a symposium sponsored by the Federal Reserve Bank of Kansas City (2001).

17. The government may secure equal access either through regulation requiring banks to offer affordable no-frills packages to poorer customers or through its agencies (for example post offices) issuing their own universally accessible e-cash and cyberbanking facilities.

18. To the extent that these portals make specific stock recommendations, they act like brokers. This poses a problem for regulators, such as the SEC, as to whether and how to bring these online portals and registered brokers under the same regulatory umbrella (see Smith and Schmitt, 2001).

19. A very interesting analysis of the online transformation of finance, stressing in particular internet-induced changes to financial-service providers and financial markets, can be found in Barber and Odean (2001).

20. The capitalization of income involves dividing the amount of income expected annually by the prevailing risk-adjusted interest rate (so-called rate of capitalization) to establish the value of an asset.

21. The concept of fictitious capital first originated over a century ago in Volume III of Marx's *Kapital* (see Marx, 1967, Chs 25, 29, and 33). It reappeared later with Hayek (1939), founder of the conservative Austrian School of Economics, who applied the concept to the money-creation process of credit-money, whereby the volume of bank credit expands without a corresponding increase in savings. See also De Brunhoff (1990) and Guttmann (1994, Ch. 2) for more detail on definitions of fictitious capital.

22. The link between e-money creation and securities is established when cybercash issuers, practicing the art of fractional-reserve banking, take unused balances in client accounts and use them to buy bonds or other marketable financial claims. Such security purchases create new money, with the profit from that action booked by the cybercash issuer as the difference between income-yielding assets (securities) and zero-interest liabilities (cash).

23. Over-the-counter (OTC) derivatives are traded within a selected group of large financial institutions (such as pension funds), banks and corporations which negotiate prices privately among themselves. They are much less regulated than options or futures traded on official exchanges which in the United States are under federal oversight by the CFTC or the SEC. The BIS estimated in June 2001 that the market for OTC derivatives involved contracts based on $100 trillion in underlying assets.

24. Credit securitization in the narrow sense involves a process of bundling similar bank loans (mortgages, home equity loans, car loans, credit-card debt) together and repackaging them into asset-backed securities which are collateralized by money flows from the borrowers. This process, which turns illiquid loans into marketable securities and links local borrowers to the global capital markets, is organized by banks as intermediaries whose loans are thus in effect prepaid by the buyers of their asset-backed securities and taken off their books. See Silverman et al. (1998) for more.

25. This idea of wealth accounts as the basis for a new type of finance emerging over the next couple of decades has been discussed by Sanford (1993).

26. For more detail on that demobilization of checks and balances by Enron, see Schroeder and Ip (2001).

27. Chaffin and Fidler (2002) point out that all the analysts, who maintained a 'strong buy' recommendation for Enron's stock all the way to the end, worked for investment banks earning huge fees from helping the energy giant to set up its partnerships. The article also shows how Enron pressured those banks to maintain enthusiasm for its stock or risk losing its business.

28. A Ponzi scheme, named after a Boston con artist who pioneered this kind of payment pyramid, involves 'a fraudulent investment scheme in which funds paid in by later investors are used to pay artificially high returns to the original investors, thus attracting more funds' (*Webster's New World Dictionary*, Third College Edition, p. 1049).

29. As Morgenson (2002) reports, even during the sky-high energy prices in the wake of California's power crisis in August 2000, Enron earned skimpy returns of only one-half percent on its trades.

30. In one instance Enron sold some excess fiber-optic connections from its broadband trading unit to one of its special-purpose vehicles called LJM2 for $100 million even though it was 'dark' fiber not yet connected to the lasers and switching equipment that transmit and route internet traffic. This one transaction alone represented a quarter of Enron's 2001 broadband sales.

31. According to Zellner (2001), Enron's bankruptcy filing in December 2001 listed $13.1 billion in debt for the parent company and an additional $18.1 billion in debts carried by its affiliates, but failed to include an estimated $20 billion in off-balance-sheet liabilities.
32. A fascinating account of Enron's collapse can be found in Eichenwald and Henriques (2002).
33. Palley (2002) has noted the increasingly self-feeding nature of such financial bubbles when rising asset prices boost the issuers' capacity for creating e-money backed by those assets. This increased pro-cyclical elasticity of private money 'production' spells, in the author's opinion, greater exposure to financial instability (see Chapter 8 for more).

Chapter 8

1. The original proposal for a single international currency, the so-called Bancor Plan, was formulated by Keynes (1943, 1980) in preparation to the Bretton Woods Conference of 1944 which ultimately decided upon a dollar-based international monetary system.
2. The United States is certainly not the only country concerned with e-policy agendas. See Fairlamb and Edmondson (2000) as well as Bremner and Ihlwan (2000) for similar debates in Europe and Asia respectively.
3. A good source of information about ongoing international developments in taxation of e-commerce is the web site www.ecommercetax.com.
4. According to a February 2002 report by the National Telecommunications and Information Agency (NTIA), the US government's technology-policy arm, web use among African Americans and Latinos grew by 33 percent and 30 percent respectively between August 2000 and September 2001, compared to only 20 percent growth among white and Asian Americans. At the same time the digital divide has widened. In 1997 only 10 percent of those US households earning less than $25,000 used the internet, compared to 45 percent of those earning more than $75,000. Four years later those numbers were 25 percent and 75 percent respectively, increasing the divide from a 35 percent gap to a 50 percent gap.
5. See Dreazen (2002) for more detail on the battle between Bush and the Democrats over the 'digital divide' and policies to close it.
6. Europeans in particular have had a hard time ridding themselves of the old habits of the brick-and-mortar economy. For instance, EU rules allow car producers to dictate retail prices and forbid dealers to compete with each other. Publishing cartels fix book prices in Germany, France, Austria and the Netherlands. The Germans prohibit price discounting on consumer goods as well as reverse auctions of the kind practiced by Priceline.com. Online auctions run afoul of century-old laws requiring the physical display of goods on the block. These are just a few examples of the Byzantine maze of rules, regulations and tax laws hampering e-commerce in Europe.
7. An informative account of the increase in cyber-attacks on online banks can be found in Junankar (2000).
8. As reported by Lemos (2001), America's newly appointed cyberterrorism czar is currently implementing a plan, dubbed GovNet, to put mission-critical private communication of federal agencies, their so-called intranets, on closed-loop networks that are less subject to attack. The US government is also going to train more computer-security personnel, make users more aware of the risks involved in not using good security practices, and encourage better security being built into information technology.

9. This question is already quite relevant today. Microsoft's new operating system Windows XP, bundled with various internet services that are centrally accessed through the Passport wallet, enables the software giant to collect and store an absolutely amazing amount of detailed information about schedules, habits and taste preferences of individual customers who have now become personally identifiable whenever they log on.

10. For more details about IASB's rule-setting efforts, see its web site www.iasb.gov.uk.

11. In recent years we have indeed seen research on intangibles explode in economics and accounting. Consultants offering advice and analytical tools for valuation of intangibles, such as pl-x.com or the New Economy Value Research Lab at the Massachusetts Institute for Technology, thrive on the internet. Both the SEC as well as the FASB are struggling with the same question.

12. For example, South Korea's massive postwar investments in education spurring rapid industrialization or India's excellent engineering schools giving the country a strong presence in software development.

13. Even the twelve European Union nations using now the euro have seen their traditional debt-monetization mechanism disappear. The European Central Bank is not allowed to conduct dynamic open-market operations which help national governments finance their budget deficits.

14. See, for instance, the Bank for International Settlements (1996b) or the European Central Bank (1998).

15. Two analyses of e-monetary policy by influential economists Friedman (2000) and Woodford (2000) share this conclusion.

16. As pointed out by Palley (2002), other sources of demand for bank reserves, related to either the public's demand for currency, tax settlement balances or international interbank settlements, may all be impacted by the spread of e-money. But these demand channels are less important to the conduct of monetary policy than the demand for reserves for clearing purposes.

17. Such reserve requirements could be raised during booms and lowered during recessions. They also operate as automatic stabilizers, not unlike taxes, by slowing down boom-induced asset price inflation and loosening when asset prices and quantities decline.

18. As indicated by Patrikis (1997), the Fed expects very significant changes in the payments system over the next decade, in particular the mobilization of large-volume ('wholesale') transfers of funds and securities on the internet rather than through Fedwire or CHIPS.

19. National regulators, such as Britain's Financial Services Authority, are currently in the process of implementing the EU Directives on e-money. Dealing with firewalls separating e-money issuance from other activities of the issuer, minimum capital requirements, asset backing of e-money liabilities, internal control mechanisms and consumer protections, these directives apply to banks and nonbank issuers of e-money alike. The Fed has yet to declare its regulatory framework for cybercash.

20. A consortium of America's top money-center banks has formed the Banking Industry Technology Secretariat (www.bitsinfo.org) to develop best-practice standards for all aspects of electronic banking.

21. The extent to which government officials are already thinking about this question is well illustrated by the Bank for International Settlements (2001).

22. Interesting discussions of globalization and the forces fuelling a growing anti-globalization movement across the world can be found in Friedman (1999) and Kapstein (1999).

23. We have already seen how fixed rules may hamper counter-cyclical policy. The Fed, given more discretion and also pursuing growth and employment objectives besides price stability, has cut interest rates much more aggressively during the latest downturn than the rule-constrained ECB was able to.

24. One of the few economists recognizing the potentially difficult coexistence between real and virtual spheres of economic activity is Tanaka (1996).
25. The Tobin tax is far too small to impede trade or long-term investments. But it will be felt quite strongly by speculators who often trade currencies and are highly leveraged. For a speculator who puts down 5 percent in his own capital, a 0.05 percent transaction tax constitutes a 1 percent tax on capital each time he turns his portfolio over (which may happen 40 times a year).
26. See Guttmann (1988; 1994, Chs 15–16) for how such a single-currency plan could work in practice.

BIBLIOGRAPHY

Ante, S. (2001) eSpeed's Trading Secrets. *Business Week*, September 3.

Arar, Y. (1999) Beam Me Up Some Money, Scotty. *PC World* (www.PCWorld.com), November 15.

Autor, D. (2001) Wiring the Labor Market. *Journal of Economic Perspectives*, **15**(1), 25–40.

Bakos, Y. (2001) The Emerging Landscape for Retail E-Commerce. *Journal of Economic Perspectives*, **15**(1), 69–80.

Bank for International Settlements (1996a) *Implications for Central Banks of the Development of Electronic Money*. Basel (Switzerland).

Bank for International Settlements (1996b) *Security of Electronic Money*. Basel (Switzerland).

Bank for International Settlements (2001) *The Implications of Electronic Trading In Financial Markets*. BIS Committee on the Global Financial System, Basel (Switzerland).

Barber, B. and Odean, T. (2001) The Internet and the Investor. *Journal of Economic Perspectives*, **15**(1), 41–54.

Barker, R. (1999) Net Banking Is Here, But Has It Arrived? *Business Week*, July 26.

Basel Committee on Banking Supervision (1998) *Risk Management for Electronic Banking and Electronic Money Activities*. Basel (Swizerland): Bank for International Settlements.

Beckett, P. (2000) Citigroup Again Makes Tracks to the Internet, Hoping Its 'Footprint' Makes a Bigger Impression. *Wall Street Journal*, July 20.

Beckett, P. (2001) Wal-Mart, Intensifying Its Fight With Visa, To Stop Using Interlink Debit-card System. *Wall Street Journal*, September 5.

Beckett, P. and Buckman, R. (2001) Citigroup, Microsoft Sign Pact Allowing Online Money Transfers. *Wall Street Journal*, May 1.

Bleakley, F. (1994) Fast Money: Electronic Payments Now Supplant Checks at More Large Firms. *Wall Street Journal*, April 13.

Borenstein, S. and Saloner, G. (2001) Economics and Electronic Commerce. *Journal of Economic Perspectives*, **15**(1), 3–12.

Borrus, A. (2000) Web Privacy: That's One Small Step. *Business Week*, July 17.

Boslet, M, (2001) Online Payment, Billing Attract Interest As Companies Assess 'Real Risk' of Paper. *Wall Street Journal*, November 28.

Bremner, B. and Ihlwan, M. (2000) The New Economy/Asia: Edging Toward The Information Age. *Business Week*, January 31.

Brown, D. (2000) Revised Crypto Rules Seen As Improvement. *Inter@ctive Week* (www.zdnet.com), January 13.

Brynjolfsson, E. and Urban, G. (eds) (2001) *Strategies for E-Business Success*. San Francisco: Jossey-Bass.

Buckman, R. (2001) Potent Program: With Its Old Playbook, Microsoft Is Muscling Into New Web Markets. *Wall Street Journal*, June 29.

Buckman, R. and Lucchetti, A. (1998) Electronic Networks Threaten Trading Desks on Street. *Wall Street Journal*, December 23.

Cave, D. (2001) Losing Faith in PayPal. *Technology & Business* (www.salon.com), February 23.

Chaffin, J. and Fidler, S. (2002) Enron's Alchemy Turns to Lead for Bankers. *Financial Times*, March 1.

Chaum, D. (1983) Blind Signatures for Untraceable Payments. *Advances in Cryptology – Crypto'82*, Berlin: Springer, 199–203.

Chaum, D. (1985) Security Without Identification: Transaction Systems to Make Big Brother Obsolete. *Communications of the ACM*, **28**(10), 1030–44.

Chaum, D. (1994) Designated Confirmer Signatures. *Advances in Cryptology – Eurocrypt '94*, Berlin: Springer-Verlag, 86–91.

Clark, D. (2001) PayPal Plans IPO, Despite Draught In Initial Offerings. *Wall Street Journal*, October 1.

Coase, R. (1937) The Nature of the Firm. *Economica*, **4**(2), 386–405.

Committee on Payment and Settlement Systems (2000) *Survey of Electronic Money Developments*. Basel: Bank for International Settlements.

Council of Economic Advisors (1990) *Economic Report of the President*. Washington, DC: US Government.

Council of Economic Advisors (2002) *Economic Report of the President*. Washington, DC: US Government.

Cox, P. (2001) When Shopping on the Web, Nothing Beats Safety of Plastic. *Wall Street Journal*, May 18.

Cringely, R. (2000) I'll Gladly Pay You Tuesday: How PayPal Has Already Won the Battle of the Internet Payment Systems. *The Pulpit* (www.pbs.org).

Davidson, P. (1978) *Money and the Real World*. London: Macmillan – now Palgrave Macmillan.

De Brunhoff, S. (1978) *The State, Capital and Economic Policy*. London: Pluto Press.

De Brunhoff, S. (1990) Fictitious Capital. In Eatwell, J., Milgate, M. and Newman, P. (eds) *The New Palgrave: Marxian Economics*. London: Macmillan – now Palgrave Macmillan.

Dorn, J. (1997) *The Future of Money in the Information Age*. Washington, DC: Cato Institute.

Dreazen, Y. (2000) Labor Secretary to Help Pursue Hourly Workers' Stock Options. *Wall Street Journal*, March 29.

Dreazen, Y. (2002) White House Spurns Efforts to Close 'Digital Divide'. *Wall Street Journal*, February 27.

Eichenwald, K. and Henriques, D. (2002) Web of Perils Did Enron In As Warnings Went Unheeded. *New York Times*, February 10.

Enos, L. (2000) E-Commerce Currency Firm Scales Back. *E-Commerce Times* (www.newsfactor.com), December 20.

European Central Bank (1998) *Report on Electronic Money*. Frankfurt.

Ewing, T. (1998) 'Open-outcry' Trading Faces Threat From Electronic Rivals. *Wall Street Journal*, December 24.

Fairlamb, D. and Edmondson, G. (2000) The New Economy/Europe: Work In Progress. *Business Week*, January 31.

Federal Reserve (2002a) *Flow of Funds Accounts of the United States, 1965–1974*. Washington (DC): Board of Governors of Federal Reserve System.

Federal Reserve (2002b) *Flow of Funds Accounts of the United States, 1975–1984*. Washington (DC): Board of Governors of Federal Reserve System.

Federal Reserve (2002c) *Flow of Funds Accounts of the United States, 1985–1994*. Washington (DC): Board of Governors of Federal Reserve System.

Federal Reserve (2002d) *Flow of Funds Accounts of the United States, 1995–2001*. Washington (DC): Board of Governors of Federal Reserve System.

Federal Reserve Bank of Kansas City (2001) *Economic Policy for the Information Economy*. Proceedings of a Symposium, Jackson Hole (WY), August 30–September 1 (www.kc.frb.org).

Ferguson, R. (1998) Implications of Developments in Electronic Commerce. Testimony before the Committee on Commerce, US House of Representatives, June 4.

Festinger, L. (1984) *The Human Legacy*. New York: Columbia University Press.

Fisher, I. (1933) The Debt-deflation Theory of Great Depressions. *Econometrica*, **1**(3), 337–57.

Ford, H. (1911) *My Life and Work*. Garden City (NY): Garden City Publishing.

Forster, S. (2000) PayPal.com Looks for Profit En Route to IPO, While Parent X.com Seeks CEO. *Wall Street Journal*, October 16.

Foust, D. (2000) The Check Is In The E-Mail. *Business Week*, October 30.

Friedman, B. (2000) *Decoupling at the Margin: The Threat to Monetary Policy from the Electronic Revolution in Banking*. Cambridge: National Bureau of Economic Research, Working Paper No. 7955.

Friedman, M. (1953) The Case for Flexible Exchange Rates. In Friedman, M. (ed.) *Essays in Positive Economics*. Chicago: University of Chicago Press.

Friedman, M. (1954) *Studies in the Quantity Theory of Money*. Chicago: University of Chicago Press.

Friedman, M. (1989) The Case for Overhauling the Federal Reserve. In Guttmann, R. (ed.) *Reforming Money and Finance: Financial Institutions and Markets in Flux*. Armonk (NY): M. E. Sharpe, pp. 39–47.

Friedman, T. (1999) *The Lexus and the Olive Tree: Understanding Globalization*. New York: Anchor Books.

Frydl, E. (1982) The Eurodollar Conundrum. Federal Reserve Bank of New York, *Quarterly Review*, **7**(1), 11–19.

Goodhart, C. (1998) The Two Concepts of Money: Implications for the Analysis of Optimal Currency Areas. *European Journal of Political Economy*, **14**(3), 407–32.

Green, H. (1998) A Little Privacy, Please. *Business Week*, March 16.

Green, H. (2000) Privacy: Outrage on the Web. *Business Week*, February 14.

Greenspan, A. (1996) Regulating Electronic Money. Speech presented at the US Treasury Conference on Electronic Money & Banking: The Role of Government, Washington, DC, September 19. Reprinted in Dorn (1997).

Grimm, B.T. (1982) Domestic Nonfinancial Corporate Profits. *Survey of Current Business*, **62**(1), 30–42, Washington (DC): US Department of Commerce.

Group of Ten (1997) *Electronic Money: Consumer Protection, Law Enforcement, Supervisory and Cross-border Issues*. Basel (Switzerland): Bank for International Settlements.

Gutner, T. (1999) E-Bonds Level the Trading Field. *Business Week*, July 12.

Guttmann, R. (1988) Crisis and Reform of the International Monetary System. In P. Arestis (ed.) *Post-Keynesian Monetary Economics: New Approaches to Financial Modelling*. Aldershot (UK): Edward Elgar, 251–99.

Guttmann, R. (1989) *Reforming Money and Finance: Financial Institutions and Markets in Flux*. Armonk (NY): M. E. Sharpe.

Guttmann, R. (1994) *How Credit-Money Shapes the Economy: The United States in a Global System*. Armonk (NY): M. E. Sharpe.

Gutzman, A. (2000) Payment Solutions: Flooz. *Business Week*, May 31.

Hamel, G. (2000) *Leading the Revolution*. Cambridge (MA): Harvard Business Review Press.

Hayek, F.A. (1939) *Profits, Interest, and Investment*. London: Routledge.

Hayek, F.A. (1978) *Denationalisation of Money – The Argument Refined*. London: Institute for Economic Affairs.

Heinsohn, G. and Steiger, O. (1983) Private Property, Debts and Interest or: The Origin of Money and the Rise and Fall of Monetary Economics. *Studi Economici*, 21, pp. 3–56.

Henriques, D. (1999) As Web Trading Soars, NYSE Seeks a Strategy. *International Herald Tribune*, July 30.

Hershey, R. (1999) Bond Market Pulls Itself Out of Dark Ages as Trading Hits the Internet. *International Herald Tribune*, June 28.

Hicks. J. (1974) *The Crisis in Keynesian Economics*. Oxford: Basil Blackwell.

Hiday, J. (1998) As Exchanges Move Towards Electronics, Open-Outcry Trading Still Has a Place. *Wall Street Journal*, March 13.

Hof, R. (2000) Who Will Profit From the Internet Agora? *Business Week*, June 5.

Hof, R. (2001) The People's Company. *Business Week*, December 3.

Ip, G. (1999) Trading Places: The Stock Exchanges, Long Static, Suddenly are Roiled by Change. *Wall Street Journal*, July 27.

Joyce, E. (2001) For Flooz, Time Was Money, and Time Ran Out. *internet.com* (www.atnewyork.com), August 30.

Junankar, S. (2000) Credit Cards Pushing e-Currency Out of the Picture. *ZDNet (UK)* (www.zdnet.co.uk), December 13.

Junankar, S. (2001) Beenz.com Seeks Buyer. *ZDNet (UK)* (www.zdnet.co.uk), March 30.

Junankar, S. (2002) Online Banks: Prime Targets for Attacks. *ZDNet News*, April 30.

Kane, M. (2001) PayPal Faces Long IPO Odds. *ZDNet News*, October 19.

Kapstein, E. (1999) *Sharing the Wealth: Workers and the World Economy*. New York: W.W. Norton.

Keynes, J.M. (1936) *The General Theory of Employment, Interest and Money*. London: Macmillan – now Palgrave Macmillan.

Keynes, J.M. (1937) Alternative Theories of the Rate of Interest. *Economic Journal*, **47**(2), 241–52.

Keynes, J.M. (1943) *Proposals for an International Clearing Union*. Cmnd. 6437, London: HM Government.

Keynes, J.M. (1980) *The Collected Writings of John Maynard Keynes, vol. 25: Activities 1940–1944: Shaping the Post-War World, The Clearing Union*, D. Moggridge (ed.) London: Macmillan – now Palgrave Macmillan.

Klemperer, P. (2000) *The Economic Theory of Auctions*. Cheltenham: Elgar.

Kuttner, K.N. and McAndrews, J.J. (2001) Personal On-line Payments. Federal Reserve Bank of New York, *Economic Policy Review*, **7**(3), December.

Lee, L. (2000) Tricks of E*Trade. *Business Week*, February 7.

Lemos, R. (2001) Defending America Against Cyberterrorism. *ZDNet News*, (www.zdnet.com), November 13.

Lemos, R. and Ricciuti, M. (2001) Can Microsoft Build the .Network? *ZDNet News*, (www.zdnet.com), October 22.

Lev, B. (2001) *Intangibles: Management, Measurement, and Reporting*. Washington, DC: Brookings.

Lucking-Reiley, D. and Spulber, D. (2001) Business-to-Business Electronic Commerce. *Journal of Economic Perspectives*, **15**(1), 55–68.

Magee, S. (1973) Currency Contracts, Pass-Throughs, and Devaluation. *Brookings Papers of Economic Activity*, 1, 303–25.

Maki, D. and Palumbo, M. (2001) Disentangling the Wealth Effect: A Cohort Analysis of Household Saving in the 1990s. *Finance and Economics Discussion Series*, No. 2001–21. Washington, DC: Federal Reserve Board.

Mandel, M. and Hof, R. (2001) Special Report: Rethinking the Internet. *Business Week*, March 26.

Marx, K. (1967) *Capital*, Vol. III. New York: International Publishers. First published in German in 1895.

Matonis, J. (1995) Digital Cash and Monetary Freedom. Paper presented at INET '95, Internet Society Annual Conference, Honolulu, June 26–30.

McDonough, W.J. (1996) The Transformation of the Retail Payments Business. Remarks to BAI Conference: The National Payments System, Washington DC, October 8.

McGee, S. (1995) Futures-Exchange Alliances Are Jilting Electronic Networks. *Wall Street Journal,* March 22.

McNamee, M. (1999) Faster, Cheaper Trading – Can the Regulators Keep Up? *Business Week*, August 9.

Miles, S. (2001) Flooz.com Says It is Seeking Merger, But Service Remain Offline for Now. *Wall Street Journal Online* (interactive.wsj.com), August 10.

Minsky, H, (1982) *Can 'It' Happen Again?* Armonk (NY): M.E. Sharpe.

Minsky, H. (1964) Longer Waves in Financial Relations: Financial Factors in the More Severe Depressions. *American Economic Review*, **54**(3), 324–55.

Morgenson, G. (2001) How Did They Value Stocks? Count the Absurd Ways. *New York Times*, March 18.

Morgenson, G. (2002) How 287 Turned Into 7: Lessons in Fuzzy Math. *New York Times*, January 20.

Morton, W. (2001) Check It Out (Special Report: E-Commerce). *Wall Street Journal*, December 10.

Moss, M. (2000) A Web CEO's Elusive Goal: Privacy. *Wall Street Journal*, February 7.

Mowery, D. and Rosenberg, N. (1998) *Paths of Innovation: Technological Change in 20th-Century America*. Cambridge: Cambridge University Press.

O'Mahony, D., Peirce, M. and Tewari, H. (1997) *Electronic Payments Systems*. Norwood (MA): Artech House.

Okamoto, T. and Ohta, K. (1991) Electronic Digital Cash. In Feigenbaum, J. (ed.) *Advances in Cryptology*. CRYPTO '91, New York: Springer, 324–50.

Palley, T. (2002) The e-Money Revolution: Challenges and Implications for Monetary Policy. *Journal of Post-Keynesian Economics*, **24**(2), 217–33.

Park. A. and Burrows, P. (2001) Dell, The Conqueror. *Business Week*, September 24.

Patrikis, E.T. (1997) Regulatory Issues – A U.S. Perspective. Speech delivered to the 'Internet Banking and Payment' Conference, UNISYS International Management Centre, Saint Paul de Vence (France), January 22–24.

Patrikis, E.T. (1998) Global Electronic Commerce – The Next Century. Speech delivered to the 1998 International ACH Conference, Seattle, March 9.

Radecki, L. and Wenninger, J. (1999) Paying Electronic Bills Electronically. Federal Reserve Bank of New York, *Current Issues in Economics and Finance*, **5**(1), 1–6.

Reed, S. (1999) Bourse Busters. *Business Week*, August 16.

Reingold, J. and Stepanek, M. (2000) Why the Productivity Revolution Will Spread. *Business Week*, February 14.

Rivlin, A. (1997) Role of the Federal Reserve in the Payment System. Testimony before the Committee on Banking and Financial Services, U.S. House of Representatives, September 16.

Rocks, D. (2001) The Net As a Lifeline. *Business Week*, October 29.

Rousseas, S. (1986) *Post Keynesian Monetary Economics*. Armonk: Sharpe.

Sanford, C. (1993) Financial Markets in 2020. *In Changing Capital Markets: Implications for Monetary Policy*, Federal Reserve Bank of Kansas City, pp. 227–43.

Sapsford, J. (2000) PayPal Sees Torrid Growth With Money-Sending Service. *Wall Street Journal*, February 16.

Sapsford. J. and Beckett, P. (2001) Visa and MasterCard Must Allow Banks To Issue Rivals' Credit Cards, Judge Rules. *Wall Street Journal*, October 10.

Sarkar, A. and Tozzi, M. (1998) Electronic Trading on Futures Exchanges. Federal Reserve Bank of New York, *Current Issues in Economics and Finance*, **4**(1), 1–6.

Schroeder, M. and Ip, G. (2001) Out of Reach: The Enron Debacle Spotlights Huge Void in Financial Regulation. *Wall Street Journal*, December 13.

Schumpeter, J. (1942) *Capitalism, Socialism, and Democracy*, London: Allen & Unwin.

Shapiro, C. and Varian, H. (1998) *Information Rules: A Strategic Guide to the Network Economy*. Cambridge (MA): Harvard Business Review Press.

Silverman, G, Sparks, D. and Osterland, A. (1998) A $2.5 Trillion Market You Hardly Know. *Business Week*, October 26.

Simpson, G. (2000a) FTC Finds Web Sites Fail to Guard Privacy. *Wall Street Journal*, May 11.

Simpson, G. (2000b) Clinton is Unlikely to Back FTC Efforts for New Power to Regulate Web Privacy. *Wall Street Journal*, May 22.

Smith, G. and Schmitt, C. (2001) Time To Reel in the Portals? *Business Week*, July 23.

Spangler, T. (1999) Start-up Touts Mobile Cash Transfer System. *Inter@ctive Week* (www.zdnet.com), November 15.

Takahashi, D. (1996) Clinton Loosens Export Policy On Encryption. *Wall Street Journal*, November 18.

Tanaka, T. (1996) Possible Economic Consequences of Digital Cash. *First Monday* (www.firstmonday.dk/issues/issue2/digital_cash).

Tapscott, D., Ticoll, D. and Lowy, A. (2000) *Digital Capital: Harnessing the Power of Business Webs*. Cambridge (MA): Harvard Business Review Press.

Taylor, F.W. (1911) *Principles of Scientific Management*. New York: Harper.

The Economist (2000) E-Cash 2.0. February 19–25.

Timmons, H. (2000) Small Is Bountiful: Merrill is Courting Business Owners – and Gaining Assets. *Business Week*, May 22.

Tobin, J. (1958) Liquidity Preference as Behavior Towards Risk. *Review of Economic Studies*, **25**(1), 65–86.

Tobin, J. (1978) A Proposal for International Monetary Reform. *Eastern Economic Review*, **4**(3-4), 153–9.

Vernon, R. (1966) International Investment and International Trade in the Product Cycle. *Quarterly Journal of Economics*, **80**(2), 197–207.

Vernon, R. (1971) *Sovereignty at Bay: The Multinational Spread of U.S. Enterprises.* New York: Basic Books.

Wachtel, H. (1997) Taming Global Money. In Guttmann, R. (ed.) *Reforming Money and Finance: Toward a New Monetary Regime.* Armonk (NY): M.E. Sharpe, pp. 198–202.

Warwick, D. (1999) *Ending Cash: The Public Benefits of Federal Electronic Currency.* New York: Quorum Books.

Wayner, P. (1997) *Digital Cash: Commerce on the Net* (2nd edn). San Francisco: Morgan Kaufman.

Wearden, G. (2001) Flooz.com Collapse Linked to Massive Credit Card Fraud. *Yahoo! Finance* (uk.news.yahoo.com), August 28.

Weber, T. (1999) E-World: Someday, a Hill of Beenz Might Be Worth a Lot. *Wall Street Journal*, December 20.

Weber, T. (2000) Recent Flaps Raise Questions About Role Of Middlemen on Web. *Wall Street Journal*, June 5.

Weber, T. (2001) Intangibles Are Tough To Value, but the Payoff Matters in Dot-Com Era. *Wall Street Journal*, May 14.

Weiner, S. (1999) Electronic Payments in the U.S. Economy: An Overview. Federal Reserve Bank of Kansas City. *Economic Review*, **84**(4), 53–64.

Wildstrom, S. (1999) Do's and Don'ts of Cyberbanking. *Business Week*, September, 29.

Wilke. J. R. (1996) Showing Its Age: Fed's Huge Empire, Set Up Years Ago, Is Costly and Inefficient. *Wall Street Journal*, September 12.

Wolfson, M. (1986) *Financial Crises: Understanding the Postwar U.S. Experience.* Armonk (NY): M.E. Sharpe.

Woodford, M. D. (2000) *Monetary Policy in a World without Money.* Cambridge: National Bureau of Economic Research, Working Paper No. 7853.

Woodford, M. D. (2001) Monetary Policy in the Information Economy. In *Economic Policy for the Information Economy.* Proceedings of a Federal Reserve Bank of Kansas City Symposium, Jackson Hole (WY).

Zellner, W. (2001) The Fall of Enron. *Business Week*, December 17.